DEEDS NOT WORDS

To Dear Marie

December 1997

From Mammy

DEEDS NOT WORDS

The Life and Work of Muriel Gahan

Geraldine Mitchell

TOWN HOUSE

Published in 1997 by
Town House and Country House
Trinity House
Charleston Road
Ranelagh, Dublin 6
Ireland

British Library Cataloguing in Publication Data. A catalogue record for this
book is available from the British Library.

ISBN: 1-86059-046-2; P/BK
ISBN: 1-860589-073-X; H/BK

Typesetting: Red Barn Publishing, Skibbereen
Printed in Ireland by ColourBooks

Contents

Acknowledgements

My thanks go first to Muriel Gahan's immediate family and close friends for their support. John and Mary Gahan put up with innumerable intrusions as I came ferreting out details of family history. Peter Gahan brought my project to life very early on with lengthy recordings of Muriel which he had had the foresight to make some years before. Martin and Mary Sheridan and Moyra Connell gave me invaluable insights into Muriel's background and family. As for Muriel's friends, had it not been for Sammy Somerville-Large I would never have embarked upon this biography in the first place. I shall never forget my excitement as I sifted through cardboard-boxfuls of jumbled papers on her dining room floor in the winter of 1992. Kathleen Delap has been equally warm in her encouragement. Brendan and Rosie Haythornthwaite were generosity personified. David Shaw-Smith was also unstinting in his help. Thank you all.

The W K Kellogg Foundation's relationship with the Irish Countrywomen's Association (ICA) goes back forty-five years. When, in Februrary 1993, I wrote to the Foundation's then Chairman and CEO, Dr Russ Mawby, outlining my project and requesting sponsorship, his response was unequivocally positive. Jim McHale, assistant to the Chairman, has been most helpful with my research. I owe the Foundation a personal debt of gratitude, but I have also been deeply impressed by the level of their belief in Irish women down the years. At a time when Muriel Gahan and her ICA sisters were hammering on closed doors at home, the Kellogg Foundation needed no convincing that women were the key to rural development and readily gave, and continued to give, the financial and moral support the ICA needed.

It is a great sadness to me that one of the good friends I made while researching this book, James McDwyer of Tralee, a founder member of Macra na Feirme and a staunch fan of Muriel's, will not see it in print. James died on St Patrick's Day 1996 and his gentle wife Una followed him only eight months later. Like Muriel, James seemed incapable of negative thought.

Ernie Sweeney, best known as a campaigner for adult literacy, made a superb guide to the Castlebar of Muriel Gahan's youth. He walked me the length and breadth of the town and introduced me to a wide variety of people whom I thank for their time and their stories, too. Judge John Garavan delivered me into Ernie's care. Mrs Rose Murray in Newport and Mrs Bessie Morrison of Thallabawn were generous with their memories. Thanks too to Mary Mullin for sharing her account of Muriel's Castlebar childhood.

Jean Haslett helped me with Alexandra College records. Susan

Harper made it possible for me to meet her aunt, Althea Hannay. I spent a memorable afternoon in St Leonards-on-Sea listening to Miss Hannay reminisce about her Westport childhood and her schooldays at Alexandra where she was Muriel's contemporary.

Michael Madden, son of Patrick Madden, has been very helpful. I also had the pleasure of meeting former basketmaker Pat O'Connor of Nenagh who evoked graphically for me the harsh realities of 1940s and 1950s rural Ireland. Special thanks too to Blanaid O'Rahilly for helping me sort out the Conor Magee Trust and to my aunt, Lillias Mitchell, for talking to me about her work.

I'd like to thank the following for sharing their memories of The Country Shop: Kay Franks, Breda Garrivan, Georgie Hamilton, Lily Harte, Mary McCarthy, the late Dorothy Moore, Eileen Neary, Stephen Pearce, Sadie Quigly, Blanaid Reddin, Judy Rogerson, Patrick Scott, Nonie Townsend, Kay Tyrell, Hilda and Robert Tweedy.

So many people helped me find out about the ICA, Country Markets and An Grianán that I can only resort to the alphabetical list once more (and again run the risk of inadvertently leaving someone out). Thank you: Kit Ahern, Karen Carleton, June Bourke, Rose Bruton, Joan Coady, Angela Coen, Mary Coleman, James Creed, Patricia D'Arcy, Patsy Duignan, Margaret Erraught, Phyllis Faris, Peggy Farrell, Alex Findlater, Sheila Findlater, Kathleen Gleeson, Jane and Louis Grubb, Adrienne Hammond, Aileen Heverin, Maureen Holden, Hannie Leahy, Marie Lewis, Mamo McDonald, Noreen O'Boyle, Sheila O'Donnellan, Mary O'Driscoll, Patty O'Flaherty, Breda O'Malley, Ann Roche and Rita Rutherfoord. Special thanks to Country Markets for allowing me to consult their minute books.

Thank you Mary Kelleher, Nancy Larchet, Veronica Rowe and Betty Searson for your help in connection with the RDS. My thanks also to Gerald Bruen RHA, Paul Hogan, Brian P Kennedy, Jim Moloney, Clara Ní Ghiolla, Harry Spain, Greg Tierney and Terry Trench who all gave me valuable background information.

My Donegal research was both fascinating and enjoyable thanks to Dunlewey friends Mary Roarty and Nora O'Donnell and their families; Manus McFaddden and his mother, Sheila; Kitty McGeady. Also the Donaghys in Kilcar, Judith Hoad at Inver; Pat Slowey and Francie O'Donnell in Ardara; Peter Sweeney, in charge of handweaving at the Magee factory; Howard and Maureen Temple of Magherabeg and Lynn and Elisabeth Temple in Mountcharles.

I fell in love with Inis Mór and could not begin to name all those who went out of their way to help me. They know who they are and they have my heartfelt thanks. A special thanks to Pauline McDonagh and Mary Brid Rua O'Flaherty. Frances Biggs and David Britton were most generous in their information about Elizabeth Rivers. Thanks to Eugene O'Kelly and Padraig Ó Céadigh of Aer Árann, to Anne O'Dowd of the Irish Folklife Section of the National Museum, to Kitty Joyce of Cleo, to Deirdre Mc Quillan.

Special thanks to Mairín Hope and Brigid Mayes who read early drafts of the book and to Neil Middleton for his unfailing moral and literary support.

I acknowledge the following for permission to quote: Anvil Books Ltd, for extracts from Ernie O'Malley's *On Another Man's Wound*; *The Irish Times* and The Board of Alexandra College.

Illustrations: Unless otherwise mentioned below, all photographs belong to the Gahan family. I am grateful to the following for permission to use their material: David Britton, Moyra Connell, Phyllis Faris, Brendan Haythornthwaite, Brian P Kennedy, Pat O'Connor, Martin Sheridan, B Somerville-Large, Denis Whelehan. Also the RDS, the National Library and *The Irish Times*.

Abbreviations

ACD: Alexandra College Dublin
ACWW: Associated Countrywomen of the World
CAO: County Agricultural Officer
CDB: Congested Districts Board
CEO: Chief Executive Officer (of County Vocational Education Committee)
ESB: Electricity Supply Board
FAO: Food and Agriculture Organisation
IHS: Irish Homespun Society
NAIDA: National Agricultural Industrial Development Association
IAOS: Irish Agricultural Organisation Society
ICA: Irish Countrywomen's Association
ICOS: Irish Co-operative Organisation Society (formerly IAOS)
RDS: Royal Dublin Society
RES: Rural Electrification Scheme
RIC: Royal Irish Constabulary
TA: Town Association
TCD: Trinity College Dublin
UCD: University College Dublin
UI: (Society of) United Irishwomen
VAD: Voluntary Aid Detachment
VEC: Vocational Educational Committee
WI: Women's Institute

Essential Landmarks in Muriel Gahan's work

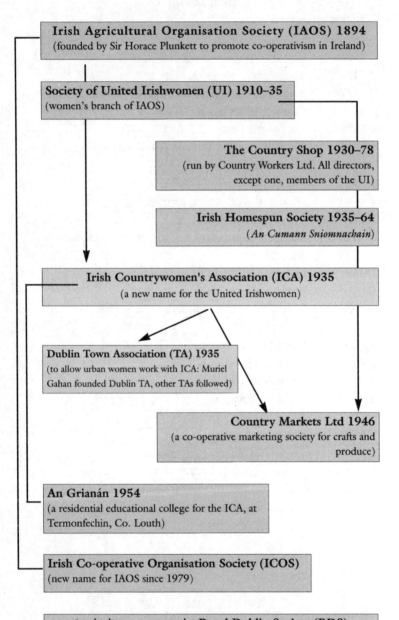

Irish Agricultural Organisation Society (IAOS) 1894
(founded by Sir Horace Plunkett to promote co-operativism in Ireland)

Society of United Irishwomen (UI) 1910–35
(women's branch of IAOS)

The Country Shop 1930–78
(run by Country Workers Ltd. All directors, except one, members of the UI)

Irish Homespun Society 1935–64
(*An Cumann Sniomnachain*)

Irish Countrywomen's Association (ICA) 1935
(a new name for the United Irishwomen)

Dublin Town Association (TA) 1935
(to allow urban women work with ICA: Muriel Gahan founded Dublin TA, other TAs followed)

Country Markets Ltd 1946
(a co-operative marketing society for crafts and produce)

An Grianán 1954
(a residential educational college for the ICA, at Termonfechin, Co. Louth)

Irish Co-operative Organisation Society (ICOS)
(new name for IAOS since 1979)

(and, always present, the Royal Dublin Society (RDS) founded in 1731)

The Weather Glass at Marylands
(on a wet morning, July 1920)

by Winifred Letts (1882–1972)

'The glass is rising' saith mine host,
Each morning though the clouds are grey.
'The glass is rising! Never mind
The showers and the gusty wind,
It surely will be fine today!'
For rain or fog or snow or mist
It rises still, the optimist!

'The glass is rising' saith mine host.
I've never known it yet to fall.
The glass is typical to me
Of this delightful family;
A happy symbol in the hall,
For tho' rain pours from sodden skies
The Gahans know the glass will rise.

Prologue

This book is about one woman's life in the service of the Irish people. When she joined the Society of United Irishwomen (UI) in 1929, Muriel very quickly adopted their motto: 'Deeds not Words'. From then on her long life (she died in her ninety-eighth year) was one of doing, not talking or writing. This is an attempt at an account of those deeds, disentangled strand by strand from the cat's cradle of interconnecting organisations she became involved with and through which she worked. It is also a tribute to the countless women and men who worked with and around her.

To challenge the biographer, Muriel (alias Miss Gahan, MG or Mu) had no enemies. She was once aptly described as 'Horace Plunkett's heir, with a greater gift for getting on with people'. She did not merely get on with people, she loved them. And while she was indeed a profound believer in the co-operative ethic which Horace Plunkett had introduced to Ireland in 1889, she also believed deeply in fun and laughter. Like any true co-operator, she invariably used the pronoun 'we' rather than 'I' and would always deflect attention or credit from herself, yet she also had that great gift of not taking herself too seriously. She did not know how to be negative and was, as someone has said, 'the very opposite of begrudgery'. One apocryphal story tells of Muriel staying in a hotel in a small town, her bedroom opening off a corridor beside the bar. She was sitting on the side of her bed, her brushed cotton nightdress buttoned up to the neck, when the door opened and a man stumbled in. 'What can I do for you, my dear?' she calmly asked.

One is loath to use that rather hackneyed word 'charisma' and yet Muriel's power over people can only be likened to the 'capacity to inspire followers with devotion and enthusiasm' which the word describes. She was a leader and a motivator. It was she alone in many situations who had the vision or simply the 'neck' to persevere where others lost heart. Horace Plunkett had once written, 'If only I could get my juniors to recognise (what came to me through finding myself pitchforked into jobs for which I had no adequate training) that nothing worthwhile can be done without going all out to do it, without failure, disappointment and endless apparent waste of time.'

Muriel's irrepressible optimism, her capacity to act as a 'benevolent steamroller', as one admirer has put it, relentlessly pressing on and always managing to enlist gangs of willing slaves, meant that while forging ahead in Horace Plunkett's wake she was spared his bitterness if her passions were not shared by those she sought to motivate.

Muriel's twin passions were the traditional Irish crafts and making rural Ireland a better place for women. She grew up in a time of unprecedented change in Ireland. And yet even though she was eighteen years old when the Easter Rising took place in Dublin in 1916 and just twenty-four when the Anglo-Irish Treaty was signed – finally signalling the severance of twenty-six of Ireland's counties from British colonial rule – the freedom struggle did not seriously impinge on her. Like the time she grew up in, her life was full of contradictions. For someone who is remembered for her role as catalyst and activist, Muriel was a late starter. She was thirty-two years old before she began to take an interest in public life and then it was by accident.

In a country given to judging people on appearance and accent she must have been a constant source of confusion. Born in 1897 to an English mother and a Church of Ireland, unionist and freemason father, Muriel's allegiances, while retaining to the end a deep love for her own church, were always beyond religion and politics. In broad terms she could be called a progressive nationalist with a firmly pluralist outlook on Irish society. Long before ecumenism had reached Ireland she would happily go to Mass wherever she found herself on a Sunday if there was no Protestant service available. As far as political parties were concerned she did business with whoever was prepared to help her in her work irrespective of labels. 'Personality feuds, political feuds, religious feuds – all the difficulties into which organisers run seem to fade away at her approach', wrote Terence de Vere White in 1977. 'It is something about her, as if the rain stopped whenever she went out or, nearer the mark, she accepted it as cheerfully as sunshine.'

There was no romantic affectation in her love for the country people she got to know in the course of her work. As far as she was concerned they were her friends and her equals. Travelling around Ireland with her towards the end of her life was like being on a royal tour, people would rush to greet her and throw their arms around her. Her voice and bearing were 'Anglo-Irish' and yet she had a total disregard for the trappings of class and an almost irresponsible personal lack of interest in money. Dressed in a tweed suit and silk blouse she might appear forbidding to a stranger, be mistaken for a 'horse Protestant' even, to use Brendan Behan's famous phrase – but anyone who worked with her knew better. Her sense of humour was unfailing and infectious. She was in her element in the restrained formalism of the committee meeting, yet she was also a person who adored games and practical jokes and whose greatest joy was the unknown adventure each new trip around Ireland at the wheel of one of her notorious cars held in store for her.

But what was she really like? 'She had the most roguish eyes I ever saw,' says Mary Roarty who first met Muriel as a small girl in the early 1930s and saw her again and again over the years, either in Dublin where she and her mother, Nancy Ferry, would demonstrate spinning or back in her home village of Dunlewey in northwest Donegal where Muriel was a frequent and welcome visitor. 'Miss Gahan had a face that you could always look at,' Mary says, 'she had a lovely, lovely face. My mother used to say, "She has such a beautiful countenance."'

Mary Roarty has a story that is typical of Muriel, generous, unconventional and totally unpatronising. Mary and another Dunlewey spinner, her friend Nora O'Donnell, were due to demonstrate in Dublin in the late 1940s at one of the many craft shows Muriel organised. She said they must come and stay with her at her parents' house outside Dublin. As they were going to bed on the first night Muriel said, 'Well girls, I'll be going off early in the morning because I have a lot to do, but don't you be in a hurry getting up, my nephew will take you into town on the elephant.' Mary and Nora didn't sleep a wink all night with worry. They had never seen a live elephant let alone ridden on one. 'Anyway we got up in the morning and we were very fidgety and we didn't know what was going to happen at all, so we looked out the window, and then outside the hall door, and we couldn't see anything but this big old-fashioned car. Then Michael, her nephew, says "All right, we're all set!" And Nora and I got into the car, it was huge, and it was stuttering and starting for as long and then it went. That was the elephant!'

Muriel adored parties and in the early days of The Country Shop would find every excuse to hold céilís there. Her great friend Olivia (Livie) Hughes shared her attitude. Thanks to them the Irish Countrywomen's Association (ICA) of the 1940s and '50s became a place where women could find warmth and laughter, an attractive haven in times that otherwise provided little cause for joy. 'As to fun', Livie once declared in her no-nonsense voice, 'I believe in it. I believe that it should be practised, that if you have fun no-one is being bitchy about each other. Fun is a tremendous ingredient in this country and God send that TV or anything doesn't do it away.' At An Grianán, the ICA's residential college, if Muriel said 'Fetch the grey blankets!' you knew you were in for a good evening with improvised drama using blankets, curtains and anything else to hand for costumes and props. She was an excellent actor herself. Self expression through drama and music had been an integral part of her childhood and had given her great confidence and a lack of self-consciousness. She wanted to share this. She once said about the ICA: 'One of the great privileges of being a member of the ICA is seeing people growing. They start timid, and then they get courage, then they start doing things. It's wonderful.' What Muriel loved most to see was a shy woman come out of her shell and drama was one way of achieving this. There was a story she loved to tell of an entertainment at An Grianán where one woman wanted to fulfil an old ambition to do the Dance of the Dying Swan. There was no-one less suited, but she did it and it made her week at An Grianán. It was Muriel who made space for her.

It was not fun all the time. Muriel believed in hard work and she was a perfectionist. Standards were everything to her: in the crafts, in staging exhibitions, in levels of efficiency or in committee procedure. If things were not up to standard she would say nothing, but her smile would vanish and she would become unnervingly silent. She could be hawk-eyed too and when she set her beady eye on you, you were done for. Before you knew where you were, you found yourself doing exactly what she wanted. The consolation was that you knew there was nothing she asked you to do that she was not prepared to do herself. The worst of it was that you would find yourself, carried along by her enthusiasm, volunteering to do impossible or hare-brained things. Ann Roche became an organiser with the ICA in 1951 and later worked full-time for Country Markets. Part of her work was setting up the Country Markets stand at the Royal Dublin Society's (RDS) Spring and Horse Shows each year. Muriel had huge talent for decorating stands and designing exhibitions. She always had to have wild flowers and greenery to offset the webs of tweed, baskets, wrought ironwork and other crafts on display. Regularly she would have family and friends scouring the countryside for marigolds or lugging in bucketfuls of bluebells and carloads of catkins.

Thus it was at one Spring Show, as Ann and Muriel were preparing the stand, that Muriel said, 'Ann, do you know what would be beautiful with this blue tweed? Gorse!' To which Ann replied without thinking: 'The very thing, Miss Gahan. I have a meeting tonight in Kildare, I'll bring some back with me.' Ann went to her meeting and promptly forgot about the gorse, but, as 'you daren't tell Miss Gahan you were going to do a thing if you didn't do it,' she knew she could not return to Dublin empty-handed. 'The show was opening the next morning and I was coming back in the middle of the night, at about eleven-thirty, driving through the plains of Kildare when suddenly I remembered Miss Gahan and her gorse.' Ann had stopped the car and was searching it in vain for some kind of cutting implement when she suddenly saw a soldier cycling along the road towards her. She stopped him and said 'Do you know where I'd get a nice bush of furze?' A look of fear crossed the young man's bewildered face. Ann insisted. 'Now I want it urgently,' she said, 'could you not do it for me?' The poor soldier had no choice but to head for a nearby clump of gorse bushes where he managed to pull off 'a big gust of it'. He dropped it at Ann's feet before leaping back on his bike and peddling furiously into the night and towards the safety of the Curragh army barracks. 'You should have heard Miss Gahan laughing when I was telling her the following day! But I was desperate – you did what Miss Gahan told you.'

No picture of Muriel would be complete without due space given to Livie Hughes, just two months her junior and her friend from the age of sixteen. Not only was she a constant presence in Muriel's life, she was also the creative inspiration behind much of what Muriel achieved. Muriel and Livie belonged to that generation of women in Ireland, many of them Protestant, who having had the benefit of progressive education unconsciously took advantage of the prevailing turmoil of identities – nationality, gender roles and class allegiance – to lead free and creative lives. They escaped the pressure to conform to middle class expectations and in many cases saw their chances of marrying disappear in the decimation of the male population in the 1914–18 war. Livie, one of whose brothers was killed in 1915 and another wounded, married in 1918 before the war ended unsure whether her young husband would ever come home alive.

Despite sharing similar backgrounds Livie and Muriel were in fact very different and it was in this contrast that their strength as a double act lay. Livie was married and living in the heart of a rural community; Muriel was single and operated from the centre of Dublin. Livie was an intellectual, widely read, highly curious and argumentative; Muriel's intelligence was also acute but she did not read very much and was not a thinker in the same way. She had excellent managerial skills, an exceptional memory and was a fine diplomat. Livie loved nothing better than a good head-on row. On a purely personal level they were different too. Muriel was always immaculately, if predictably, turned out; Livie had a total disregard for dress and her appearance. She sometimes wore odd clothes, often second-hand. Once she was wearing a peculiar sort of gym-slip on a group outing. A woman turned to Jack Hughes, her husband, walking some paces behind her and said, 'Who is that extraordinary woman?' 'I'm afraid I haven't a clue', he replied without turning a hair.

What Muriel and Livie had in common were strong personalities and common aims. Often their approach in reaching those aims differed in emphasis and this could cause tension between them. Although Livie was often domineering and was wont to give out orders, it was out of impulsiveness. At the same time she held a very principled belief in democracy and within the ICA would always to go back to the grass roots before taking any decision. In her eyes, Muriel tended to behave autocratically and, being Livie, she did not hesitate to tell her so. She would constantly complain about Muriel's bossiness. And yet they were devoted to each other. 'We both enjoy ourselves very much when we go off together and she extracts all sorts of notions from me.' she said once, adding, on another occasion, 'MG and self are best separated, unless we are alone together when we get along famously.'

It did not occur to either Muriel or Livie that women were not equal to men. Like many women of their class and generation, they found the idea absurd. At the same time, they recognised inequality when they met it and set out to change things. Again, their perspective was revealingly different. Muriel immediately saw all the positive aspects of women's lives: the strong role they played in the west of Ireland, for example, often because of the men's prolonged absences from home as migrant labourers; the fact that it was the spinners who traditionally controlled the weaving trade. She built on those strengths, always on the alert for areas where women could be backed up and encouraged. She was thrilled, for example, to find one or two women weavers still working in the 1940s. Livie was far more militant and politically aware. She was enraged when she saw how Irish society kept women and girls back. An angry outburst in 1960 is typical. Livie was involved in Macra na Tuaithe, the rural youth movement today called Foróige, and had persuaded a bacon factory to let a group of girls have some pigs to fatten as a project. When the County Agricultural Officer went to inspect the pigs he found that they were doing well but reported that he thought pigs were an unsuitable project for girls. Livie was furious. 'Girls and women must not do anything really profitable on the farm', she wrote to a friend. 'They may do the hens (of course at a loss). They may milk the cows and feed the calves, but they may not handle the creamery cheque. Let women and girls do embroidery, and perhaps house decoration, if not too expensive.'

Personal growth, empowerment, interactive skills, assertiveness... None of these words or phrases had been coined when Muriel and Livie took up the cause of rural Irish women, yet that was what their work was all about. Nor were the traditional crafts or their makers held in any esteem in Ireland at that time. 'Ethnic' was not yet cool. And yet Muriel's belief in and respect for traditional craftworkers was implicit and complete and never wavered.

This is the story of her life's work.

— *1* —

Wild and Woolly in Castlebar

The Gahans are an old Ulster family, descendants of the princes of Limavady, in Co. Derry. The name O'Cathain or O'Cahan first appeared in family records in the seventeenth century[1], and the origins from O'Cahan, later O'Kane, probably account for the family's pronunciation of their name as 'gain' rather than 'gan' or 'ga-han'. Muriel was born in October 1897 in a house called Magherabeg on the outskirts of Donegal town, an elegant ivy-clad building which was then entirely thatched. Her grandfather, Frederick Gahan, was county engineer for Donegal. His mother had been a Cork Townsend and he married a Townsend too.[2] He and his wife, Jane Townsend, had eight children: one daughter (the eldest) and seven sons. Two boys died young and Muriel's father, born in 1866 and named Frederick George Townsend Gahan, was the eldest of the surviving sons. He followed in his father's footsteps by becoming a civil engineer; three of his four brothers became Church of Ireland clergymen. Townsend Gahan, known as 'Townie' to his friends, worked first with the Cavan and Leitrim Light Railway Company, but when the Congested Districts Board (CDB) was established in 1891 in an effort by the government to improve living conditions in the poorest areas of the west of Ireland, he was offered a job there. He worked for the Board until it was dissolved in 1923, when he was transferred to the Land Commission. Townsend Gahan's fourth brother, Reginald, who was thirteen years his junior, also went to work for the CDB. By 1906 he was paymaster of the Board's estates but was 'suspended from duty owing to certain irregularities in his accounts.'[3] He was bailed out by Townsend and packed off to Canada where he compounded his disgrace by marrying a Roman Catholic.

In January 1892 Townsend Gahan married an English woman, Winifred Mary Waters, whom he had met in Ireland where she had come to work as a governess. The wedding took place in the bride's home town of Haddenham in Cambridgeshire, England, where her father was a brewer and master bricklayer. The couple, both aged twenty-six, moved into the Gahan family home in Donegal town and in July 1894 their first child, Mary Kathleen Grania, was born. Two years later twin boys, Charles Frederick Townsend (Carlie) and Edward John Beresford (Teddy) were born. Just nineteen months after their arrival, on 27 October 1897[4], came Winifred Muriel Françoise. The twin brothers were delighted with their little sister and according to Muriel were soon playing with her like a doll, one putting her up on a low wall, for example, and the other retrieving her when she fell off on the other side. She was given the pet name 'Wee Dove' and was late starting to speak. When she finally did decide to talk, her first words were, fittingly enough, 'Opie that door!'. In January 1900 there was a terrible tragedy. Carlie, by then aged three years and ten months, was killed, having climbed onto a chair beside the fireplace in the nursery at Magherabeg and fallen over the fire guard into the fire.

Not long after Carlie's death, in the autumn of 1900, the family moved to Castlebar, Co. Mayo. Family legend has always explained the move by a desire to leave painful memories behind but in fact it was a professional decision taken by the CDB in the previous year. During 1899 Townsend Gahan was sent on several field trips to Mayo where the pressure on CDB staff was steadily growing. The redistribution of estates bought up there was proving more complicated and more time-consuming than anticipated and sending their Donegal inspector on missions outside his home area was also proving expensive. At a committee meeting in Dublin in November 1899 it was decided therefore that Mr Gahan should transfer his headquarters from Donegal to Mayo. His salary was to be increased by one hundred pounds a year, the rise being justified by the fact that 'the Board expect to save at least that sum under the head of subsistence allowance.'[5]

The move to Mayo was certainly well-timed, helping the young couple put the traumatic and heartbreaking loss of Carlie behind them. As far as Muriel was concerned there is no doubt that, along with the extraordinary influence which her father and his work had on her, the ten years she spent as a small child in Castlebar played a crucial part in her later development. These were intensely happy times ('We had the happiest of childhoods I would think of any children ever') and laid the foundations for a long life fuelled by boundless reserves of energy. It was here too that Muriel's enduring love for the west of Ireland began.

Mayo is a county of wide open spaces and elemental extremes. Visitors are either troubled by the county's desolate beauty or profoundly moved by it. The many writers and artists who have been seduced over the years by its landscapes, light, sea and sky find that their adjectival resources are soon strained. Mayo's extraordinary beauty was imprinted on Muriel Gahan's psyche at an early age. The poverty which was everywhere and extreme marked her deeply too. At the end of the last century Mayo was one of the poorest regions of Ireland, where those who had survived the famines and clearances of the nineteenth century still struggled hard simply to survive. Frequently they depended upon one or more members of the family spending several months of the year in Scotland or England as seasonal migrant labourers. The Gahan children were never shielded from this reality. On the contrary, their father used to take them with him on work trips into the countryside whenever he could.

But it was in the urban setting of Castlebar, not rural Mayo, that the family was to live and in 1900 Castlebar was a busy, relatively comfortable town with a population of over four thousand and a substantial middle class. It had been a market town for nearly three centuries and was geographically centred around two symbols of power: the military barracks built on the site of the old castle and Castlebar House, residence of the local landlord family, the once infamous but by 1900 well-liked Lucans.[6] More importantly though for the life that Muriel Gahan and her family were to enjoy there, it was both a garrison town and the county capital. As Mayo's administrative centre Castlebar housed the county courthouse, the gaol, the lunatic asylum, an infirmary and workhouse as well as being the seat of the urban and district councils, which were elected bodies since the Local Government Act of 1898. It was also the county headquarters of the CDB. These institutions provided a middle class made up of members of the liberal professions and the civil service who mixed with the landed gentry and military officers to make the town's social life lively with concerts, balls and garden parties.

With hindsight we know that the days of that world were numbered. Its final passing would be marked dramatically in Castlebar by the burning of the barracks and gaol in 1922. But in

1900 the townspeople, especially the better-off landless families like the Gahans, had no reason not to enjoy the present. Political tensions did not impinge in any serious way on their lifestyle. Despite Castlebar's strong associations with Michael Davitt and the Land League (the famous founding meeting of the League had taken place in Castlebar in 1879), the established order of the old garrison town stood firm, with the Earl of Lucan at the apex of its social hierarchy. The 'soporific Ireland of the late 'nineties', described by Elizabeth Bowen in *Bowen's Court*, had lingered on in Castlebar into the first decade of the twentieth century.[7]

An elegant Green, once the Lucans' cricket field, formed the heart of the town. A leafy Mall had been laid out along its northwestern edge leading from the gates of the Lucan estate to the Church of Ireland church, Christ Church. It was along this Mall each Sunday, if he was in residence, that the Earl of Lucan and his retinue would proceed. On Sunday mornings the town would be bright with military music, full of the sounds of harness and hoofbeats and the tramp of boots as soldiers marched in full regalia through the town delivering men to the different places of worship: the Presbyterian kirk on Charles Street, the new Roman Catholic church on Chapel Street, the Methodist meeting hall on the Mall and finally Christ Church on the corner of the Green. In the afternoon the different regimental bands would take turns to play for the townspeople.

Ernie O'Malley, who was later to play a prominent role in the Anglo-Irish War, was born in Castlebar in the same year as Muriel Gahan. His youngest sister, Kay Hogan, would later become a close friend and co-worker of Muriel's. The Malleys left the town for Dublin when Ernie was nine or ten years old, but Muriel remembered him well as a small boy in a blue velvet suit at children's parties. Ernie O'Malley's father, Luke Malley, worked for the Crown Solicitor for Mayo, Malachy J Kelly, and they all – Kellys, Gahans and Malleys – belonged to the same social circle. The Malley home was directly opposite the RIC barracks on Ellison Street, part of the main market street of the town, and thanks to Ernie's reminiscences we have a vivid picture of a scene with which the young Gahans would have been familiar too:

> On market days we could sense the roughness of country people. Awkward men drinking pints of frothy porter, using wiry ash plants on each other in daylight or being dragged and sometimes carried to the barracks by police. Bullocks

beaten through the streets, the shrill complaining of pigs, a steady waft of speech and smells of cow dung and fresh horse droppings. Shawled barefooted women selling eggs and yellow, strong salty butter in plaited osier baskets, salty dilisk in trays, or minding bonnovs with a súgán. A ballad singer with an old song or one of a recent happening, stressing his syllables, rushing a long line into a short singing space whilst the people gathered in a circle, following the words eagerly. They bought his broadsheets and hummed the notes as they walked around. Old women with pleated frills to their white caps, the more wealthy with black bonnets shaking from a spangle of flat beads; boys in corduroy trousers and bare feet; rosy girls in tight laced boots, which some had put on at the entrance to the town. Through all, talk, laughter, hot-blooded sudden blows, a sense of the bare breath of Mayo, backed by rounded mountains and sea, frayed lake-edges and the straight reach of Nephin mountain.[8]

The house the Gahans rented on arriving in Castlebar was out on the Westport road, less than a mile from the town centre and the market hubbub. Yet although it was close to the town it had all the advantages of a country house. It was called Creagh's Villa (known simply as 'Creagh' to the family) and was right on the shore of Lough Lannagh. It was one of a small number of 'gentlemen's residences' close to Castlebar town and a suitable home for a CDB inspector with three young children and a passion for tennis and fishing. In an advertisement which appeared in the *Connaught Telegraph* when the house was put up for sale some years later, it was described as

'beautifully situated, being a 2–storey slated and spacious house and in first class state of repair. There is a fine yard to the rere, also first class out-offices, consisting of stables, coach-houses, sheds, motor house etc all enclosed by a high stone wall. There is a fine garden attached to the house with reproductive fruit trees in same, also croquet and tennis grounds in front of the house. The dwelling house commands a splendid view of Croaghpatrick, Nephin and other mountain scenery and adjoins Loch Lannagh Lakes. The house and lands are within 5 minutes' walk of Castlebar town and within a reasonable distance of Lochs Conn, Cullen, Mask and Carra, famous for trout and salmon fishing.'[9]

Croquet and tennis grounds were to become the hallmark of all the Gahans' homes and one of Townsend Gahan's first preoccupations on moving house was organising these. It was he who first laid them out at Creagh.

The exact date of the move is not known, but by the night of the Census on March 31 1901 the house was full. That Sunday night eleven people slept there. As well as the five Gahans there were three visiting relatives and a live-in staff of three: a governess, a housemaid and a cook. In 1901 the Gahan family income would have been between five and six hundred pounds a year. Canon J O Hannay (alias George A Birmingham, the novelist, playwright and member of the Gaelic League Executive from 1904 to 1907) was rector of Westport, eleven miles west of Castlebar, from 1892 until 1912. He was a contemporary of Gahan's and the families, both with young children, knew each other well. Although Townsend Gahan's salary would not have been considered particularly 'small' at the time, it is nevertheless interesting to read what Hannay, with a lifestyle and outlook similar to the Gahans', had to say about the cost of living in Mayo at the turn of the century. In his autobiography, *Pleasant Places*, he says that his clerical income 'did not amount to £400 a year' and he writes: 'It was possible to live comfortably in Mayo on a very small income. Food prices were low. The wages of a servant began at eight pounds a year for an untrained girl, and for a cook sixteen pounds a year was considered a high wage. It must be remembered that an unskilled labourer earned no more than nine shillings and sixpence a week, so that the wages paid to a servant corresponded pretty closely to the general average of earnings.'[10]

The Gahans, like the Hannays and all the better-off families in the county, both Protestant and Catholic, employed a succession of governesses ('that anaemic form of spinsterhood', wrote O'Malley). The Church of Ireland ran primary schools in both Westport and Castlebar but they were attended by the children of the poorer parishioners. Although her brother Teddy was sent for a short time to a prep school in Tunbridge Wells, Kent, in England where his aunt Susanna lived, neither Muriel nor her sister Grania attended a formal school before the age of eleven or twelve. Nor did their little brother, 'Mac', born in Castlebar in 1902 and christened Dermot Owen Townsend Gahan. Teddy's secondary education was at Sligo Grammar School. Having paid his black sheep brother's debts to the CDB, Muriel's father could no longer afford an English boarding school for his eldest son.

Muriel remembered little about her tutoring at Creagh and any account of her childhood invariably highlighted escapades and outdoor activities. Her sister Grania was referred to as the 'literary member of the family', the 'bookworm', while Muriel and Teddy spent as much time as permitted out of doors. Sometimes they would get out the long ladder and climb on to the roof of the house, licking their feet first to prevent them from slipping on the slates. The view across the lake to Croagh Patrick and the Nephin Beg range was even better from so high up. But bicycles were their greatest source of pleasure. As soon as they were old enough they would think nothing of cycling on long summer days to Westport to visit friends, or beyond Westport to climb the holy mountain of Croagh Patrick before cycling home again to Castlebar in the evening. The dreaded punishment, the only effective form of punishment within their parents' power, was the removal of the valves from their bicycle tyres to prevent them from using them. Even when deprived of their bikes, climbing trees, swimming and fishing, or building bridges and dams on the lakeshore always took precedence over reading or learning from books. Muriel even hated sewing, which her mother tried in vain to teach her and which required a modicum of sitting still. As for knitting she claimed never to have got beyond one sock. Her only strong memories of an enjoyable indoor activity were of sitting around the fire in the evening listening to their father read aloud. To his annoyance Grania would stand behind his armchair, looking over his shoulder to make sure he was not skipping too much. Muriel loved stories and being read to and the books in the house ranged from collections of Irish myths and legends to novels by Jules Verne. She would blackmail her sister into reading to her at bedtime by threatening to tell their parents of some minor misdemeanour committed by Grania during the day.

Teddy and Muriel would run barefoot all summer from May to September just like the local children. Their feet hard as leather, they would show off to visiting town children by tramping barefoot over piles of nettles. Ernie O'Malley, who was 'not allowed to go with other children; few were "good enough" for us', remembers watching with envy 'a boy who could use stilts and a tomboy who could walk on her hands'.[11] When the Gahan children cycled ten miles south for tennis with the Blosse-Lynch children at Partry House, they were looked on as rather 'woolly and wild' by their more sophisticated friends.

There were family outings too which Muriel always remembered with great pleasure. Each Saturday the pony, Dolly, would be harnessed and they would all set out in the trap to Cloonkeen, three miles down the road, to get their week's supply of butter from Mrs Walsh. The children had nicknamed it 'Cabbagetown' because of the rows and rows of cabbages growing near the people's houses. Family picnics were a regular feature often combined with fishing on Lough Mask or picking blackberries for jam in the autumn. Pontoon, on Lough Cullin, was their favourite picnic destination and they would make an annual outing there on Grania's birthday, the twelfth of July.

Muriel's memories of growing up in Castlebar were not just of physical freedom (Hannay, remembering the 'wild and independent' life of his own children, wrote: 'I can imagine no better way of bringing up children'[12]), but of social freedom too. Unlike Ernie O'Malley, she was never aware of being different from other people, a tribute to her parents and their lack of social pretension. She was neither too rich nor too poor, permitted by virtue of her age to slip from one social class to another and thanks to her father had far more opportunities to do so than other children of the same social group.

The Gahan parents though devoted to one another had very different characters. Muriel's mother was a thrifty, careful housekeeper. The children were dressed inexpensively in home-made homespun clothes and anything else that could be made at home was. Her father, a talented amateur artist and great lover of poetry and plays, was generous to a point of extravagance. He would buy his wife expensive jewellery, upsetting her economising instincts. On one occasion the children found their mother crying behind the kitchen door because their father had bought her a diamond ring. But she was by no means a kill-joy and they both enjoyed joining in the social life of the town. Muriel remembered Castlebar as 'a great place for doing things *together*', full of 'happenings', as she called them, such as concerts and plays in which both Gahan parents were keen to take part. Muriel's mother played the organ and the piano and her father made an excellent judge in Gilbert and Sullivan's *Trial by Jury*. The children soon became used to going on the stage. The plays and musical events would take place either on the high stage of the Town Hall or in the smaller parochial hall on the Mall. Muriel remembered playing the lead role in *The Sleeping Beauty* and causing some parental jealousy. Lord Lucan's agent, A C Larminie, a pillar of the urban council and justice of the peace, was overheard to say 'I don't know why *she* was called the Beauty when my daughter Christobel was there and could have been chosen.' Children's parties would be organised, especially during the long winter months, in any of the 'respectable' houses where there were young children. Catholic and Protestant children mixed on these occasions where social status overrode religious affiliation. But the freedom of the first ten magic years in Castlebar came to an end when in 1910, just before her thirteenth birthday, Muriel was sent to join her sister at St Winifred's school for girls near Bangor, North Wales.

Notes

1. See O Hart, J. *Irish Pedigrees or, the Origin and Stem of the Irish Nation*, Dublin, 1881.

2. The rather complex family history with intermarriages and recurring names is typical of a certain social class in Ireland. The friendship between Gahans and Somerville-Larges, for example, which persists to the present day, stems from their being related through the Townshends of Castle Townshend, Co. Cork, described by a biographer of authors Somerville and Ross as being 'a nest of cousins'.

3. Congested Districts Board, Minutes of Proceedings, 21 September 1906.

4. For years Muriel's birthday was celebrated on 28 October, but her birth certificate states that she was born the day before on 27 October 1897.

5. Congested Districts Board, Minutes of Proceedings, 24 November 1899.

6. The callous behaviour of the Earl of Lucan towards his tenants during the Great Famine of the 1840s made him a justifiably hated man in Mayo. He has been described as 'perhaps the greatest depopulator in all of Mayo, who cleared some 2,000 people and destroyed 300 houses in Ballinrobe parish alone between 1846 and 1849.' (Donnelly, J S Jnr. 'Mass Eviction and the Great Famine: the clearances revisited', in Póirtéir, C. *The Great Irish Famine*, Mercier Press, Dublin, 1995.)

7. Bowen, Elizabeth. *Bowen's Court*, London, 1942, p 316.

8. O'Malley, Ernie. *On Another Man's Wound*, Anvil Books, 1979, pp 11–12. Some words in this passage may need explanation: *porter*: dark ale brewed from black malt; *ashplant*: a walking-stick made of ash wood; *osier*: willow; *dilisk*: an edible seaweed; *bonnovs*: piglets; *súgán*: the Irish word for a rope made from twisted hay.

9. *The Mayo News*, 27 September 1919.

10. Birmingham, George A. *Pleasant Places*. London, 1934, p 100.

11. O'Malley. op. cit. pp 10–11.

12. Birmingham. op. cit. p 99.

— 2 —

The Elite

Of St Winifred's, an Anglican school at Llanfairfechan on the Welsh coast, Muriel chose to remember very little except the beauty of the Welsh mountains and her discovery of hockey. 'I enjoyed *doing* things more than being erudite and learned', was her unsatisfactory explanation. True, she never complained of having been unhappy. A collection of books won as school prizes show that she had no problem with learning other than that of priorities: games came first. Neverthless it cannot have been easy to leave behind the freedom of Castlebar, her parents and her young brother Mac, even if her sister was already at the school and may have helped to soften the blow of her first introduction to institutional discipline. There were quite a lot of other Protestant Irish girls at the school. Muriel remembered how the Irish group would be mocked for their accents, for pronouncing 'with' as 'wit' instead of the soft English way and aspirating their '*wh*en's and '*wh*ere's. The other girls there would also wonder at the fact that the Irish girls all seemed to know each other or be distantly related. What a tiny country Ireland must be, they would say.

Holidays were what counted, when Muriel and Teddy could resume their outdoor life in Mayo. Creagh had been given up once Grania, Teddy and Muriel were all at boarding school. The remaining family, Mac and his parents along with just one live-in servant, had moved into quarters in the military barracks which had temporarily been discontinued as a military station and was let out to private families at low rents. The Gahans' move would have been primarily for economic reasons, as a means of cutting down on costs in order to meet school fees more easily. The quarters were not cramped, however, with eleven rooms and no fewer than thirty windows in front. There were huge courtyards and vast expanses of wall to bash balls against.

In 1913 when Mac was ready for secondary school and Grania was about to enter university, it was decided that Mrs Gahan should take a house in Dublin, since that was where all four children would now be undergoing some stage of their education. Townsend Gahan would move into a room in the house of Castlebar's Church of Ireland rector and his wife, the Reverend and Mrs Lendrum, and travel to Dublin at weekends.

By September 1913 Grania was nineteen years old and went to Trinity College Dublin (TCD) to read history and political science. In the same year and reading the same subjects was Theodosia (Theo) Hannay, Canon J O Hannay's elder daughter, who had remained a good friend since Mayo days. Both young women did well, gaining 'first rank' results in their annual exams and graduating in 1917. Grania took up Irish and won prizes for it in 1916 and 1917. Both were awarded gold medals on their final results. Despite her brilliance as a student it is ironic that later in her life Grania would come to envy and admire Muriel who without any academic qualifications at all had built such a career for herself. Grania once told her daughter-in-law that if she had to name the one person she most admired in the world it would be her sister, Muriel. On another occasion, however, when Grania wrote from her Castlebar home to her sister in Dublin expressing envy for the freedom and excitement of Muriel's busy life, Muriel replied rebuking Grania sharply. What right had she to be dissatisfied with her lot when she was fortunate enough to have a husband and children, Muriel asked.

Teddy was to have followed Grania to TCD in 1914 to study engineering, but when war broke out in August 1914 he felt it was his duty to enlist. He joined the Royal Leinster Fusiliers, but was rejected for active service because of flat feet and served instead with the Royal Army Service Corps in France, reaching the rank of captain. He was not demobilised until 1920 when he took up his studies again. Mac went to St Columba's College, an old Protestant school for boys in the foothills of the Dublin mountains. As for Muriel, she was not quite sixteen in the autumn of 1913, but she did not go back to St Winifred's. Instead she was enrolled at Alexandra College, then at Earlsfort Terrace in Dublin, in January 1914.

Alexandra College had been founded in 1866 thanks to the efforts of a remarkable Quaker woman from Co. Offaly, Mrs Anne

Jellicoe, whose initial ambition had been to provide a training college for governesses – that poorly paid, barely respected yet sizeable group of young women. She wanted to ensure that women in Ireland could have a 'sound and systematic education, one which should fit them to adorn an exalted position, or enable them, under adverse circumstances, to enter on a career of usefulness and independence.'[1] From the start Alexandra College had strong Church of Ireland and Trinity College links but it was open to all religions. Its work to have girls' education taken seriously was outstanding for its day and by 1880 it had become a women's university college, preparing students for external degrees from the Royal University of Ireland. (The RUI disappeared when the National University of Ireland (NUI) was founded in 1908.) Its determined efforts to be recognised as a women's college attached to the more prestigious TCD failed and when the latter started admitting female students in 1903 Alexandra College's function changed to that of a preparatory college for university entrance exams. It then expanded to provide training for secondary teachers, secretarial courses and instruction in hygiene and housecraft.[2]

Muriel always recognised that it was 'the Alexandra' that provided any education she got. 'They taught us to be leaders,' she would say, adding with a mischievous smile, 'leaders of what, I'm not quite sure.' Although radical and progressive in educational matters, the College's politics were conservative and unionist. It is an indication of Alexandra's unique character, however, that Padraic Pearse, one of the leaders of the 1916 Easter Rising, was employed to teach Irish there from 1904 to 1907. Later Dorothy Macardle, author of *The Irish Republic* (1937), who lived for a period in the house of republican and feminist Maud Gonne MacBride on St Stephens Green, was a very popular and inspiring teacher of English at the College and was known as 'Maccy' to her students. Her involvement in the nationalist struggle was no secret and as she put it herself, 'it was in 1922 that I was suddenly translated from the position of lecturer in Alexandra College to that of a military prisoner in Mountjoy Jail.'[3] Muriel had been on the committee of the Dramatic Club with Dorothy Macardle in 1915 and 1916 and shared her passion for plays and acting. Just before she left the College, Muriel was one of a cast of three in 'a capital performance' of *A Pot of Broth* for the Soldiers' Wives Club.[4]

Dorothy Macardle was just eight years older than Muriel and

speaking at a reunion of old Alexandrans in 1952 she paid tribute to the Anglo-Irish traditions embodied in the old Alexandra. Looking back to the Alexandra of 1914 and before, she said:

> It looks, in truth, like a simple garden of Eden, open to sunlight and sheltered from storm. It looks like a citadel of a golden age. It looks like the microcosm of that world of the Anglo-Irish ascendancy, with all its extraordinary privilege, with its talent and creativeness, its social conscience, its grace, vigour and charm. The tide of change, the surge of revolution, was gathering and beating about the walls – but we did not know.
>
> We lived in a dream of security: I and my fellow-students believed we had only to equip ourselves well and do our work earnestly and we were bound to be rewarded with a life of expanding interest, opportunity and delight. The woman's cause was advancing and we meant to be in the vanguard; our inherited privileges were ours by some divine right but had to be justified by service, and we were more than willing to serve. Confidently we looked forward to honourable, progressive and happy lives.[5]

The Gahans moved into a rented house at 20 Leinster Square in Rathmines, a genteel and predominantly Protestant southern suburb of Dublin. The house was and still is a fine, tall house looking down on to lower Rathmines Road. At once Townsend Gahan set about laying out a tennis court in the back garden. This was quite a feat since the garden could not accommodate a full-sized court. He would have had to settle for a rather under-sized single court, doubling up as a croquet ground. At 1 Prince Arthur Terrace, only a few houses away from the Gahans' home, lived Susan Mitchell (member of the United Irishwomen (UI), poet, feminist and co-editor of *The Irish Homestead* with George Russell, better known as AE, the poet, artist and mystic who had joined Horace Plunkett's co-operative movement in 1897). Susan lived with her nieces, the Brabazon sisters, who had been close friends of the Gahans in Wesport where their father worked for the Bank of Ireland. She was renowned in Dublin for her parties. Muriel remembered some of these even though as an unbookish teenager she was only peripherally aware of the stature of the guests. She retained a clear memory of being at one of them – with Susan Mitchell 'sitting on the floor in her drawing room surrounded by a crowd of men, including Yeats, AE, and all those people of those times who were poets and writers. And there she was sitting on a stool, down on the floor, singing.'[6]

Muriel started at Alexandra College in January 1914 and stayed there until June 1916. After the hiatus of Wales, the good times began again for her in Dublin. She was reunited with her family and had the freedom of the city thanks to her beloved bicycle. The College was also within easy cycling distance. She made good and lasting friends there, nearly all of whom were more academically inclined than she was but then it was, as Muriel was to comment much later, 'a year of outstanding scholarship'. This was where her lifelong friendship with Livie Hughes, then Olivia Crookshank, began. Livie won a bronze medal in 1914, a medal in English in 1915 and went on to read history in TCD in 1916, breaking off her studies to marry in July 1918. Enid Starkie, later to become a prominent French scholar, was another classmate. She had won the Pfeiffer entrance scholarship to Alexandra College in 1913 and in 1916 won an entrance scholarship to Somerville College, Oxford, where she went on to become a Fellow. In the same group of friends were Mabel Thomas, who twice won the Jellicoe Memorial Prize and who, according to Enid Starkie, 'was considered an intellectual prodigy',[7] and Kathleen (Bi) Preston, who won the prize for science in 1915 and was later to return to the College to lecture in mathematics after taking a degree at Newnham College, Cambridge. Muriel remembered being good at history and coming first in an all-Ireland history competition or exam, but there is no trace of this in the school records. She also had a better memory for poetry than the other students and remembered poems her father had taught her. This won her some good marks in English. But it was hockey and all other sports that Muriel unashamedly confessed to loving best and where she excelled. She developed a passion for both gymnastics and the gym teacher, a Miss Tempest. The only honours recorded in her name in the school magazine are twice coming second in tennis championships and winning a first prize in the Potato Race at the College Sports in 1915.

Muriel Gahan's memory of Enid Starkie at Alexandra was of an extremely musical, clever girl who was also quite unhappy, 'a sad person'. She would often come to visit Muriel at home and play the Gahans' piano, finding that Muriel, being 'less erudite' (Muriel's own term) than the other girls, could see the importance of 'enjoying other sides of life', such as music, and was therefore easier to be with. Enid Starkie had suffered greatly from the College's attitude to her passion for music. 'You are too clever a girl,' the principal had said to her, 'to waste your talents on music.'[8] Muriel also remembered how Enid Starkie used to powder her face using white flour and how she and the other girls used to look down on this. In her autobiography, *A Lady's Child*, Enid Starkie corroborates this memory but gives reasons for the white powder which her friends may not have understood at the time. She was 'bitterly self-conscious' of her bad skin and hated the successive crops of pimples which would appear on her face. 'My mother used to insist that they came because I did not clean my face thoroughly. She advised me to use a hard loofah and a rough towel. With a loofah hard enough to scrub a pig's back I rubbed my chin with characteristic fanatical zeal until I had rubbed the skin off, but I did not rub the pimples away. They appeared more luxuriant than ever. I was not allowed to put powder on my face to disguise the ravages caused by my fierce facial treatment, but sometimes, ashamed to appear at school in this guise, I used to powder my chin with tooth powder.' [9]

Enid Starkie does not mention Muriel Gahan by name in *A Lady's Child*, but we know that they belonged to the same small circle of friends. 'During my last year at school,' Enid Starkie wrote, 'I was, I believe, more popular than I had been earlier in my course. My schoolfellows seemed to consider me less peculiar than formerly, now that I was an official of many of the clubs and played tennis in the school matches. [Mrs. Starkie would not allow her daughter to play hockey in case it thickened her ankles.] I had by then many school friends besides Kathleen Preston and Mabel Thomas. There was a large gang of us which called itself the *Elite* – I had nothing to do with the choice of this name – and its most important members were Kathleen Preston, Mabel Thomas and Olave (sic) Crookshank; there were a few other girls as well and myself.'[10] Muriel Gahan was one of these 'few other girls' along with Hetty Micks, Frances Steen and Althea Hannay.

Althea Hannay, Theo's younger sister, had a special affinity with Muriel on two counts: she was from Mayo and she was not interested in school. 'We sat side by side and we used to be the torment of our teachers,' Althea Hannay remembered, 'the two of us together, as you can imagine, both keen on talking. I remember Muriel coming in like a breath of fresh air into that school. I was stodging along, never a good pupil, and she wasn't at all interested in being a good pupil either. She wasn't at all a model pupil, any more than I was. We were rather written off as "those West of Irish".' [11]

It was Muriel's strong friendship with Livie Crookshank which was most to influence the future course of her life. Even at this early stage, Livie was sensitive to social issues and interested in co-operation as a way of encouraging people to help themselves towards a better life. She remembered Horace Plunkett coming to lecture at Alexandra College. He disappointed her because he was 'a dullish speaker, not a very good lecturer', but she found him impressive nevertheless for what he had done. 'He knew what he was up to, that was the kind of feeling he gave you.' Livie Crookshank's expectations of Plunkett had been high because she had already become acquainted with the co-operative library in Plunkett House in Dublin and used to go there quite frequently. 'Why co-operation interested me was that I collected rents: some of the elder girls at the Alexandra were taken to collect rents in the slum houses which the Alexandra had reconditioned and looked after. It always seemed to me that the people there bought things like coal at a ridiculously high price.' How much better it would be, eighteen-year-old Livie thought, if the people joined together to buy a ton of coal and then distributed it amongst themselves.

Many years later, in 1953, Livie Hughes wrote to her friend and fellow-ICA worker Sarah Ryan, a Yorkshire woman who had married the Irish historian Desmond Ryan, defending her social work at Alexandra College:

> It may have been 'fashionable' to collect rents in slums for the teenagers in England, but I think that A.C.D. is the only school that attempted anything of the kind in Ireland. At any time there can have only been about two girls helping to do it, and certainly not because of fashion. I think that at any rate in those days it was a sensible and helpful thing to buy up some of the slum tenements, and make a job of making them less dreadful and more sanitary. You never saw the slums in those days...I suppose it was Noblesse Oblige, and a lot of outdated ideas, but if I had a daughter I wouldn't mind at all for her to get some of the training which I got...A violent Christian as I was then did not like having two coats when other people had none, and in fact has hardly been reconciled to it from that day to this.

The Alexandra Guild, which ran the scheme described by Livie and had become affiliated to the National Union of Women Workers shortly after it was formed in 1911, was just one example of the College's pioneering ventures. Within the school too were extra-curricular activities, such as the many clubs, which were of immense educational value to the students. The clubs were run by the girls themselves and meetings were held after school hours. This was to be Muriel's first introduction to committee procedure, a skill she was to develop into an art form later in life. The club committee would organise everything from the tea and biscuits for ordinary meetings to inviting outside guests and speakers. Girls were encouraged to stand up and express opinions.

'There seemed very little point in thinking of any future as long as the war was on',[12] wrote Enid Starkie referring to her final year at Alexandra College and the First World War. The 1916 rising had not impinged on most of the girls' lives except as something exciting to observe from a distance. Muriel remembered climbing on to the roof of the rectory of St Stephen's Church in Upper Mount Street in the centre of Dublin during Easter Week, to see what she could see. The Great War, on the other hand, had touched them all very closely: Muriel's brother was away in France; Livie's adored brother Artie, a close friend of her future husband, Jack Hughes, was killed in the Dardanelles in 1915, aged twenty-one, and another brother, Henry, was wounded in Gallipoli; Mabel Thomas' brother, who had joined the newly formed Flying Corps, was killed; Kathleen Preston lost two cousins in France and her brother was badly wounded; Enid Starkie's brother, Walter, had not been able to enlist because of a weak chest but many of his closest friends were killed. During the war a great many girls from Alexandra College joined the Voluntary Aid Detachment (VAD) and served as nurses, cooks and ambulance drivers in Ireland, England and France. Althea Hannay worked in a base-camp canteen in France. Muriel made her contribution to the 'war effort' much closer to home. She and several other Alexandra girls got jobs at Sir Howard Grubb's munitions factory in Rathmines. Muriel was vague about what she did at the factory, but remembered working at a machine turning out shell cases 'or something ghastly like that'. She cannot have worked there for very long because after 1916, Grubb's works were gradually transferred to England.[13]

At some point, perhaps in 1918 or maybe earlier, Muriel accepted the invitation of an old and wealthy friend of the family,

May Batterscome, now Mrs May Talbot, to come and look after her young son, Patrick. The original plan had been that Muriel would accompany the mother and son on a trip to East Africa where Mr Talbot was posted. Muriel was excited at the idea of travelling but Mr Talbot died in Africa before the journey began and Muriel went instead to help the young widow at her home in Wales. She had a very good time nonetheless. Her job was far from taxing and once the war was over it involved some enjoyable European travel by chauffeur-driven car as well as an entertaining social life in Wales with lots of tennis.

Then in the summer of 1919 news reached Muriel in Wales that her brother, Mac, had had an accident at school and was very ill in hospital. She rushed home. Mac had been playing 'cloister cricket', a game traditionally played by the boys of St Columba's College outside the school chapel, when he had fallen and hit his head on the flagstones. He developed meningitis and died in hospital three weeks later on 19 July. He was not quite seventeen years old and had been an outgoing, happy and popular boy. It was a devastating blow for the family. Muriel did not return to Wales. It was decided that she and her mother would move back to Castlebar.

Notes

1. Alexandra College Magazine, June 1916.
2. Information about Alexandra College from O'Connor, A V and Parkes S M. *Gladly Learn and Gladly Teach*, Blackwater Press, Dublin, 1984.
3. Alexandra College Magazine, June 1952.
4. Alexandra College Magazine, June 1916.
5. Alexandra College Magazine, June 1952.
6. Muriel in conversation with her great-nephew, Peter Gahan, 31 July 1986.
7. Starkie, Enid. *A Lady's Child*, Faber and Faber Ltd, London, 1941, p 216.
8. ibid p 241.
9. ibid pp 221–222.
10. ibid p 239.
11. In conversation with the author, St Leonards-on-Sea, July 1995.
12. Starkie, E. op cit, p 239.
13. Information about Sir Howard Grubb from Burnett JE and Morrisson-Law AD *Vulgar and Mechanick: the scientific instrument trade in Ireland 1650–1921*, RDS and Scottish Museums, 1989.

— 3 —

'The Time of My Life. . .'
Castlebar 1919–26

Ireland's War of Independence began in 1919. The Soloheadbeg ambush, in which two policemen were killed, had taken place on 21 January, the day the first Irish parliament, Dáil Eireann, met. They were the first members of the British forces to have been killed in Ireland since the Easter Rising in 1916. Two-and-a-half years of guerrilla warfare were to follow. By September, around the time the Gahans were moving into their new house in Castlebar, Dáil Eireann was outlawed and before the end of the year the first Black and Tans, the notorious irregular force engaged by Britain to combat the Irish Volunteers, were being recruited.

The Gahans moved into a house called Maryland, a surprising choice for such a small family since it was even bigger and grander than Creagh. At most there can only have been four of them, excluding servants, because Teddy was still with the British army in France. For most of the time, indeed, Muriel may have been on her own with her parents. Grania took a one-year teachers' training course in England on graduating from TCD and then took up a teaching post near Windsor, Berkshire in England. She probably only came to Castlebar during the school holidays. The man she would later marry and to whom she had been engaged in secret for several years, Dr Alfred ('Naultie') Sheridan, was Assistant Medical Officer at the mental hospital in Castlebar. Muriel was very fond of him too. 'He used to be one of our great dancing pals. I was very attached to Naultie', she remembered, 'and I had a rag round my wrist for ages, belonging to Naultie, I'd found it someplace and I'd wrapped it round my wrist and kept it there for a long time.'

Despite his rather grim job, Naultie Sheridan was much appreciated for his droll sense of humour and was considered a great asset to any party. But although Grania was by now twenty-five years old and Sheridan ten years her senior the marriage was constantly deferred. The relationship did not meet with parental approval, Grania's father being particularly concerned with the match. Despite the fact that the Sheridans were a prominent Castlebar family of socially impeccable background (Naultie Sheridan's father had been registrar of Mayo County Court for thirty years and his brother Joseph, a TCD graduate, was Chief Justice in East Africa and would be knighted in 1932), they were Catholics. While Castlebar was justly proud of the excellent relationship which existed between the two religious communities in the town, getting along well together was one thing, marrying was quite another. Townsend Gahan was clearly unhappy about the discriminatory rules and regulations his daughter would have to comply with in marrying a Roman Catholic.

Maryland, built on a rise between Castlebar railway station and the military airfield, was a seven bedroom house on twenty-eight acres. Townsend Gahan immediately arranged for three tennis courts to be made. A section of the second battalion of the Border Regiment, the principal regiment garrisoned in Castlebar, was stationed at the airfield until it was closed in November 1920. 'I had the time of my life' is how Muriel summed up her memories of this her second period in Castlebar, which was to last until her father's retirement in 1926 and the family's return to Dublin. She remembered standing 'for hours' at the upstairs windows of the house gazing down towards the air base hoping to see some of her officer friends coming along the road past Maryland. 'The soldiers were in Castlebar and, with our tennis grounds, we were very popular with the officers.' The huge hall at Maryland was ideal for dances, which also made the Gahans a popular family. 'We were always having dances, because it was perfect for that. Castlebar was one of the calmest places.'

This may seem a curious remark to make about a garrison town during one of the most convulsed periods of Irish history. And yet for some of the time and for some of the people Castlebar was a very calm place between 1919 and 1921. Indeed in national and relative terms it was quite calm a lot of the time for most people. Between the signing of the truce in July 1921 and the signing of the Anglo-Irish Treaty five months later the atmosphere in Castlebar was positively euphoric. It was after the departure of the

Crown forces in January 1922, in the lead up to and during the Civil War, that the town, strongly pro-Treaty, lived through its darkest hour.

Even at the height of the war the regular British troops based in Castlebar, amongst them Muriel's 'pals', were rarely the butt of local anger or hatred even though by definition they were associated with the repression of Irish Volunteers. In 1921 some soldiers stationed in nearby Foxford were responsible for horrendous outrages against local people.[1] But the 'Crown forces' as a whole were not yet looked on as a foreign army. After all an estimated 200,000 Irishmen had taken part in the 1914–18 war and thousands were still serving with the Imperial army abroad. In a garrison town like Castlebar, the soldiers had long been an integral part of urban life and a source of livelihood to the town. As elsewhere in Ireland it was the Black and Tans and the Auxiliaries who were responsible for the worst atrocities in the area.

In spite of everything the Christmas editorial message in the *Connaught Telegraph* in 1919 was optimistic: 'Another memorable year for Ireland is drawing to a close, but black as the prospect is, weighty as the oppression, and harsh as the power of the rulers, there is strong indication that the dawn of freedom is at hand. World-wide public opinion is on our side, the power and prestige of the tyrant is going down before it and growing weak, and with God's help, 1920 will see the realisation of our aspiration.' Townsend Gahan and other prominent members of the Church of Ireland community in Castlebar were prompted to express their own hopes and fears about the political situation in Ireland. In August 1920 Muriel's father took part in a meeting where they 'let it be known that they were not adverse to a settlement of liberal self-government' as a means of bringing about 'a settlement of the differences that bid fair to bring Ireland to ruin.'

Anxieties lessened when the truce came in July 1921. While the Gahans had held house parties and tennis afternoons before the truce and the officers passing along the Gahans' garden wall on their way to and from the airfield would sing out to Muriel, 'She's the sweetest girl in Maryland. . .', it was in the second half of 1921 that she really had the time of her life, 'a *gorgeous* time'. Teddy was back in Ireland and had taken up his studies again at Trinity. He had taken lodgings with the Hay family on the northside of Dublin and soon was engaged to Vera, the daughter of the house. Vera's father was secretary of the Midland Great Western Railway and Teddy and Vera were able to travel free of charge from

Dublin's Broadstone Station to Castlebar, Westport and even on to Newport, Mulranny or Achill, wherever the fun was. Muriel, on the other hand, did not need to depend on the railway to get to the parties. 'We used to travel to all kinds of dances in the cars belonging to the army – they were vans really, some sort of peculiar vans [presumably armoured cars]. And whether it was to Mulranny where we had gorgeous dances, or to Ballinrobe, or whether it was to Castlebar, it was all the same, and Teddy and Vera would join us.' Friends from Dublin would also travel to Castlebar and all seem to have been blissfully unaware of the political situation. 'All our friends would want to come and stay with us, particularly one friend, who had a young man in Dublin, and he disapproved of her (coming to Castlebar) very strongly, but we couldn't get her away. We used to have parties where we'd all arrive and bring all the things, everyone brought food and so on – "surprise parties" we called them.' By this stage Muriel was 'great pals with a lot of officers in the army, I never knew which one I liked the best.'

There was one with whom she got on particularly well and who was equally fond of her. 'We had more or less planned to get together later, but it never happened. Our lives just sort of divided, we went our different ways.' This was 'Prid', the only one of her many officer friends to be immortalised in the family photograph album. 'He borrowed the Colonel's horse and would bring me riding up the mountains. One desperate day I remember we were going up the mountains across the bog when suddenly the horse stuck in the bog and the next thing I knew, we couldn't get the horse out. The Colonel's horse! Luckily there was a house not very far from us and so Prid went over to get the owner of the house and they dug the horse out. So we were able to get back and we had to wash the horse before the Colonel got him again.

'I kept hens in those days, and ducks, because I really had nothing much to do. I was really rather a lady of leisure then, except for enjoying myself at the dances and playing hockey and tennis. My pals from the army and the air force used to come and "help" me look after my ducks and hens.' Once some hens were stolen and it turned out to have been some of the air force crew who were duly punished. At the beginning of September 1921 Muriel was busier than usual as Maryland was given over to a two-day fund-raising exercise in aid of the Christ Church Repair Fund. On Wednesday and Thursday, 7 and 8 September, a Fête was held, ('entrance by ticket only 3d.'), between three and seven o'clock each afternoon. Included in the Fête were 'Garden Produce, Competitions of all kinds, Concerts, Fortune-telling etc., Tea 1s.' and each night there was dancing from 8.30 pm until one in the morning.

The Fête was a huge success and over a hundred pounds was raised. 'Music emanating from a grove in the demesne' was provided by the Border Regiment brass band. The two-day festivities were open to everyone and anyone who had the price of an entry ticket could go. In 1995, Agnes Fahey, born, like Muriel Gahan, in 1897, the youngest daughter of the Breaffy blacksmith, still remembered tea and dancing at Maryland. 'In those days there wasn't that much going on for us in Castlebar,' she said, 'only the silent movies and card games, so you went to everything that was going.'

There had been nine months of dry weather in 1921 and the good weather combined with the truce gave rise to an explosion of shows, sports, carnivals and dances in the Castlebar region the like of which had not been seen for some years. But as the weeks went by and the peace negotiations dragged on, the mood began to darken. The tone of the *Connaught Telegraph's* editorials moved from optimism ('the prospects of peace are bright', 3 September 1921) through anxiety ('the peace negotiations have reached a critical stage', 17 September 1921) to exasperation ('when the crisis is reached the Cabinet should have the wisdom enough to realise the folly of giving Ulster her way and the paramount necessity of ending for ever the long-standing Irish trouble', 3 December 1921). Finally, when 'after a weary and disappointing sitting' the Dáil approved the Anglo-Irish Treaty by a majority of only seven votes, the voice is tired: 'and now the hope of all is that the members of An Dáil will compose any little differences that may exist and settle down to have the terms confirmed by the law as soon as possible.' (14 January 1922)

The passing of the Treaty meant the end of the British military presence in Castlebar. A final 'grand concert and dance' was held in the Barracks on 12 and 13 January, 'by kind permission of Colonel Pakenham and the officers of the 2nd Border Regiment.' The organisers were once more from Christ Church and there must have been a huge feeling of sadness and foreboding amongst those who like Muriel had grown to enjoy the officers' company so much. The commanding officer was the first to put the contents of his quarters up for auction. Next came the auction of military stores, 'hundreds of Bedsteads, Palliasses and Bed Covering,

Chairs, Forms, Tables, Basins, Baths, Buckets, Bins, Cups and Saucers, Plates and Bowls. . .' Then came further auctions of military and RIC men's furniture. Finally they all left and the barracks were handed over to the IRA. 'Following the departure of the 2nd Border Regiment from Castlebar at six o'clock on last Monday morning (13 Feb), a guard of the 1st Battalion of the West Mayo Brigade IRA . . . took over possession of the Barracks . . . The tricolour flag now floats over the building.' A month later the Mayo RIC left Castlebar jail and headed for Dublin.

Castlebar, having managed to escape turmoil and violence until then, was severely shaken in 1922. The feeling within the town was pro-Treaty but rural Mayo, where the brigades of the Irish Volunteers had fought hard and at great personal cost during the 1919–21 war, was vehemently opposed to compromise with Britain. Michael Collins, nationalist leader and signatory of the Anglo-Irish Treaty, attempted to address a crowd on the Green in Castlebar in April but the meeting had to be abandoned as armed hecklers made it impossible for him to be heard. The stormy meeting is still vividly remembered by older people in Castlebar.

Reports began to appear of attacks on Protestants. The Brownes of Breaffy House were ejected from their home for six weeks and left Castlebar for England. The newspaper denounced the 'indignity' placed on Dixon, the county engineer, whose windows were smashed and noted with approval that the Irish Republican Police took prompt action against those responsible. A week later the house of Dr Browne, son of the popular Judge Dodwell Browne of Rahins, and a good friend of the Gahans, was attacked. 'Dr Browne, who is a public benefactor,' read the newspaper report, 'is extremely popular in the Castlebar district and there is the utmost indignation that he should be subjected to this annoyance.' 'Here in Mayo', the editor remarked, 'the people even in the height of the Black and Tan terror, were not so alarmed or anxious for the future.'

Neither during the War of Independence nor during the Civil War, however, did the Gahans have any trouble or feel intimidated in any way. Townsend Gahan continued his work for the CDB unhindered. 'In those days all the bridges were blown up, we had to drive to Athlone to get any train, but whenever there was any sort of problem, they knew exactly where the CDB offices were and would get someone to go and mend everything so that my father was *never* at any time during that Civil War not able to go where he wanted to go.' Muriel put this down to the fact that 'he'd done such a marvellous job round the countryside and they all knew him so well and thought such a lot of him. He was never, never, never,' she insisted, 'in any way impeded from carrying on his work.'

In July 1922 the National or Free State forces 'delivered' Castlebar from the IRA or the 'bolshies' as they were known locally. For those who remained in the town, the night the 'bolshies' burnt down the gaol and the barracks before being driven from the town was one they remembered all their lives. Muriel did not remember it. Many people, including very possibly Muriel and her mother, had left for the seaside in the preceding weeks fearing an impending battle. Having been persuaded, after protracted discussion, not to blow the two buildings up, thus causing structural damage to the town, the IRA set the buildings alight instead and they 'went down in the Moloch of destruction', according to the next day's newspaper report. The IRA forces left the town and the Free Staters took over.

Life in Castlebar slowly got back to something like normality but it was a much quieter life for Muriel than what she had been used to since 1919. There were concerts and picture shows, fund-raising whist drives and the hockey club to which both she and her father belonged. In August 1923 her sister Grania finally married Naultie Sheridan though without her father's blessing. Muriel and Teddy travelled with the couple to England where they were married in the sacristy of St Raphael's Church in Kingston-on-Thames, since Roman Catholic rules did not then allow mixed marriages in the main body of the church. Neither of the Gahan parents attended the ceremony. In September 1924 Teddy married Vera Hay.

Gradually Castlebar was changing. Lord Lucan sold Castlebar House along with its grounds, known as The Lawn, to the Sisters of Mercy who planned to expand their convent and open a girls' boarding school there. Immediately there was consternation in the town because the nuns put a notice on the gates to the Lawn saying it was closed to the public. Lord Lucan had allowed it to be used as a park. In June 1924 the contents of Castlebar House were put to auction. The CDB had been dissolved in 1923 and its new functions divided between the Land Commission and the departments of fisheries and industry. The materials from its offices in Castlebar were sold. 'The new land act having obliterated the CDB,' the local newspaper announced, 'the Castlebar offices are to be discontinued. Most of the officials have left for Dublin, but we understand that the present arrangement is that Mr Gahan and his staff will continue'. He would remain in Castlebar and work for the Land Commission until his sixtieth year, 1926.

One by one the Protestant pillars of old Castlebar disappeared from public life. Lendrum, who had done so much for the town during his nineteen years as rector, not the least by collaborating closely with his Roman Catholic counterpart, his friend and ally Canon Lyons, had been promoted to the position of Dean of Tuam at the end of 1923. Dixon retired from his post of county engineer after thirty years' service just a month later. Larminie, Lord Lucan's agent, had already been fifty years in public office. The Fitzgeralds of Turlough House sold the contents of the house and moved to England.

Finally the Gahans' turn to leave came. The furniture and 'effects' of Maryland were sold at auction on 30 March 1926. Two months later Townsend Gahan was presented with a gold hunter watch by the Land Commission staff in a ceremony where he was praised for his record of 'fair dealing and consideration of the tenantry that any public official might well be proud of'', the *Connaught Telegraph* reported. 'Mr Gahan, who was visibly affected, spoke in feeling terms of his cordial relationship with the staff, and said he felt deeply the sundering of the ties a quarter of a century's association had cemented. In thanking his colleagues for their tribute, he referred to the happy associations he had formed in Castlebar and throughout the province generally, and said he felt some gratification in knowing that the staff and himself had been instrumental in planting hundreds of thousands of peasant proprietors on the soil and in healthy happy homes.'

Notes

1. *Seventy Years Young*, Memories of Elizabeth, Countess of Fingall, Dublin 1991 pp 397–399.

— 4 —

Benevolent Intelligence –
F G Townsend Gahan

'You'd always know a house your father built – it would have a lovely view.' Muriel Gahan often repeated with great pride this remark made to her by a man who had been rehoused by the CDB under Townsend Gahan's direction. In south west Mayo, where the last CDB houses were built as late as 1922, there are still people who remember him as 'a lovely man'. But he cannot take all the credit for giving people houses with views. With the total restructuring of land holding carried out by the CDB, the new houses tended to be built alone and on elevated sites, in stark contrast to the traditional *clachan* or village grouping of houses, often positioned in the shelter of a hollow. It is nevertheless true that Muriel's father cared deeply about the welfare of the people he was helping and probably paid extra attention to the location of houses. The way Muriel used to tell the story, however, spoke chapters about her admiration for him. In order to understand the extraordinary energy with which she launched into a project to help preserve the traditional crafts in 1929, and how that idea led to a further sixty years of commitment to the people of rural Ireland, one must take a closer look at her father's work with the Congested Districts Board. His influence on her was profound.

Arthur James Balfour, who was made Chief Secretary for Ireland in 1887 and who from 1902 to 1905 was British Tory prime minister, was responsible for setting up the Congested Districts Board. It was a scheme to tackle rural poverty and the enduring inequities of land ownership in Ireland while at the same time, it was hoped, defusing agrarian revolt. It came into being as a result of the Purchase of Land (Ireland) Act of 1891. This act set out a system for evaluating poverty in terms of an area's capacity for supporting the people living in it. It stated that when more than a fifth of the people of any given area had a per capita rateable value of less than thirty shillings, then that area should be designated a 'congested district' and given special treatment to alleviate conditions. After the necessary calculations had been made, the congested districts were found to include most of Connaught and part of counties Clare, Cork, Kerry and Donegal, the 'congestion' referring not to density of population but to the inadequacy of the land to support the people living on it. Mayo, Donegal, and Galway turned out to be the worst off.

Balfour was not a popular man and the CDB was seen by many Irish nationalists merely as a means of 'killing Home Rule by kindness' and stamping out the seeds of revolt sewn by the Land League. Others have since argued that urban poverty was in fact far worse than rural poverty in the Ireland of the 1880s and have suggested that by attacking rural poverty the British government was in fact taking a safe option. Had they tackled urban conditions in Ireland with the same verve they would have been opening themselves up to demands for a similar policy at home.[1] The fact of the matter is that twenty-five years before the Russian revolution, the State had intervened on a massive scale, submitting landlords to compulsory purchase of their lands and redistributing them to the landless poor.[2]

The Board's first aim was to improve rural living standards and conditions by increasing the size of smallholdings. It also set out to explore the possibilities of voluntary migration to better land, or even emigration. It planned to improve livestock and methods of cultivation and to aid and develop all sorts of local industry, including fishing. The CDB was very keen from the outset to distinguish itself from the many relief committees and similar enterprises that had succeeded each other without lasting effect throughout the second half of the nineteenth century. In its first report, published in 1892, it stated that it was 'constituted with a view to bringing about a gradual and lasting improvement in the poor districts of the west of Ireland and not for the immediate "relief" of exceptional distress.' Four committees were set up to deal with Land, Industries, Fisheries and Finance.

Over its thirty-two year life-span the CDB passed from initial optimism and enthusiasm for innumerable schemes to weariness and exasperation as much energy was absorbed in legal wrangles involved in the purchase, division and fair redistribution of land amongst tenants. Along the way it did a great deal of good work, bringing about enormous improvements in housing conditions[3], setting up local industry and providing practical training in skills for women and young people as well as putting huge energy and resources into developing a fishing industry along the western seaboard, perhaps its most controversial endeavour. In all, it bought up and redistributed over two million acres of land. Inevitably it was often the butt of satire and derision, on occasion being alluded to as 'one of our pier-building Boards'.[4] The creation of boards to tackle given problems, not unlike the creation of employment schemes today, had become a government reflex and public opinion, or rather tax-payers' opinion, tended to be sceptical when another one appeared. There was also the Victorian concern that distributing government money might be 'detrimental to (the) moral erectness and manly perseverance' of 'people too indolent to help themselves'.[5]

Whatever the political motivation or public perceptions, the CDB had some remarkable members, including its first secretary, later to be appointed to the Board, William L Micks, who was also Grania Gahan's godfather and the father of Muriel's school friend, Hetty Micks. The Micks and the Gahans remained lifelong friends. There were also such indefatigable social reformers as Horace Plunkett who founded the Irish Agricultural Organisation Society (IAOS) in 1894 for the promotion of co-operatives, and Father Denis O'Hara of Kiltimagh, Co. Mayo. The execution of the Board's decisions was – mercifully – in the hands *not* of politicians but of extremely dedicated and hard-working civil engineers.

Townsend Gahan was one such engineer. His career is perhaps best summed up in the words of W L Micks in his account of the Board's work, published in 1925.[6] There he wrote:

> The earliest appointment made to the outdoor staff when the Board began its work was Mr F G Townsend Gahan, Civil Engineer. He had acted with me in 1890–91 in connection with Relief works in Co. Donegal. His energy and efficiency then attracted much notice from Colonel Peacock and all with whom he worked; and, owing to his knowledge of his native County Donegal, he was employed first in making most of the 'base-line' reports in 1892 on districts in that county, and subsequently in the construction of piers and roads. At the same time he acted as General

Inspector in connection with all the operations of the Board in the County Donegal. Subsequently he was transferred to the County Mayo, where his time was occupied in connection with the Estates work of the Board and the designing and carrying out of various engineering operations. He was the first to be appointed a Senior Inspector, an office which he continued to hold until the dissolution of the Board in 1923, when he was transferred to the Land Commission. He was then the senior outdoor official in the Board's service; and from intimate official and personal knowledge of Mr Gahan for more than thirty years I consider that his intelligence, knowledge, independence of character and absolute trustworthiness make him one of the most valuable public officials in Ireland.

The first task before the CDB was to work out exactly what the problems were and in what order they should be tackled. It was Balfour himself who suggested the usefulness of base-line reports. 'While engaged in dealing with the distress last winter,' he wrote in a memorandum to the CDB in November 1891, 'I was furnished, through the kindness of Mr Micks, at that time Local Government Board Inspector in Co. Donegal, with a most interesting "budget" of an average family in different parts of the country.' Balfour suggested that the principle of such a minutely detailed report could be extended to every congested district in the form of base-line studies. The information thus collected would not only allow the Board to allocate resources equitably; it would also provide a yardstick against which to measure progress.

Six men were given an elaborate questionnaire on which to base their enquiries and then each was allotted a geographical area to research. The thirty-two headings (*see* Annexe I) show the scope and thoroughness of the survey and give an idea of the depth of knowledge Muriel Gahan's father would have possessed. He was to report on the southern divisions of his home county, Donegal. Most of the reports were finished by the end of 1892, but a few hung over until 1895 and 1896 and Tory Island was not covered (by Gahan) until February 1897. There were eighty-four reports in all.

The base-line reports provide us with a fascinating and detailed insight into how people lived in the 1890s. Gahan wrote up seventeen of the districts and his reports are particularly detailed and lovingly compiled. Indeed from the point of view of wealth of detail, Gahan's reports bear closest resemblance to the one 'model' report Micks himself wrote, dealing with The Rosses in Co. Donegal.[7] Reading Gahan's reports and contrasting them with some of those by other inspectors we can learn something about the man himself. George A Birmingham (alias Hannay) in his novel *Spanish Gold*, in which the CDB figures prominently as the target of gentle satire, speaks of the 'look of benevolent intelligence which is always to be found on the faces of men connected with the Government.'[8] Benevolent intelligence is exactly the quality which comes through Townsend Gahan's reports. Unlike some of the other inspectors, Gahan never uses a tone of superiority nor shows contempt for the people he visits and invariably looks for an explanation for behaviour patterns. In Glencolumcille, under the heading 'Character of the people for industry', for example, he writes: 'In this district the people are not, as a rule, industrious, and though one cannot but blame it as a fault, it is to a certain extent their misfortune, for, until lately, they had no interest to better themselves as they feared an addition to their rent in consequence, and even to the present day, though the fear of the rent being raised is a thing of the past, yet they have the same feeling over them still, and until they get some violent stirring up will remain so.' Commenting on the people of a district in north-west Mayo, another inspector states baldly, 'The people in this district are decidedly idle and lazy'.

In his base-line reports, Gahan repeatedly shows concern for the health and welfare of the people in the districts he visits. Tea is one of his hobbyhorses. 'The quantity of tea taken cannot but be injurious to the people and one may often see children of five or six years drinking tea strong enough for any adult.' He calculates that an average family must get through thirty-nine pounds of tea a year. In Glenties, 'tea is not "drawn" in the ordinary fashion, it is regularly boiled and is not considered good unless it is almost perfectly black.' The result, he says, are large numbers of people who suffer from stomach complaints and 'the dispensary is crowded every dispensary day.' Compounding the problem of too much strong tea is the fact that women are too often paid in kind for any goods they produce. 'It is on tea that the small dealers make their greatest profits, and it is tea principally they make the women take in exchange for their eggs or knitting.' In his report on Brockagh, where women knit and sell socks, his indignation returns: 'The rate of wages is very low, and the system of payment most objectionable, the work being always paid for in tea, sugar, tobacco etc., never in money, the value besides in many cases being only a nominal equivalent for the low wages. Although the price paid for socks is nominally 1s 6d, yet since that is generally taken in tea and always in goods, 1s 2d is about the actual money value, and not only that but very often women are almost forced to buy goods they do not want at all.' The same criticism of the exploitation of knitters crops up in Gweedore: 'The shopkeepers who distribute the yarn get a commission and are paid in cash for the stockings when returned, but they only pay the people (the knitters) in kind.' One exception is singled out for praise in Glenties, the centre of the Donegal knitting industry where the women 'all knit, down to the tiny children of five or six years of age; they knit in the fields, knit in the houses, knit as they walk along the roads – in fact, unless their hands are otherwise employed, they are always knitting.' Here McDevitts, a knitting firm set up to provide a livelihood after the Famine, 'pay cash always where others pay only in kind and at lower rates.'

Gahan describes clothing with a painter's eye for detail and colour, as this report about the people of the Rosguill area shows:

> Trousers and Sunday suits of the men are almost always bright. The vests, shirts and drawers etc are home-made flannel or tweed; the socks are knitted at home. The petticoats and vests worn by the women are home-made, and sometimes the dresses of the older women. The dresses of the younger women are almost invariably of bought stuffs, made either by themselves or by the local dressmakers. A dress is made up for from 3s 6d to 5s, and 3s for trimmings. Nearly all wear hats or bonnets which cost from 3s to 7s 6d according to the fancy of the wearer. The men and women are fond of bright colours, red and blue being the favourites. The women generally go bare-footed, except when going to market or to chapel, when the boots are carried in the hands until nearing the village or chapel, when they are put on, and taken off at the same place going home; women's boots cost 5s 6d; men's 9s 6d. Women's last three years with care; men's one year with one soling. The men wear two shirts generally, and in winter sometimes three; except when going anywhere, they do not, as a rule, wear coats. The Sunday shirt is always bought and is white or some fancy check or stripe; 3s or 3s 6d is generally paid for one of these shirts. The Sunday coat and trousers when

too bad for Sunday wear are used on weekdays. A good many, both men and women, obtain garments at a very low price from the itinerant clothes vendors, who attend the different fairs.[9]

We can feel from Townsend Gahan's accounts that he loves being with the people, watching them, listening to them. When after elaborate description of the interior of a cottage in Rosguill he adds of its inhabitants, 'they sit up late at night telling tales round the fire', we can imagine him sitting with them, a 'look of benevolent intelligence' on his face, and deriving as much pleasure from the experience as his daughter Muriel would many years later when she too travelled around the country.

Of course Muriel's travels first began as a small girl with her father. He would quite often allow the children to accompany him when he set off to visit projects in the far reaches of Co. Mayo. 'Of the many happy memories of those early days, standing out most clearly in my mind are the trips with our father on his official visits to out of the way places in the county's isolated and desolate countryside north of the Nephin mountains, stretching from the Belmullet, Erris district coast line in the north west to the Foxford area in the east. Our method of transport was always the same: for short distances, our own pony and trap, and on longer journeys Mr. Ainsworth's hired "outside car" with a tougher horse than our poor old Dolly. No feeling of cold because we were well wrapped up in our favourite Foxford rugs.'[10]

As they travelled along, Gahan would have talked to the children about the CDB's attempts to develop the crafts at the turn of the century. It was no easier at this time than when Muriel tried to revive them forty years on. 'The aiding and developing of spinning, weaving, knitting and other industrial handicrafts,' wrote Micks in his first annual report on the activities of the CDB in 1892, 'must be recognised, even after a little reflection, as being the most difficult duty entrusted to the Board.' What emerges from the base-line reports is that, with the possible exception of hand-knitted socks, the other local craft industries – homespun weaving, sprigging (embroidery on linen), lace-making, basket-weaving, and so on – were in decline in 1892, just as they were once more in 1929 when Muriel Gahan's personal crusade to save them began. Several phrases recur frequently in the inspectors' reports: 'There is not the same demand now as there used to be'; 'Hand-knitting, spinning and weaving are still carried out, but only for home use and by the passing generation'; 'The younger people generally don't approve of (the homespun flannel or tweed) and only those who cannot afford to buy cloth use it'; 'The trade has suffered a great deal from the machine-made work.' Such phrases were to become all too familiar to Muriel Gahan in the 1930s and 1940s.

Long before Muriel and her friends had the idea of opening The Country Shop in Dublin as a sales depot for craftworkers she would have learnt from her father of the many women who, like the founder of the Foxford Woollen Mills, Mother Morrogh-Bernard, did pioneering work to create employment in the traditional crafts and to provide an income for the people of the west of Ireland, especially the women. Philanthropy had flourished in nineteenth century Ireland as a response to dire poverty and conditions. The revival of the lace industry was the direct result of relief work at the time of the 1840s Famine. In the 1880s several remarkable women were trying to generate income for the poor by promoting the crafts and cottage industries.

The best known is no doubt Lady Aberdeen whose Irish Home Industries Association was set up in 1886 becoming the Irish Industries Association in 1892. She also founded the Women's National Health Association in 1909 in a crusade against tuberculosis, with particular focus on the health of mothers and their children. Her belief in the importance of the survival of handcrafts in an increasingly mechanised world was to be echoed many times by Muriel Gahan. 'We believe that although machinery has transformed the whole face of the country,' Lady Aberdeen wrote in 1893, 'yet there is still a place for the manufactures of the hand which machinery can never displace, and that the proper organisation and development of these is full of moral as well as material good to the country that possess them.'[11]

Many individual women worked alongside the local people they were trying to help without the backing of any wider structure, nor the aura of a grande dame like Lady Aberdeen. There was a Miss Sturge in Letterfrack, Co. Galway, an Englishwoman from Birmingham who had tried to get a basket-making factory going there in 1888. She planted willow beds and had a building erected to serve as the factory. Ill-health forced her to retire in 1897 but the CDB undertook to try to keep the factory going as a commercial concern. At Moneygold, Co. Sligo, Mrs Eccles had started home industry classes with a view to reviving tweed and linen weaving and embroidery. In 1881 a Miss Fitzgerald began to teach the women and girls of Valentia Island, Co. Kerry, to knit stockings, socks and jerseys. By 1892 up to eighty knitters were employed. Miss Fitzgerald providing the materials, paying fixed rates and finding a market for the goods produced, including a contract with a steamer company, the White Star Line.

One of the most ambitious and far-reaching ventures by a woman, and one which Muriel Gahan was to attempt to revive fifty years later, was Mrs Alice Hart's Donegal Industrial Fund. Mrs Hart had visited north-west Donegal after the 1879–83 famine. Appalled by the poverty and conditions she saw, Alice Hart studied the possibility of reviving the traditional local wool-related industries of weaving and knitting and then finding a market for the articles produced. She set up the Donegal Industrial Fund to finance classes in the Gweedore area and carried out experiments in vegetable dyeing with local Donegal plants. She also arranged for a Glenties weaver, Daniel Tighe, to travel to Harris in the Outer Hebrides of Scotland to learn about colour in homespuns and then share his knowledge on his return. By 1884 she had opened a shop in London as an outlet. Using shows and exhibitions to publicise her venture, she was not only successful in marketing Donegal tweeds and natural dye socks but soon extended her area of interest to the rest of Ireland and to wood carving and embroidery, introducing a new type which she called 'Kells Embroidery' (the patterns inspired by the Book of Kells and other illuminated Celtic manuscripts). By 1886 she was operating from Donegal House, a new larger shop in fashionable Wigmore Street, and in 1887 she succeeded in securing a government grant of £1000. 'Managed on sound economic principles, though philanthropic in aim, with all profits being devoted to the furtherance of technical teaching, Alice Hart's cottage industries were one of the great successes of the Irish Revival,' writes Paul Larmour in his exquisite book *The Arts and Crafts Movement in Ireland*.[12] Unfortunately where Donegal homespuns were concerned, the enterprise did not outlive Mrs Hart's return to England in 1896. Nevertheless in the 1930s when Muriel made her own efforts to keep the homespun tradition in northwest Donegal going, she found that Mrs Hart's legacy lived on in the beautiful colours produced by dyers Sophie Ferry and Nancy Ferry, for example, and in the designs of such weavers as Micky Sally Gallagher and Manus Ferry, all of Dunlewey.

Townsend Gahan's own contribution to the development of the traditional crafts was not insignificant. Gahan put his mind to the question while carrying out the base-line reports. Before it was taken up and expanded by Lady Aberdeen in 1894, it was Muriel's father in May 1892 who had first come up with the idea of establishing a tweed depot and quality control centre for webs of flannel and tweed at Ardara, Co. Donegal, where an important wool fair was held monthly. At that time there were an estimated 410 spinners and thirty-four weavers working in the area, but according to Gahan weavers would often rush their work to make the maximum amount of money and would produce bad cloth. His inspection and quality control scheme was adapted and expanded by Lady Aberdeen to include 'the establishment of a technical weaving school upon a small scale in the village of Ardara, so that weavers who visit Ardara on fair and market days might receive an object lesson as to the value of modern looms.'[13] This was the start of a significant development of the woollen industry in south Donegal ensuring that despite many ups and downs over the years the deeply rooted tradition of weaving has never been allowed to die. Muriel would later make her own contribution to its survival.

Notes

1. Lecture by Mary E Daly to the Merriman Summer School, 1994.
2. Talk by Dr Kevin Whelan at a symposium on the work of the CDB in Clare Island, July 1995.
3. Mary E Daly, Merriman Summer School 1994: 'By 1914, the Irish rural labourer was the best-housed in the United Kingdom.'
4. Birmingham, George A. *The Lighter Side of Irish Life*, T N Foulis, London, 1911, p 127.
5. Harris Stone, J. *Connemara and the Neighbouring Spots of Beauty and Interest*, London, 1906, p 62.
6. Micks, W L. *History of the Congested Districts Board*, Dublin, 1925, p 194.
7. ibid pp 241–258.
8. Birmingham, G A. *Spanish Gold*, London, 1911, p 4.
9. Report on Rosguill, 1 September 1892.
10. Letter from Muriel Gahan to Mary Mullin, 1983. The Foxford Woollen Mills had been established by Mother Morrogh-Bernard in 1892 and this, along with a less successful knitting factory at Ballaghadereen, also in Co. Mayo and also started by the Sisters of Charity, were two of the very first initiatives the CDB had supported. When the Gahans lived in Castlebar they visited Foxford frequently and Townsend Gahan remained a friend and admirer of Mother Morrogh-Bernard until her

death at the age of ninety in 1932.

11. Quoted by Paul Larmour in *The Arts and Crafts Movement in Ireland* from Ishbel Aberdeen, 'Ireland at the World Fair', *The North American Review*, 1893, pp 18–21.

12. Larmour, P. *The Arts & Crafts Movement in Ireland*, Friar's Bush Press, Belfast,1992, p 24.

13. From *Third Report of the CDB for Ireland*, 12 October 1894.

— 5 —

The Road to Ballycroy

Townsend Gahan's time in Castlebar came to an end with his retirement from the Land Commission in 1926. The Gahans moved to Dublin where Townsend began to do valuation work for the ESB, working on the preparation for the 1940 Poulaphouca hydro-electric scheme, which involved the reclamation of much land to create what we know today as the Blessington lakes, and on the Portarlington turf-fired power station.

Muriel and her parents moved into Rathmines once more, this time to 26 Leinster Road, one of several houses on the street owned by great-aunt Bertha Townsend. Muriel now twenty-nine was without employment other than chores about the house, which were minimal. 'I did darned all,' she confessed later in life, 'because my mother was very efficient and we always had a helpmeet of some kind.' She continued to live an enjoyable but idle life, learning to drive and keeping up her hockey with the Maids of the Mountains, a sister club to the Three Rock Rovers. She also joined a tennis club. Any money she needed was provided by her father. She travelled a lot, often staying with her old school friend, Livie Hughes, now settled at Annsgift, her husband's family farm in Fethard, Co. Tipperary, or visiting her sister Grania and other old friends in Mayo.

Even though Grania had gone to university and then trained for a career as a teacher, Muriel, who had no interest in studying, was not expected to find a job. There was no financial need for it. Travelling about and staying with friends was considered a suitable occupation. 'We girls of the Edwardian age used to spend a good deal of our time paying visits,' wrote Clara Vyvyan, an English writer, 'for when we had been "finished" at our respective schools we would return to a home life that was strangely empty; further book learning was not encouraged, yet we were not given any regular occupation. These parentally inflicted visits would in some cases lead to marriage, or at any rate to the formation of new friendships which, in their turn, might lead to marriage; more often they would just pass the time.'[1]

Unlike Clara Vyvyan's visits, however, much of Muriel's travelling involved outdoor activity. Although she was not particularly keen on fishing herself, many of the family's closest friends, including Livie's husband, Jack Hughes, and the Somerville-Large brothers Paddy and Becher were, like Muriel's father, near fanatics. They all saw a lot of each other and Muriel became increasingly attracted to Paddy. Several fishing trips a year to the west of Ireland would have been the norm and Muriel went along for the company and the fun. Sometimes a group of a dozen or more friends would combine camping and fishing. These were major expeditions by car involving several army-type tents, hefty camp beds, cooking utensils and full fishing gear. Men and women shared the cooking and washing up and slept out under the open sky when weather permitted.

Muriel must have been feeling less than totally fulfilled with this life of fun and leisure, however, because when, as she was cycling down Harcourt Street one day, she spotted two young women dressed in painters' overalls wheeling a cart loaded down with ladders and pots of paint, she did not hesitate for a moment in following them. She was no stranger to painting herself having had plenty of experience doing up the family's last house in Castlebar, but never until this instant had she thought of it as a potential job. The girls left their ladders and disappeared into a house. Muriel drew up alongside the handcart to examine the contents more closely and found a name and address painted on the side: *The Modern Decorator*, she read, *24 South Anne Street*. History does not relate the exact date of this providential discovery but it is most likely to have been sometime in 1927 since before then there is no trace of a firm called The Modern Decorator operating from that address.

When Muriel turned up at 24 South Anne Street the next day and announced to the 'very respectable-looking person' who opened the door that she would like to come and work with the company, she received a cool welcome. 'Oh, well,' came the reply, 'you'd have to *pay* if you're an apprentice.' Muriel explained that she had no money but that she did have decorating experience and would be prepared to come and work for nothing. In the end she was taken on and found herself in the most unusual and exciting decorating company, made up entirely of women. The boss, Miss Ivy Hutton, was a perfectionist and demanded very high standards of her team who worked hard and were increasingly in demand in the whole Dublin area. Before long, Muriel introduced two of her friends, Joan Stoker and Nora Ringwood, to work in the firm. The young women's job was not simply that of advising on interior decoration and then calling in painters to do the work, as one might imagine. Muriel and her co-workers in The Modern Decorator did everything: preparing and painting ceilings and walls, putting up wallpaper and stripping paint as well as working out colour schemes and mixing the paints. 'It was that training which was so good,' Muriel said later, 'because we had to mix all our own paints: you got a white paint and you mixed everything with it to get your other coloured paints. No question, like today, of buying your paints ready made.'

By early 1929 Muriel was already confidently introducing herself to people as 'a painter by trade'. Given the sequence of events which was to follow, one can be excused for believing that the hand of providence had been involved in crossing Muriel's path with that of The Modern Decorator: it was Muriel's skills as an interior decorator which were to lead her in the Spring of 1929 to Miss Lucy Franks, to the Society of United Irishwomen (UI) and to the RDS, and those meetings in turn determined a lifetime dedicated to the people of rural Ireland. The UI had been founded in 1910 out of Horace Plunkett's co-operative movement to give women a role in the social transformation of Ireland and in January 1929 a paragraph on the UI's page of the *Farmers' Gazette* expressed the hope 'that 1929 may bring in new members with enthusiasm for helping themselves and their districts, in organising centres for work, as well as for social and educational welfare.' The appeal went on, 'Women to lead are badly needed; women of wide understanding and vision, who know what country conditions are, and not what one would like to imagine them to be.'

A couple of months later Muriel's 'call' came. Livie Hughes wrote to her saying that the UI was to have a stand at the RDS Spring Show and Miss Lucy Franks, UI honorary secretary since 1928 and a cousin by marriage of Livie's, could do with some help getting it ready. It so happened that The Modern Decorator had added 'Painted Furniture' to its list of services that year and that was exactly the skill most urgently needed. Livie Hughes had joined the UI in 1928, helping to revive the Fethard branch which had been started in 1914, and she had instantly been engaged by the aims and principles of the society. Muriel on the other hand alleged never to have heard of it, and still less of Lucy Franks, until Livie's letter reached her. Towards the end of her life, Muriel, in one of her many tributes to Livie Hughes, said, 'Throughout my adult lifetime, every kind of thing has resulted from Livie Hughes getting in touch with me and saying, "I'm thinking of doing this", or "should we do that?"'[2] This was just the beginning.

Lucy Franks (affectionately referred to as 'Franksie' by her friends) is a key figure in the Irish countrywomen's movement and was responsible for its survival and revival after Irish independence. A niece of the famous socialist and feminist Charlotte Despard, she was twenty years older than Livie and Muriel and had been a member of the UI since 1917 when she had helped to found a branch in Castletown, Co. Laois. In 1923 the family home, Westfield House, in nearby Mountrath was burnt down. Lucy's father was an invalid in his late eighties and was only just removed from the house in time while her dog was killed in the fire. Her father died in October 1924 and some time later Lucy Franks left Ireland for a while, travelling first to South Africa where she stayed with some cousins and then to England. She returned home in September 1926 to find a very weak Society of United Irishwomen, only eight branches left and fewer than a hundred members.[3] The years of political upheaval had taken their toll and, as AE put it at the UI AGM in 1929, the Society had been 'rather like a small kitten in an arena full of infuriated elephants; it had nothing to do but lie low'.

But it was safe to come out now and Lucy Franks was immediately full of energy and ideas for injecting new life into the organisation and making it immediately *useful* to Irish women, her prime objective. She had learnt basket-making herself while in England and one of the first projects she set up was basket- and tray-making classes, encouraging UI members to sell what they made. By 1927 she had become a member of the RDS and was organising a stand at the Spring Show to sell the women's work. (Her brother, Harry Franks, who had rebuilt Westfield House, was a keen RDS supporter and was vice-president from 1925 until his death in 1942 and president from 1935 to 1938.) The stand was in the name of 'Countryside Workers', taking its title from an ambitious 'Country Side Exhibition' which the Reverend Peter Conefrey PP of Cloone, Co. Leitrim had held in 1920 and for a few years after. In 1920 Reverend Conefrey brought no fewer than sixty demonstrators to the RDS from Galway and Longford to show how flax and wool were prepared, spun and woven.[4] The RDS had a long tradition of supporting rural industry and traditional crafts going back to its foundation in 1731. A scientific interest in the development of industries, coupled with support for numerous philanthropic ventures in the nineteenth century, led it to stage regular competitions and shows. In this way not only was a market promoted for all sorts of crafts but the Society saw to it that standards were constantly monitored and improved through the encouragement of prizes and publicity.

At the 1928 Spring Show, 'the entire South Gallery was allotted for the Countryside Workers Exhibit which attracted so much attention that the promenade space was inadequate', according to an RDS report. There were daily demonstrations from 11 am to 6 pm and the 1928 programme read as follows:

> _United Irish Women's Society._ Established 1910, Sister Society to the IAOS, to encourage and establish Countryside Industries and Hand Work in the homes of the people. Exhibition of products.
>
> _The Slaney Weavers, Spinners and Mat Makers._ This industry was started by Mrs Harold Lett[5] in 1925 to give employment to girls in their own homes.
>
> _Basket Makers_ from Camolin, Co. Wexford; Gortlamon, Co. Clare; and Castletown, Laois.
>
> _Chairmaking and Seat Weaving_ by Camolin Workers.
>
> _Donegal Homespun Weaving_ by native Irish-speaking weavers.
>
> _Montessori School Children_ from Waterford Schools. The work the children and the two pioneer teachers will present will illustrate the development in Crafts, Art Design and Mathematics secured by the Montessori system of teaching.
>
> _Roebuck Industries._[6] Shell and Felt Flowers. Shells gathered by children from many different strands in Ireland – Kerry, Donegal, Wexford and Dublin – as well as shells from the Southern Seas. Flowers for Altar Decoration, Millinery, Table Decoration, Confirmation and Funeral Wreaths.

The Modern Decorator also had a stand, in an annexe to the Main Hall, advertising 'Interior Home Decoration, Furnished Room Cretonnes and Lamp Shades etc.'

In 1929 there was a record attendance at the Spring Show: 93,922 people came, an increase of 8,000 over the previous year.

This success was put down to the 'up to date methods of publicity adopted. In this direction the broadcast talks of the Director prior to the shows were an achievement of far-reaching consequences and undoubtedly responsible for the increased patronage accorded.' The Countryside Workers Exhibit in 1929, this time in the East Gallery of the Main Hall, was Lucy Franks' most ambitious so far. The programme read as follows:

> *United Irish Women Society.* The Society of United Irish Women, established 1910, in connection with the IAOS to promote co-operation among rural women for social and industrial betterment, and to revive rural craftsmanship.
> *Tipperary Basketmakers* – a Real Cottage Industry.
> *Longhill Knitters, Co. Limerick* – An Association of Workers in Machine Knitting.
> *Camolin Workers* – Chairmaking and Seat Weaving.
> *United Irish Women's Branches in Counties Sligo, Wexford and Clare* – Cane Basket Workers
> *Straw Mat Maker* – a Home Craft Worker from Tipperary.
> *Weaver and Spinner from Co. Kerry*
> Two Cottage Rooms – Furnishings by Amateur Craft Workers.

It was with this last exhibit that Muriel Gahan became involved. With only weeks to go before the Spring Show opened on 8 May, the cottage rooms – one of them a model kitchen – were far from ready. Time was running out, volunteers were thin on the ground and help was urgently needed. One evening after work Muriel rode along to the address Livie had given her, 19 Pembroke Road, where she was told she would find Miss Franks 'out the back', painting furniture. Lucy Franks, who was quite deaf but notorious for her selective use of this disability, understood at once why Muriel had come and thrust the paintbrush and pot of paint she was using into her hands saying simply: 'How wonderful!' Muriel took over painting a dresser.

The Spring Show itself was an eye-opener for Muriel. There she got to know people like Mainie Jellett, the modernist artist, no doubt also mobilised at the last minute by Livie Hughes, her first cousin, and put in charge, somewhat incongruously, of the model kitchen display. Mainie Jellett would continue to design stands and textiles for the UI in the future. Muriel was introduced to Vida Lentaigne, an active United Irishwoman who lived in the house at

Termonfechin, which twenty-five years on would become An Grianán. Mrs Lentaigne had organised a small glove-making industry there and encouraged basket-making too, planting willow beds to supply a local blind basket-maker. Josie Mangan, a 'poultry instructress' from Cork, came up to the stand and was instantly won over by the UI's aims. A year later she would open Cork's first branch, in Clonakilty. Later she was to be one of the main movers behind the creation of Country Markets. Muriel also met the traditional craftworkers from Kerry, Wexford and Tipperary who had been invited to Dublin to demonstrate. Their world, which she loved, was already familiar to her from her childhood. What was new and exciting was her encounter with the collective enthusiasm of the United Irishwomen.

After the 1929 Spring Show Muriel at once became a member of the UI and continued to help Lucy Franks, working with her in the temporary office used by the UI at the Employment Bureau for Women at 33 Molesworth Street in Dublin. She used to remember with amusement the first UI meetings she attended: 'I couldn't even get up to say "I beg to propose. . .", I'd be shivering with fright.' In the course of her work with Lucy Franks, which involved one-finger typing on a huge typewriter, the organisation of the 1930 Spring Show came up for discussion and it became clear that the Kerry weavers would not be able to return to demonstrate. It was now autumn and Muriel was planning a trip to Castlebar to stay with Grania. Lucy Franks asked her if, while she was in Mayo, she would try to find a weaver willing to demonstrate the weaving of homespun tweed (that is to say woollen cloth made entirely of handspun yarn, warp and weft, and woven in the weaver's own home) for the 1930 Spring Show.

The story of Muriel Gahan's search for a weaver is a much-told one. She loved to tell it herself – to her friends, to journalists, in ICA publications, at public functions. She was right to tell it too, because that search for a weaver and her eventual discovery of Patrick Madden in Ballycroy, Co. Mayo was what led directly to the idea of setting up a craft depot in Dublin to provide an outlet for isolated craftworkers. That in turn developed into the creation of The Country Shop, for years the nerve-centre for so much that was being achieved in the country, both for the crafts and for women. The weaver story is a good story and like all good stories it is worth the retelling. Here is how Muriel Gahan herself told it to her great-nephew, Peter, in 1986:

I started searching for homespun. I kept asking all the local people: 'Do you know any weavers? Have you got any weavers round here?' And they'd say, 'Oh, you mean Foxford!' And I'd say, 'No, I don't mean Foxford, I mean homespun.' I remembered when we were children in Castlebar, we used to walk along by Lord Lucan's house and all along by their yard, on the wall, were laid out lots of pieces of homespun. It was Lady Lucan who revived the industry in Mayo. Then one day I was in Westport, with another friend of ours, and she had on a lovely tweed skirt. And I said, 'Where did you get that skirt? That's a homespun skirt.' 'Oh, I bought it from a woman who came from Buckagh, the other side of Newport.' So that gave me the clue. So another day Grania and I started off in their nice little car, which Naultie had very kindly lent us. We drove off to find the weaver. When we got to Newport we asked for Buckagh and were told it was up the mountains, out this road, up that road, up towards the Nephin range. So we drove on and then we turned up the roads they told us to turn up. I asked somebody where the weaver lived and they said there's one up the hill there. So up we went. It was a lovely day and the woman came to the door and there was a big loom straight facing us from the door and so I said, 'I hear the husband is a weaver. . .' 'Oh,' she said, 'yes he is, indeed he is.' And then I saw the husband rushing away to hide behind his loom. 'Will you come in?' said she.

From childhood days visiting cottages around Mayo with her father, Muriel had developed the reflex of looking straight up to the rafters as soon as she entered a house to seek out the straw St Brigid's crosses which more often than not adorned the base of the thatch, going from the oldest and most blackened to the brightest and newest which was still nailed directly over the door since the last St Brigid's Day, 1 February. Here in the first weaver's house in Buckagh, there were no St Brigid's crosses but Muriel's eye immediately spotted something up in the roof that interested her even more.

There was a lovely roll of bright scarlet frieze, the heavy wool, so I knew there was something going in that house. I saw himself just then. 'Do you think he'd ever come to Dublin to weave at the Spring Show?' 'Would you go to

Dublin, John?' He came out. 'Go to Dublin? Is it go to Dublin? What would I go to Dublin for?' 'Well,' I said, 'we'd love it if you'd come and weave up there.' 'Weave up in Dublin?' he said, 'Sure I've never been beyond this place, what would I go to Dublin for?' 'Well,' I said, 'maybe you'd know another chap, another weaver round about who might come to Dublin?'

So off Muriel set, a beautiful roll of scarlet frieze bought from John Murray under her arm, but no agreement on the Dublin question. On she went to a near neighbour, Edward Mulchrone:

A very nice woman with her hair down her back, the way all the country women wore it in those days, came to the door. 'I hear himself is a great weaver,' I said, 'would he come to Dublin, I wonder?' 'He's out there weaving in the shed, won't you come out to see him?' replied Mrs. Mulchrone. So we went out to the shed and there he was, weaving away. 'This lady wants to know would you go to Dublin?' 'Go to Dublin is it?' he said, 'Oh, sure I couldn't go to Dublin!' 'Well,' I said, 'would you have a length of frieze or flannel or anything?' From him I got a lovely web of plain grey flannel. Anyway Mrs Mulchrone was a terribly nice woman and she said, 'Will you come in? Will you have a cup of tea?' So in we went into her little house and we were sitting down and there was a little tiny window the side I was on, looking out at Nephin mountain and every time I think of that little house I think of that view of the mountain we used to climb when we were kids. She gave us a lovely cup of tea and something to eat too, potato cakes or something, which she cooked for us on the fire.

Edward Mulchrone's daughter Rose, now Mrs Rose Murray (her late husband was distantly related to the first weaver) was a small girl that autumn of 1929, but she remembers well the visit of the 'very down to earth' Miss Gahan from Dublin. Rose was the youngest of seven children, two of whom had already gone to America and two to England. She would always help her father set up his loom, handing the threads through the heddles. She would also be sent out with an old wooden spoon or a knife to scrape the 'moss', a lichen, off the rocks to make dye. As well as blankets and tweed for suits, her father used to weave flannel for underclothes

Six-year-old Muriel stars as Bo-Peep in a family production at Creagh. *Left to right:* Little brother Mac, Muriel, Teddy, Grania and visiting cousin Nell Jones.

Castlebar, 1904. Muriel and Teddy looking wild while a more sedate Grania holds the dog and Winifred Gahan restrains baby Mac.

Tennis and croquet at Maryland in 1922.

Maryland, 1922. Muriel with Prid, the man she did not marry.

Kingston-on-Thames, August 1923. Grania marries Naultie without her father's blessing. Muriel was bridesmaid, Charlie Allen was best man and Teddy gave the bride away. *Left to right:* Muriel, Teddy, Grania, Naultie and Charlie.

Townsend and Winifred Gahan with the cat sitting in front. Standing behind: Grania, Naultie, Vera, Teddy and Muriel, *c.* 1925.

1927. Camping at Lough Mask. Muriel does her washing while the menfolk fish.

1929. Lisheen was the place, November the month, when Muriel and her friends decided to set up a sales depot in Dublin where isolated craftworkers could market their goods. *Left to right:* Paddy Somerville-Large, Livie Hughes, Jack Hughes, Muriel Gahan and Becher Somerville-Large.

Lucy Franks poses proudly in front of an array of traditional crafts brought together for the 'Countryside Workers' stand in the late 1920s.

Long before Lucy Franks' time, the RDS promoted home industries. Here are four of the sixty wool workers brought to the 1920 Spring Show to demonstrate the production of linen and woollen cloth.

1930. Seventeen-year-old Nenagh basketmaker, Patrick O'Connor, and his father demonstrate their craft in Dublin.

A thatched cottage became the street sign for The Country Shop and was a familiar sight hanging outside 23 St Stephen's Green.

The Country Shop

DEPOT FOR IRISH COUNTRY
INDUSTRIES.
Work done by U.I. Branches.

LIGHT LUNCHEONS AND TEAS.
Fresh Honey—Home-made Jams.
Pickles and Bottled Fruit.

CLUB—Reading and Writing Rooms.
Parcel Room for Use of Country Members.

Annual Subscription, One Guinea.

Applications to The Secretary,
THE COUNTRY SHOP,
23 STEPHEN'S GREEN, DUBLIN.

The Farmers' Gazette was a vital medium of communication for the United Irishwomen, later known as the ICA. It was an excellent place to advertise the newly opened Country Shop.

Muriel used every inch of The Country Shop to show the best of Irish crafts. The ultra modern had its place too. Stacking stools by Alvar Aalto line the walls under sketches of traditional craftworkers by Elizabeth Rivers.

and white flannel for quilts which would be dyed after it was woven. Rose remembers being disappointed that her father turned down the invitation to travel to Dublin since she would have gone with him to help, but she says his reasons were very sound. Already in his sixties, he was worried about how his loom – his source of livelihood – would survive the experience. It would need to be dismantled and reconstructed twice and the living he made as a weaver was precarious enough as it was without running the risk of losing it altogether because of a broken loom. He was a well-educated man who had worked in England before he married and it was not timidity that stopped him from going, as Muriel's telling of the tale sometimes implied.

Muriel and her sister left the Mulchrones with the a web of plain grey flannel and from there they were directed to a Mr Mulgrew on the Mulranny road:

> When we got to Mr Mulgrew's he was there standing at the top of the steps up from the road to his little house. I called up to him the same question I had asked the others, but the answer was the same too. Then I said, 'Have you anything at all. . .have you any frieze or any flannel in the house at all?' His weaving was beautiful, it wasn't the plain weave, it was these crooked grains going this way and that way and it was a mixture of the grey and the crottle brown. The very dark colours they dyed from the bog 'mud'[7], the browny colours they got from the lichen off the rocks[8] and the scarlet, of course, was most likely not a natural dye. Then the wife would walk to the town, about fifteen miles, to sell her frieze or her tweed.

It was Mr Mulgrew (in another version of the story described as a patriarch with a flowing white beard) who directed Muriel to Patrick Madden:

> 'There's a young fella now beyond in Ballycroy, maybe he'd go to Dublin. . .' By this time it was too late for us to go on anywhere else. But another day, we started out to go right across beyond Mulranny and we went to a pub in Ballycroy and we said 'Do you know Mr Patrick Madden the weaver?' They did, of course, and we were directed back along the road we had just come along and down towards the sea. I can always remember the lovely view from there, it was

Croagh Patrick, the other side of Clew Bay and the beautiful waters of Clew Bay down in front of us. It was, again, a lovely sunny day. So back we went and then down by the sea road, this tiny little road. . .

Thus are legends built. It was, of course, Slievemore on Achill Island, not Croagh Patrick that Muriel could see to the west of Ballycroy, across, not Clew Bay, but the narrow channel separating the Island from the mainland, the tail-end of Blacksod Bay. The weather has improved with time, too. When Muriel wrote an article for the *Christian Science Monitor* in 1933, just four years after her first meeting with Patrick Madden, she began thus: "In Mayo again, further west, on a day of driving rain and mist . . ." But let the story continue:

There was no sign of a house in the bog at all and suddenly there was a plume of smoke coming out, out of the bog it looked to me. We got out of the car and we walked down this little muddy boreen and there at the bottom, sunk down, was this tiny little house. The water was streaming down the walls, the thatch looked as if it had never been rendered for years on end and there was a great cow lumbering around the yard with its bones sticking out. The yard was full of stones. And then this rather wild-looking, tall man suddenly appeared at the door. 'Are you Patrick Madden, the weaver?' I asked. 'I am', he said, 'won't you come in?' So we went in the door and there was this huge loom buried deep in the floor, I can still see the great thick sides to it, and opposite was a bright light burning. And he'd just put turf on the fire which was why we had suddenly seen the smoke. So he said, 'Will you come and sit by the fire?'. So we sat by the fire and I started – by this time I was getting a bit exhausted – 'Would you ever come to Dublin to weave for the Spring Show next year?' 'I would!' he said. 'And what will you do for a loom?' I asked because I knew he wouldn't get the loom out of the house. 'I'll make a loom!' There was *nothing* I asked Patrick Madden that he couldn't do. And as we were going out the door, he pointed at the red light I had seen. 'You know', he said, 'I have that light burning to St Anthony, the poor man's friend, and it was he sent you here today.'

That was the beginning of a long and fruitful friendship between Patrick Madden and Muriel Gahan which lasted until his death in 1968. Even before Madden came to Dublin with his new loom to demonstrate at the Spring Show in May 1930, he was writing long letters to Muriel about the state of the homespun industry, the quality of yarn, the drawbacks of home dyeing and a host of technical questions to do with weaving (*see* Annexe II). As Muriel wrote in 1933, 'the fire of a Zealot burned in his eye, and he had visions of all Ireland being carpeted in his rugs.' After her visit he crossed out Drumslide, the name of his townland, on his headed notepaper and wrote in St Anthony's Place instead, later having the new name printed in purple ink on the letterhead. So struck was he by Muriel's understanding of his craft and her encouragement of him that in one letter he even asked her to marry him. Patrick Madden came of a long line of weavers and the loom which Muriel had seen embedded in the floor of the Ballycroy house had been built there by his grandfather. Madden was highly skilled, articulate and like Muriel he had a strong personality. A fellow craftsman once described him as an 'angular' person to deal with. He was a well-established weaver who sold to wealthy tourists and also received orders directly from England. He told his son, Michael Madden, also a weaver, that in his father's time buyers used to come to Ballycroy from the Queen of England. Tweeds would be shipped out to the Queen's Regiment and the Royal Family.

It was above all the contrast between the quality of the man and his skill on the one hand and the conditions in which he was obliged to live on the other that angered Muriel and fired her determination to do something to restore to craftworkers the dignity their social function deserved. The story of the search for Patrick Madden is emblematic of Muriel's whole life's work, involving as it did intrepidness, love of adventure, recognition of skills and a great deal of determination. Childhood training in the company of her father had come into its own.

Notes

1. Vyvyan, C C. *On Timeless Shores*, Peter Owen Ltd, London, 1957, p 9.
2. From 'Heroes and Heroines', a radio interview of Dr Muriel Gahan by John Quinn, RTE Radio 1, 21 July 1988.
3. From Lucy Franks' speech at the 1952 AGM of the ICA as reported in the *Farmers' Gazette* 29 March 1952.
4. Meenan J and Clarke D (eds). *The Royal Dublin Society 1731–1981*, Gill and Macmillan, Dublin, 1981.

5. Mrs Harold Lett, Vice-President of the Wexford Farmers Union, founded the first branch of the Society of United Irishwomen at Bree, Wexford in 1910.

6. Roebuck Industries was set up in 1924 by Maud Gonne MacBride and Charlotte Despard in Roebuck House, Clonskeagh, Dublin as a means of raising money for destitute republicans and providing some employment. Charlotte Despard was in charge of a jam-making venture while Maud Gonne ran the shell-making part, 'making intricate ornaments of varying size from sea shells', closer to 'art deco designs than the gruesome seaside souvenirs which one might have imagined.' see Ward M. *Maud Gonne: a life* , Pandora, London, 1990, p 143.

7. The bog 'mud' or 'ink' was a white, putty-like substance which was found in seams or veins in the bog and when boiled up with dark coloured wool would produce the colour black, much in demand for older women's clothes in particular. The wool had first to be 'barked', ie dyed a dark brown with imported chip wood or the root of the water lily. From author's conversations with Mrs Bessie Morrison, spinner, Co. Mayo.

8. Lichen dyes: '*Parmelia omphalodes*, the crottle for dyeing in Co. Donegal, for a tan brown colour. *Parmelia saxatilis* grows near the sea on rocks in Connemara. Used by the countrywomen for a brown colour.' From Mitchell, L. *Irish Spinning, Dyeing and Weaving*, Dundalgan Press, Dundalk, 1978, p 22. In Mayo and Connemara it is known as 'the moss'.

— 6 —

'Why Not Serve Lunches
and Teas as Well?'

With four rolls of cloth in the back of the Sheridans' car (Patrick Madden had sold her some natural grey homespun) Muriel and Grania drove back to Castlebar. The following weekend Muriel joined her friends, Livie and Jack, Paddy and Becher Somerville-Large at Lisheen, the cottage which they, along with Muriel and her father, had had built on the shores of Lough Corrib. It was one of those mild Novembers, soft and still, the autumn colours stunning; this time it was the shooting that had brought the men there. Muriel could contain neither her excitement nor her indignation as she showed her friends the beautiful webs of tweed and told them of the hard time the weavers were having marketing their goods. Soon they were discussing the idea of setting up some sort of depot in Dublin where real homespun could be sent from the country and then sold on by Dublin-based people like the Gahans or Paddy Somerville-Large. Immediately Muriel wrote to Lucy Franks not only to tell her that she had found a weaver for the 1930 Spring Show, but also to share the new idea of a depot in Dublin. Lucy Franks replied 'Why not sell lunches and teas as well?' This apparently throwaway remark was to prove the key to The Country Shop's future success. When Lucy Franks died in 1964 Muriel acknowledged the fact that 'over the years we have more and more realised that it is only because of the restaurant that we are able to carry out the purposes for which we founded the company.'[1]

Muriel lost no time when she got back to Dublin. She handed in her notice at The Modern Decorator and set about looking for suitable premises to rent. Because of the idea of turning the depot into a restaurant as well, Muriel's searches centred round the Dawson Street area where she remembered a small restaurant called The Sod of Turf existing some years before, with creels of turf outside the door. There were already a number of small eating houses in the vicinity and several craft outlets.

By the end of January 1930 Muriel had spotted the basement of 23 St Stephen's Green, a handsome Georgian house built in the 1790s between the top of Dawson Street and the fashionable Shelbourne Hotel. The rent was to be £60 a year. It took a lot of imagination and plenty of Gahan optimism to envisage opening a restaurant there but then her friend Joan Stoker had already nicknamed her 'The Botch Queen' because she revelled in rescuing extreme situations. When Muriel visited the basement for the first time it was dark and dank, not having been used for years. Traces of former occupants were strewn around the dusty, stone-floored rooms. 'It was desperate,' she remembered, 'littered with inkpots. As we went on a bit further, right down to the back which was later our kitchen there were . . . bodies!' These turned out to be tailor's dummies, left behind by Joseph Cavenagh, a gentleman's tailor who had owned the building at the beginning of the century. As recently as 1924 Cooper, Dennison and Walkden Ltd, ink manufacturers, had occupied space there too. 'The whole place was so neglected and desolate as to fill one with that elation which the prospect of any desperate venture evokes', she told an American reporter from the safe distance of the 1960s.[2]

At the time there was more desperation than elation. One reason for this was Muriel's relationship with Paddy Somerville-Large. She had with time grown deeply in love with him and much of her pleasure at the proposed restaurant and craft depot was being involved in them with him. But as the project began to take shape it became clear that Paddy did not reciprocate her feelings and in February 1930 Livie Hughes noted in her diary: 'MG very miserable about basement, P T S-L etc.' It was a very painful time for Muriel since she had entered into the adventure with the hope of having more than a business partnership with him. Still she did not abandon the project. Giving up was not in her nature. Instead she threw herself even more energetically into the conversion of the basement and sheer hard work carried her through the crisis.

There was also the Spring Show to cheer her up, with Patrick Madden contributing to the success of the UI exhibition. 'The Countryside Workers Exhibit on the Gallery of the Main Hall was well patronised and visitors were much impressed by the demonstrations given in basket and rush work and the making of cane furniture, toys, and hand woven tweeds, by native labour, thereby demonstrating what is possible in stimulating an interest in small cottage industries.' When Muriel met Patrick Madden in 1929 he was already weaving 'floor rugs of great beauty and original design out of homespun wool which he dyed himself', but she nevertheless took him to see Miss Emily Wynne in Avoca[3] while he was in Dublin so that he might find further stimulation for his naturally strong sense of design. Muriel had an unfailing instinct for the saleable and knew that with the right encouragement Madden's rugs would become highly popular.

Later in life, when the more difficult moments had faded in her mind, Muriel would remember those months preparing the basement of 23 St Stephen's Green as pure adventure: 'It was just a kitchen when we went in to it, with its old stone floor. We had to put in new steps from the street and turned the first part into our "Cottage". We did it up and we enjoyed ourselves enormously painting everything: the walls, and the floor and our tables and chairs. I was going to paint them all green and then one day we had a red chair out and so we decided we'd have a mixture of red and green. We only had that whole bottom floor, we had nothing further, we had no stairs upstairs as we had in later days.' The question arose of what to call the depot-cum-restaurant. 'When we started we thought we'd call it The Thatch, because it had been The Sod of Turf that had brought me along the Green. But dear Joan (Stoker) had a desperate lisp, she couldn't say "thatch", all she could say was "tatch". When we were working at the painting she would always go home for lunch – her father was a dentist in Westland Row – but I stayed and had lunch on the spot. So while I was sitting there having my lunch and brooding over the name I suddenly found myself writing T-h-e C-o-u-n-t-r-y S-h-o-p. When Joan came back I told her and that was that.'

It soon became apparent that they must form a limited company if they were to proceed with the business and in May negotiations started with the solicitors. After much to-ing and fro-ing, during which time Muriel got cold feet and began to balk at the prospect of becoming managing director of the fledgling company, Country Workers Limited was incorporated on 16 October 1930, the name inspired by Lucy Franks' and Vida Lentaigne's Countryside Workers Exhibits at the 1928, 1929 and 1930 Spring Shows. Muriel had accepted the role of managing director.

The opening of The Country Shop was set for Monday, 1 December 1930 and preparations went ahead feverishly. With the paint barely dry on the last chairs, there was a party for family, friends and well-wishers on the preceding Saturday. This was organised by Winifred Letts, author of the poem, 'The Weatherglass at Marylands', about the Gahans and their irrepressible optimism. 'Then, on the Monday, we opened. We'd had a cook in and she'd put in a lot of eggs, preserved in waterglass the way we did in those days. We also had plenty of jam. On the Monday we had lunch on, at 1/6d, and the friends poured in and, after lunch, there was nothing left, not a thing for tea.' An emergency consultation with the cook was held. 'I knew we had eggs and I knew we had jam so I said to our cook, we can make potato cakes and they can have scrambled eggs if they like and they can have tea and they can have jam of course and we'll call it The Country Tea – and that's how our Country Tea started.' It was to remain one of the great attractions of The Country Shop until it closed in 1978.

In those very early days, Muriel looked after people as they came into The Country Shop, in the part called The Cottage where she had on sale a small selection of crafts: the homespuns she had collected; handwoven, vegetable-dyed tweeds from Avoca; a lot of baskets (both rod baskets and rushwork) and some iron work. As managing director, Muriel's starting salary was 30/- a week, the same as the cook's. Joan Stoker (before long to be made cashier) and Nora Ringwood looked after the restaurant part, the cook cooked, a helper helped her and a young lad who had been employed as a painter's boy in the decoration phase was kept on to do the washing up. When it closed The Country Shop would have a staff of fifty, serving 700 meals a day. Still it didn't get off to a bad start. By 8 December 1930, after just one week in operation, Livie Hughes noted: 'Charmed with The Country Shop. So far great success.'

The aims of Country Workers Ltd, unchanged until 1967[4], were set out at the first company meeting held on Thursday 11 December 1930. Those present were 'Mrs Lentaigne and Mrs Hughes, directors, Miss Franks and Miss Gahan.' Muriel was appointed secretary, a position she held, in addition to that of managing director, until September 1959. Lucy Franks, Paddy Somerville-Large and Muriel all became directors. Vida Lentaigne resigned in 1933, but Lucy Franks remained a director until she died in 1964 and Muriel and Livie were still in place when

Country Workers Ltd was wound up in 1978. Paddy Somerville-Large, who married Grace Orpen in 1933, ceded his position as director to her in 1938, but retained a place on the Board of the company as a shareholder. The objects of the company were to be as follows:

> 1. To help the people in the poor districts in the west by encouraging and supporting home industries such as hand spinning, weaving and knitting.
> 2. To encourage individual craftworkers such as smiths and carpenters in the country, and all other country industries and country products.
> 3. To promote and assist the work of the United Irishwomen in the country.

Several points emerge from these rather vague and simplistic aims. Firstly, priority is given to 'the west', Muriel Gahan's home region, over the rest of the country and within the west to woollen-related crafts, these also being what Muriel was most familiar with at this stage. There is also a strong overall emphasis on 'the country' which was to make The Country Shop a unique embassy in Dublin for isolated rural communities and individuals. This might at first appear a statement of the obvious, since creating an outlet for country crafts had after all been the whole point of establishing the depot and shop in the first place. But had not the founders' commitment to rural Ireland been so strong, it might easily (especially given those founders' social background) have become nothing more than a fashionable place for Dublin's middle class to pick up quaint furnishings for their houses or lengths of homespun tweed to take to their dressmakers and have made up into conversation-piece clothes. There were plenty of places already operating in Dublin which offered just this version of 'the country' to city-dwellers. From the Misses Reid, at 19 Clare Street, for example, one could buy 'beautiful work by Peasants, including Hand-made & Embroidered Robes, Shawls and Underclothing, in Silk, Crepe de Chine, Cashmere, Linen etc.' The novelty of The Country Shop was not that it was Ireland's first craft shop – it wasn't – but that it existed primarily for its suppliers, not its customers, and that as a non-profit company in true co-operative spirit it redistributed money to the country craftworkers as well as to its restaurant staff.

The premises at 23 St Stephen's Green, which housed not only

The Country Shop but also the Irish Homespun Society (from its inception in 1935 until 1965) as well as the ICA (from 1937 until 1964) and later Country Markets Ltd (from 1946 until 1975), with *all* of which bodies Muriel Gahan's work was so inextricably involved, soon became a sort of commando headquarters, a centre of operations for rural Ireland. This priority was fiercely guarded. Once, Muriel herself was suspected of putting Dublin first and the reprimand was not long in coming. Livie Hughes rapped the table sharply during a Country Workers directors' meeting in 1941 as suggestions made by Muriel for alleviating distress caused in Dublin by the war were being discussed. Muriel had brought three worthy schemes to the other directors' attention but 'Mrs Hughes wished it to be noted in the minutes that Country Workers was a company to help country districts, and she would support any scheme for the town only on the understanding that some corresponding efforts were being made in the country.' By the next meeting, held two weeks later, Muriel had come up with an ingenious compromise which unfortunately did not meet with approval. 'A special meeting held to discuss question of mobile canteen. It was agreed that Miss Gahan's idea was not practical of lending the caravan to the St John's Ambulance Brigade for the Emergency, and then giving it to the ICA. It was decided that nothing further should be done at the moment.'

In her contribution to the third Triennial Conference of the Associated Countrywomen of the World[5] (ACWW) which she attended in Washington in 1936, Lucy Franks spoke of the newly renamed United Irishwomen, since 1935 known as the Irish Countrywomen's Association (ICA)[6]: 'The young society has done well in its first year. It has been sponsored by a group of godmothers in Dublin who have formed themselves into Town Associates. Their functions are to organise a summer school; to arrange for hospitality for country members coming to Dublin for meetings or the Spring Show; to keep the country guilds in touch with good designs; to shop for them; to raise funds for the Association and to keep their needs before the public.'

In their infancies, Country Workers and the Dublin Town Associates of the ICA shared many of the functions listed by Lucy Franks. It was no coincidence that Muriel was the chief engineer of both. And 'godmothers' is certainly a good way of describing the first directors of Country Workers Ltd. Of the five original directors of The Country Shop, Paddy Somerville-Large, the only man, was more of a godfather anyway, supplying as he did the vital capital to get the business going.[7] But whatever about personal relationships, he shared Muriel's, Livie's and Lucy Franks' commitment to improving Irish society and had a lifelong involvement with the unemployed through the Mount Street Club. It was thanks to him too that four of the ICA's staunchest early members joined the Dublin Town Association. After his marriage to Grace Orpen, her three sisters – Cerise (Parker), Kathleen (Delap) and Bea (Trench) – were soon, like Grace, fully committed to the Association's work.

Country Workers' early concentration on the *west* of Ireland can be explained in part by another remark Lucy Franks made in her 1936 address to the ACWW conference. Speaking of The Country Shop's contribution to Irish country women she said: 'All Irish country crafts come within the scope of The Country Shop, not only those of the ICA, for there are many parts of Ireland, such as Donegal, Connemara and Kerry, where it would be a great practical impossibility to organise countrywomen's guilds.' Without the benefit of local ICA structures, it is implied, the craftworkers in the west were most urgently in need of support.

With our double-glazed mentality it is hard for most of us to imagine what life was like in rural areas of Ireland in the 1920s and 1930s, especially in the more remote parts of the west. Not that everything was rosy and rich in Dublin in 1930. Far from it. After all this was the Dublin of Behan's childhood and O'Casey's plays. A 1938 survey found that 68,000 of Dublin's poor were living in inhumane conditions.[8] But today as we blast westwards along EU-funded highways or take a six-minute hop by air to the Aran Islands, staying at our destinations in warm and tastefully decorated B&Bs often boasting 'en-suite facilities', we should perhaps pause to exercise our imaginations. To conjure up the countryside that Muriel began to visit in 1929 when she carried out her epic search for weavers in Mayo, or the Connemara she scoured for homespun in 1930, or again what she saw in the summer of 1931 when she and Livie Hughes set off for the Aran Islands for the first time, we must begin with some simple arithmetic: take life as we know it today and subtract the following: tarred roads, street lighting, running water, electricity and telephones in the home, entertainment at the push of a button or twist of a knob, supermarkets, instant food, disposable nappies. . . the list goes on. One must then translate those external conditions into individual lives: women up before dawn to haul water from the pump or well, working by poor light in the evenings, their life an endless grind of cooking, washing clothes and battling to get them dry. Farmers on the road at two in the morning to drive their cattle to the nearest market town on fair day, and driving the animals home again in the evening if they were not sold. It was a life of ceaseless drudgery from which there was no way out short of emigration.

None of the founders of Country Workers had any romantic ideas about rural Ireland. Muriel and Livie, whose future roles were to be so dominant, were both aware of how harsh life was in the country. They also saw in urban areas that life was moving on, becoming increasingly mechanised, and that the demand for craftworkers' goods was diminishing. They recognised that with the death of the traditional crafts a whole way of life in the country was threatened. More pressingly, they saw poverty and an untapped source of extra income in the shape of crafts. They saw that only new markets for the crafts would sustain their makers' livelihoods. Their attitude to the crafts was and remained pragmatic, if different in emphasis. Livie, inspired by Lucy Franks, was most interested in any craft new or old that women and young people in the country could turn their hands to. Muriel cared passionately about the traditional crafts and their makers. But tradition did not mean standing still and even less harking back to so-called better days. 'Tradition,' Muriel believed, 'is not just resting on the past, but is ever starting afresh and moving onwards.' It was no mere chance, for example, that one of Muriel's hobby-horses throughout her life was improving standards and design.

Proof of both women's pragmatism was their enthusiasm for the two 'new' crafts developed by the UI for its members in the 1920s and 1930s. These were rush work, introduced by Livie after she had seen a rush basket for sale in a Belfast shop, and lumra – from *lomra* the Irish word for a fleece – a method of making rugs, cushion covers and tea-cosies from carded but unspun wool. This craft grew up in New Zealand during a slump in wool prices and was introduced to Ireland in the early 1930s. Both techniques were simple to learn. The raw materials for these two crafts – rushes and wool – were readily available and free. The wool for lumra work was at first collected from hedges and hawthorn bushes, not bought; the rushes were in the rivers for the taking.

Above all, rushwork baskets and lumra rugs *sold* well. 'It is important that we should consider in what way the handcrafts should be approached to make them worthwhile', Muriel once said in a lecture. 'Two things are sure, they must be linked with the countryside, and they must have quality. But,' she went on, 'the economic value of handcrafts has been recognised from famine days: self-sufficiency, the making of clothing, of household or farm implements which otherwise must be done without, or the making of goods for sale. As an old Mayo spinner said to me one day, "There's more in it for me out of a web of frieze than out of a bullock." This economic value is of first importance to us in Ireland where so many of our holdings are uneconomic or bordering on it, and the struggle with circumstances strangles all other considerations.'9

What also struck Muriel and angered her from the very beginning of her work in the crafts was the low esteem craftsmen were held in by people in general, and their resultingly low self esteem. Today, thanks to the efforts of the Crafts Council of Ireland (another brainchild of Muriel's) and the department of industry and commerce, craftworkers are given a high profile and seen as cultural ambassadors abroad, their annual (collective) sales reaching many millions of pounds. In 1930 the picture was very different. 'The sad part was that nobody took the slightest interest in them, with the result that they took no interest in themselves. They didn't realise that they were doing something very valuable. People looked down on people who worked with their hands. All that mattered was if you were a priest, or if you were a poet, or if you had a job in an office, but never, never, never if you were turning out the most beautiful crafts. Whether they'd be basketmakers, whether they'd be weavers and spinners, any of the traditional crafts, they were looked down on, always.' On another occasion, making a plea for respect for the craftworkers' skills, Muriel, referring to early Celtic art, spoke of them working 'not in gold or silver but in white sheep's wool and grey lichen, in green sallies and the red heart of the elm. We have to make our country craftsmen see that we are proud of them too. We have forgotten for so long that they *are* skilled craftsmen that they are near to forgetting it themselves, and one of the chief joys of creation is seeing that it is good.'

It took twelve years for The Country Shop to establish itself and find its way. By then it had moved on from a rather amateur, philanthropic first decade into a militant phase when Muriel, as managing director, would use all the societies and associations she had become involved in – ICA, RDS and Homespun Society as well as Country Workers Ltd – to their utmost possibilities. Muriel had learnt a lot during the teething crises of the alarmingly fast-growing baby she and her friends had given birth to. She lost no time in putting the income of The Country Shop to good use.

1943 stands out as the year when Muriel's work for the crafts and for the people of rural Ireland took off. She took some major decisions, instigating an all-Ireland craft survey and seeking to involve state bodies in a structured craft improvement scheme. She also began to approach national educational authorities, an early indication of the direction her work for the crafts would take in future years. In 1943, for example, Muriel asked the director of the National College of Art, Michael Bourke, to set up a school of weaving, a demand she would doggedly reiterate year after year until 1951, when Lillias Mitchell was finally appointed by General Richard Mulcahy, then minister for education, to a newly-created department of spinning, weaving and dyeing. By January 1943 Country Workers was in a position to allot 'up to £200 in prize schemes and grants to increase production of crafts and produce.' It was in 1943 too that Country Workers bought a silver cup to be held as a perpetual challenge cup for ICA members. Further ideas for spending the money generated by The Country Shop included holding an architects' competition for a design for an ICA hall and for 'a country cottage with all practical details'.[10] In July 1943 the germ of an idea was sown which was to blossom three years later as Country Markets Ltd: 'some co-operative effort such as market stalls'.

But the most important achievement of 1943 was when Country Workers presented the ICA with a grant of £750 to be matched by £250 raised by the ICA themselves. 'The £1,000 so raised to pay for two full-time, or one full-time and other part time organisers for two years.' Phyllis O'Connell of Fethard was able to start immediately, in January 1943, as general organiser and Muriel Kehoe as craft organiser. Mairin McDonald was also paid a salary from the grant for her secretarial work for the ICA. This was truly a crowning moment for The Country Shop, which had been founded by Muriel and her friends virtually on goodwill alone twelve years before.

Muriel's job was not all office-bound and had its compensations, as she candidly admitted herself. 'It fell to me, employed by the company as managing director, to travel round the country in search of craftsmen who were in need of help and sale of their work. No assignment can ever have given anyone more happiness than that search of mine for country crafts. In those nine years before the war, I, and various ICA friends who came with me, travelled to every county in Ireland, north and south. We went up mountains, into remote valleys, into the heart of the boglands, around the coast and out to the Aran Islands.' It was a labour of love too. 'Wherever we went, our hearts went out to the craftsmen we found, men and women full of zest for life, carrying on their craft with skill and, especially the women, with boundless energy and utmost enjoyment. My admiration for the countrywomen on the small farm was unbounded and has never lessened.'[11]

Notes

1. Country Workers Ltd, 34th Annual Report, 7 December 1964.

2. Article by Nell Giles Ahern in *The Boston Globe*. One of a series on 'Women of Ireland' written shortly after John F Kennedy's visit to Ireland.

3. Emily, Winifred and Veronica Wynne took over the Avoca Woollen Mills in 1927. Emily and Veronica worked on colours and design for the weaving while Winifred grew plants for sale and ran a toy workshop. Visiting friends would immediately be put to work finishing the various articles in the Wynne drawing room. Emily died in 1958, Winifred and Veronica in 1969.

4. In 1967, the aims of the company were revised as follows:
    1) To help people in small farm areas by encouraging and supporting their home industries and other economic projects.
    2) To encourage craftworkers in the country and generally to promote Country Crafts and Country Products, with special emphasis on developing their co-operative organisation.
    3) To promote and assist the work of the Irish Countrywomen's Association.

5. ACWW began in 1927 and from 1933 Lucy Franks represented Ireland, ranking as a founder member. She devoted much of her energy to the international association until her death in 1964, sadly just one year before Ireland hosted the ACWW's eleventh Triennial Conference, held in Dublin.

6. The Society of United Irishwomen was renamed because of a fear that it might be taken for a political party. In 1933 General Eoin O'Duffy, a man with fascist sympathies who was later to fight for Franco in the Spanish Civil War, had formed the short-lived United Ireland Party, a legal version of the Blueshirts. The United Ireland Party was soon reconstructed to form Fine Gael.

7. Paddy Somerville-Large had initially taken a £300 share in the company but it was not publicly known that he had paid both builders and

architects in the initial renovations to the basement premises of 23 St Stephen's Green. In 1944 it was discovered that he had in fact put up £791 to get The Country Shop off the ground, more than £20,000 in today's money.

8. Foster, R F. *Modern Ireland 1600–1972*, Penguin, London, 1989, p 538.

9. From 'The Irish Countrywoman and Adult Education' a paper read at the Annual Congress of the Irish Vocational Education Association in Dublin in June 1950 by Muriel, then vice-president of the ICA.

10. The competition took place in 1944 and was judged by Vincent Kelly B Arch, President of the Institute of Architects and Dermot O'Toole B Arch, President of the Architectural Association. To the £50 prize money proposed by Country Workers Ltd, the Royal Institute of Architects added a further £50. Thirty-one designs of cottages and eleven of community centres were submitted. Best cottage design was won by Patrick Sheehan, Limerick; best hall by Brian Coughlan, Dublin. The plans were exhibited in Dublin and then in various towns throughout the country.

11. From the original manuscript for an article which appeared in edited form in the booklet *Co-operation: The Story of Slieve Bawn Co-operative Handcraft Market* , 1968.

− 7 −

Aran, 1931 − A Legend is Born

It would be difficult to exaggerate the importance of Muriel's first visit to the Aran Islands. She and Livie Hughes took the steamer to Inis Mór, the largest of the Aran Islands, one sparkling day in August 1931. On a personal level it was an exhilarating trip but it was also to have far-reaching effects for the people of the islands and for the image of Irish crafts abroad. Muriel was to be the first person ever to offer Aran women money for their knitting or, more precisely, for the patterned jerseys that they knitted. Out of the economic incentive she provided grew the intricate and beautiful white Aran knitwear which has become as much a symbol of Ireland abroad today as the shamrock itself, copied and adapted in countries all over the world but still best understood by the native hand-knitters of the islands many of whom to this day knit from pictures in their heads and not from patterns. Here was a craft which Muriel, more commonly remembered for her work in the preservation of crafts, helped directly to develop. In her intuitive response to the exceptional creative skills of the Inis Mór women she met on that first trip, she was acting out her belief that tradition is 'not just resting on the past, but is ever starting afresh and moving onwards.'

Muriel often spoke of the three principles governing country crafts: necessity, economy and beauty. She found these working together in harmony on Inis Mór as they once had all over Ireland. 'The Aran Islands are a perfect illustration of our three principles, with their boat builders, their basketmakers, their weavers, their knitters, their blacksmiths, their carpenters − every kind of craft you can think of. These crafts are necessary to them; money is scarce so economy also counts; their need for expression shines out in the beauty of all they do.'

It was an extraordinary and lucky coincidence that Muriel chose the summer of 1931 to make her first craft-finding trip to Inis Mór. What was perceived as the unspoiled primitivism of the island way of life was beginning to attract international attention once again – the Aran Islands' romantic appeal is cyclical – and 1931 became a pivotal year for the latest surge of popularity. The fact that Muriel had spotted and encouraged Aran knitting just before the international spotlight snapped on once more gave the incredible skill and inventiveness of the knitters a head start. Publicity, free and unsolicited, was just around the corner. But first of all, in June 1931, a long and fully illustrated feature on the Aran islands had appeared in the *National Geographic Magazine* under the heading 'The Timeless Arans'.[1] It may well have been this article, as well as a chance encounter with an Irishman on the liner to Europe, that decided Robert J Flaherty to take a closer look at the Aran Islands with a view to making a film there. He arrived on Inis Mór for his first 'recce' in November 1931, returning in January 1932 to spend the next two years making *Man of Aran*. Even before the finished film was screened in 1934, arousing huge curiosity about the islands, Flaherty's own presence at Kilmurvey on Inis Mór attracted many hangers-on from the arts world who would not otherwise have come to the island. Also on the island in 1931, quite coincidentally but seduced too perhaps by the *National Geographic* article, was a young and cocky Orson Welles. Like Livie and Muriel he preceded Robert Flaherty by several months, arriving in summer. He was a precocious 16–year-old, 'tall, broadly handsome, ingenuous, eloquent, filled with the blarney' and ostensibly in Ireland to learn to paint. Legend has it that he was obliged to take the ferry from Kilronan back to Galway sooner than planned because, as well as being short of cash, 'some of the older islanders began to worry about the fates of their daughters'.[2] He left towards the end of August at the same time as Muriel and Livie Hughes, as the following extract from a letter which Muriel wrote to her old school friend Frances Steen, reveals:

> Never have I enjoyed anything so much since the day you &
> I set off at 7 o'c one fine morning, our bicycles insecurely
> roped on the top of a rickety taxi, & whirled madly through
> the streets to catch a train which was even then due to leave
> for the west.

It was just the same exquisite feeling of not knowing where or what we were going to do next – & not caring. We started off with not the slightest idea of where we were going to stop, how long we were going to stop or how we were going to get there. From the moment we landed at Galway Quay, we were in a different land – a jabber of Irish all around – women in their red petticoats & beautiful patterned shawls like the Keating poster – fine looking men wearing the most perfectly coloured indigo blue homespuns – gaily coloured woven belts, black squashed in hats · & their absurd pampooties.

There had been a fair at Galway the day before & all the animals had to be shipped. Horses, cows, donkeys, sheep and pigs, they were all there – squealing, bleating, teaming and stampeding, their owners standing calmly by while a swearing, stravaging little sap of a mate struggled to fix ropes and pulleys on to his obstreperous cargo. The cargo, I may say, got slightly mixed and we wondered what would be the result of a struggling horse being let down in a sack of flour or a box of groceries. Nobody else seemed to mind, however, and we felt we were being finicky.

We made great friends on the boat & one of them happened to be the nearest and dearest neighbour of the woman we had hopes of stopping with – he'd see us there all right, he had a car, he always drove people to Mary Faherty's. As he had found us a most comfortable seat in the boat we felt we would be churlish to refuse his offer, so we allowed ourselves to be driven to Mary Faherty's though we had been looking forward to a good walk. Everyone seemed much disappointed by the way that we had not been ill coming over, it seems to be the thing, & certainly it was quite rough and took 3 hours – 30 miles – to return to Aran. . .[3]

But everything was made up for when we got to Mary Faherty's. She beamed a welcome to us at the door – of course she had rooms – & wasn't it lucky we hadn't come the week before when she had the house packed out with schoolteachers & priests & all sorts. We walked into the cleanest, whitest kitchen I have ever seen in Ireland – a grand turf fire blazing in the hearth & two sleek white cats sitting contentedly by. That was one of the nicest things about the island – all the animals – horses and cows, cats and dogs, looked so well cared for & well fed, not like so many other parts of the West. We saw no real poverty either, and apparently there is none. They are all self-supporting and have enough to spare.

Well, I could go on dithering like this about the place for pages, but suffice to say we walked and we walked and we saw the great stone forts Dun Oghill & Dun Goghan & Dun Aengus[4], & I have never seen anything so wonderful as the last. Perched on the top of a cliff 300 ft. high, with its great triple ring of massive walls, it is like some great Gargantua keeping guard over the sacred isle and one wondered what strange, what amazing tales it could tell. The whole island of course is nothing but a sheet of rock, but there are the most exquisite flowers springing up wherever a speck of earth can lie: real maidenhair fern, gentians, saxifrage – all sorts of things that grow nowhere else in Ireland. And the weather was perfect: bright sun, blue sky & and the bluest of blue seas.

You will be tired of all these eulogies by this time, but the half is not told you. However I will spare you. Sufficient to say that the finishing touch was our stumbling by accident on the island tragedy: Liam O'Flaherty & Edmund Curtis' divorced wife. He had brought her there for the first time just a month before & there he had her in the very centre of the most rigid tradition holding ultra Catholic stronghold in the country – and the O'Flahertys the head and centre of it all. The very first thing we did when we arrived was to ask for Mrs O'Flaherty. I wanted to see her about the homespuns and Livie was at College with her. But little did we know what we were putting our feet into – head foremost. It is too long a tale to recount here but we had it all by nightfall from our hostess – trust Livie. The wretched girl, we felt terribly sorry for her, but it was madness to bring her there. We caught sight of Liam one day. A ruddy attractive looking youth, 'just a little boy', Mrs Faherty kept saying.[5]

The journey back was not the least amusing part of the trip. Again somewhat rough, the captain going round succouring sick and sorrowing passengers. The mate and steward, very much the worse of a farewell party, struggling to cut bread and butter and make tea for the hungry ones. (The party was with a lively young American who turned out to be Orson Welles). It was just like a boat in a pantomime & we should

not have been a bit surprised to see one of the cows coming
up and dancing a hornpipe. We helped the stricken steward
to get our tea in the end & had the reward. He fixed me
with a watery eye: 'You're a fine girl you are, & I've seen lots
of fine girls too, and you've game in your eye.'
Fran, you have got to go to Aran.

The purpose of Muriel's trip was to locate craftworkers and offer
them The Country Shop as an outlet. Although her enthusiasm
for the crafts never diminished throughout her long life, in that
summer of 1931 the keenness with which she set out to discover
what Inis Mór had to offer must have been particularly intense.
Added to the pure adventure of the trip there was the excitement
of seeing the traditional Aran clothing at first hand. It was Michael
Donoghue who drove them to Corruch, two miles west of
Kilronan, where his neighbour Mary Faherty took in guests.
Muriel would have been curious about everything, she would have
touched and smelt and felt the different textures of the clothes and
would have asked about the different dyes[6] and the sources of
wool. There was the diversity in the use of homespuns for the
men's various shirts, waistcoats, trousers and undertrousers and
the beautiful woven belts which held them up. Muriel would have
examined the older women's thick, heavy petticoats (often up to
four or five yards of material in one skirt), the under one made of
white flannel and the outside one of red, blue or black brushed
frieze with two tucks all the way around the lower half and black
ribbon trimmings between the tucks. She would have admired the
pretty, close-fitting blouses some women still wore with the skirts
and seen how they wrapped their shawls tightly over the blouses
and tied them behind their backs. She would have taken a closer
look at the 'absurd pampooties' made of cow hide and left
steeping in water overnight to keep them supple.

But it was the knitting and the colourful crioses which caught
Muriel's eye as potentially saleable. Though never hitherto sold
outside the islands, the crios – a multicoloured belt, two to three
yards long, woven without a loom, which the men wound round
their waists to hold up their trousers – was commonly bought by
tourists prior to 1931. Visitors to Dun Aengus and the Seven
Churches of Eoghanacht, for example, would call at houses in the
village in the hopes of coming away with a souvenir of the
islanders' distinctive dress. One person Muriel was directed to very
soon was Annie Mullen, 'Naneen Mhicilín', the wife of red-

bearded Patch Ruadh who would star in *Man of Aran* and who was a skilled basket-maker. Naneen was an outgoing sociable woman who was used to tourists calling. She lived in Eoghanacht, in the 'far west', where both she and her neighbour and sister-in-law Brid Rua Dirrane were expert crios weavers.

The only knitting those early tourists might have sought to buy were stockings, navy-blue knee-length socks with white heels and turn-downs and a white diamond pattern round the toes. The women's stockings often had delicate patterning running in panels up the shaped calf. Muriel would have seen the dark fishermen's ganseys the men wore, made out of naturally grey wool or knitted in white yarn and then dyed navy so that they would not show the dirt and would blend in with the traditional colours of the men's dress. She would have noticed the intricacy of the patterned sections, often only across the upper part of the body and, as someone who had never managed to knit more than half a sock herself, would have marvelled at the dexterity of women and even small girls knitting furiously as they walked to the beach or herded the cows, controlling up to nine steel knitting pins used then to knit the ganseys in the traditional way, in the round and all of one piece.

By 1931 when, ironically, hand-knitted fishermen's ganseys had virtually disappeared elsewhere, superseded by machine-knits, there had developed on Aran a variation on the classic dark pullover which would at once have alerted Muriel's instinct for what was essential in a given craft. In the west end of Inis Mór, not far from where she and Livie were staying, the knitters had let their skill and inventiveness run riot, not just with their menfolk's dark ganseys. There was something even more exciting in store. Whether it was brought to her attention or whether she spotted it for herself one Sunday morning, a smaller version, knitted in natural white wool and left undyed for young boys' confirmations and then worn by them to Mass, must have struck her at once as an original and very special garment. Knitting these jerseys for such important days, the women gave freer rein to their imaginations, competing with each other, making each white 'geansaí' a work of art in itself. In the tightly spun creamy-white wool, the stitches, less well-discernible in navy or brown, stood out in crisp relief. It is not hard to see how, with a little encouragement, both artistic and material, the knitters lost no time in producing intricately patterned white adult-size jumpers for sale.

There has been much speculation and debate about the origins of the Aran stitches. There is no historical evidence for their existence on Inis Mór further back than the turn of the century. Once fishing had been developed by the CDB (their 1892 report had stated that all piers on Inis Mór were unsuitable for big boats, that there was virtually no fish curing done and that the steamer called only once a week) the influx of fishermen and sailors from elsewhere in Ireland and from further afield in the British Isles would have increased significantly, introducing the knitted gansey to the traditional Aran wardrobe. Were 'the stitches', as the complex combinations of patterns are still referred to on Inis Mór, spotted on the back of a visiting fisherman at Mass one Sunday or did they simply develop out of the cable stitch commonly found on the Scottish fisherman's gansey? Were they brought back from America by returned emigrants or across the water from Co. Clare with a load of bonnavs? The English-born artist Elizabeth Rivers, always known on the island as Betty Rivers, lived for nearly ten years in the back-to-back cottages Flaherty had built for the interior shots of *Man of Aran* and had heard yet another explanation shortly after she first arrived on Inis Mór in 1934:

> Most of the women and girls are remarkable knitters, and one notices the handsome patterned jerseys that the men wear. No two are alike though the same stitches appear in different permutations and combinations. I had always supposed the varied designs used to be traditional – since they have much in common with the early Celtic ornament. Most of them have probably been handed down for generations but I have also been told of an obscure genius. . .This man had a passion for knitting and a furtive and inventive mind. Disliking cold and storm, with the coming of winter he would go to bed and stay there for weeks at a time. 'Divil a pattern but he knew it and had more of his own than all of the others again', one man told me. 'But he went away to America afterwards. Many of the patterns that you see now were his at first.'[7]

More interesting than where the basic patterns came from is what the women in the west of Inis Mór did with them next. There was a latent reserve of creative talent and outstanding mathematical ability awaiting stimulation. Repeatedly, in talking to the older women on the island, two names recur. Firstly that of Nora Gill, 'Nora Mhairtin', of Eoghanacht – a dressmaker widely renowned for her craftsmanship – for teaching 'the stitches' to both family and neighbours. And secondly Naneen – the crios-maker – for first organising knitters for Muriel. While Elizabeth Rivers was living on the island – she left in 1943 – she too played a vital part in getting the finished garments up to The Country Shop, making up the brown paper parcels with the women and addressing them to 23 St Stephen's Green. She also made sketches of individual stitches which today hang at An Grianán.

By 1934 elaborately patterned white sweaters, until just a few years before for small boys only, had become the fashion for the young men of the island. They would be worn on Sundays and special occasions under a dark jacket, another innovation in style. When Clara Vyvyan recorded her first visit to Aran in the late 1930s, staying in the *Man of Aran* cottages with Elizabeth Rivers, she wrote eloquently of the women's knitting:

> They knit or weave and fashion their own woollen and homespun garments for themselves and for their menfok, but for all the simplicity of their needs and their material, they execute their work with the devotion of an artist. The jerseys that the women knit are white or indigo but they obtain their rich effects in the variety of patterned stitches and on these square shaped garments with round necks they improvise, as a musician will improvise on some simple melody, their own individual fancies. There are circles and ellipses and zigzag lines and dots like a chain of pearls, and loops and lovers' knots and lines like rippled water. These garments are like gothic architecture that combines with simplicity of form a lavish richness of adornment on capital and column, on architrave and transom. Like those medieval craftsmen, those women put their own personal ideas in to their work, so that no two jerseys are alike.[8]

By September 1933 Muriel had Aran knitting on display in Dublin, in a 'Country Industries' exhibition in the Gallery of The Country Shop. All Aran crafts were well represented. 'The most original exhibit', wrote Livie Hughes in a report on the exhibition, 'is the collection of objects from the Aran Islands. The beautiful knitting and variegated belts, the pampooties, the wooden vessels and baskets, the photos of the islands which would make anyone want to visit and revisit them.' The *Farmers' Gazette* reported 'beautiful and elaborate knitting from handspun wool'. Mary Faherty, with whom Muriel and Livie had stayed, won a prize.

Three years later The Country Shop dramatically contributed to the future of Aran knitting. Heinz Kiewe, the Oxford-based German textile journalist, was in Dublin and bought an Aran gansey there. He described it later as 'a peculiar whiskery looking chunk of sweater in "Biblical white". . .it looked too odd for words, being hard as a board, shapeless as a Coptic priest's shirt, and with an atmosphere of Stonehenge all around it'.[9] It smelt strongly of oil and turf smoke. This did not stop him from bringing the object to a knitting specialist in England, Mary Thomas, who photographed it for her 1943 book of knitting patterns and gave a description of some of the stitches. This was to be the very first time anything approaching a 'knitting pattern' for the Aran stitches was worked out. The rest is history.

In 1945 Muriel became worried about how Aran knitting, by now well known and popular, was being exploited. Already unhappy about how Gaeltarra Éireann, set up to promote rural industries in the Gaeltacht regions, had taken over the homespun industry in Donegal during the war and was encouraging quantity rather than quality, she reported to her fellow Country Workers directors that 'Gaeltarra Éireann were sending bad designs and materials to Aran to be knitted. She thought Country Workers should do all in their power to preserve the traditional designs.' It was agreed that a competition for Aran knitters should be held in The Country Shop, with substantial prizes for the best jerseys[10]. There would be a special prize for girls under sixteen. The competition, which was judged in April 1946, was a huge success with fifty jerseys entered, *all different,* many with different patterns back and front. The judges, Frances Burroughs from the National College of Art and Gerty Grew of the Cluna Studio in Dublin, were bowled over by what they saw. They described the collection of knitwear as 'quite unique'. 'The craftsmanship displayed is excellent, the knitting wonderfully even, and the patterns very varied, showing great originality in their different arrangements; all making it very difficult to judge. The standard of the jerseys in general was very high, and the knitting extremely good and firm, a very essential point as regards their use. Suitability for its purpose is the root of good craftsmanship.' Typically, Muriel did not let the matter lie there. In the Spring of 1947 she sent her newly engaged craft organiser, Miranda Scally, out to the islands. Miranda spent six weeks there and as a result The Country Shop 'now had 80 knitters on its books', each knitter with her own number. In the spring of 1953 another Aran competition was held, this time in the Mansion House in Dublin and three years later, still worried about the abuse of the term 'Aran', The Country Shop introduced 'Handmade in Aran' labels for the jumpers and cardigans sold by them.

Mary Villa Dirrane remembered well the role The Country Shop came to play in her life. Like many of the older knitters still alive today, the words 'Country Shop' have a special resonance for her. She too lived in Eoghanacht, six miles west of Kilronan, which along with the other western townlands of Sruthan, Creig an Cheirin and Bun Gowla, as Muriel had quickly discovered, produced the finest and most inventive knitters on Inis Mór. Until Muriel came along, though, there was no reason to knit for anyone outside one's immediate family and any extra wool would more usefully be put into weaving extra blankets or more flannels and tweeds for the family's clothes. But, although Muriel was right when she had observed in 1931 that there was 'no real poverty' on the island – insofar as there was no hunger and the people in their hard-wearing homespuns looked well turned out and strong – life was nevertheless extremely hard, especially since the 1929 Crash in America had virtually dried up emigrants' remittances. As Breandán Ó hEithir wrote of his childhood on Inis Mór in the 'thirties, 'while I have no memories of real poverty around us, I have vivid memories of real deprivation. . .the introduction of the dole was hailed in places like Aran as a definite social revolution.'[11] The chance of earning some extra money through knitting was seized upon avidly. The pay from The Country Shop was not much at the beginning but even so, after a long day working at home and on the shore or in the fields, women would sit up half the night and knit and knit by the light of a paraffin lamp in order to earn that extra pittance for their family. Muriel Gahan was the first to pay Mary Villa to knit, she was emphatic about that, remembering it in the same breath as the introduction of the dole as an equally revolutionary event. Then Robert Flaherty who, after offering her the main female part in *Man of Aran* which she refused[12], asked her to knit some ganseys for members of his crew. Unlike Muriel, who from the start favoured white wool, Flaherty's people liked the natural grey best, making Mary Villa's nighttime knitting in a poor light even harder.

Once their knitting had a saleable value and the fashion was catching on in the island, there was no holding back the knitters. By the mid-1930s young girls were bitten by the knitting bug. Pauline and Peggy McDonagh would sit at the back of Eoghill church on Sunday where they'd be sure to get a good view of the men's jumpers so that they could then rush straight home after Mass and try to work out new stitches. The most exciting stitches were on the backs of men from 'the far west', from beyond Kilmurvey (there was no church west of Eoghill then, Eoghanacht chapel was not built until 1958). This too was where Muriel's first commissioned knitters lived and from where a steady supply of Aran handknits for The Country Shop was to come. In the 1946 Aran knitting contest, twenty-three of the thirty-two knitters who won prizes or were commended were from Kilmurvey and points west. Four of Nora Gill's grand-daughters were highly commended or commended and Mary Villa Dirrane's daughter won first prize for the under-sixteens. The mother of the poet Máirtín Ó Direáin won third prize overall.

One of Muriel Gahan's rules was that she would never sell an Aran jumper which had not been knitted on the islands. This rule held until The Country Shop closed in 1978. She was equally intransigent about crioses. Crioses for The Country Shop had to be made of handspun, home-dyed thread. Producing a crios of shop yarn was much faster and might be sold through other outlets but it did not cross the threshold of The Country Shop. Una Dirrane, originally from Inis Meáin (home, it is said, of the most beautiful crioses), but living on Inis Mór, remembers making crioses for The Country Shop as if it was yesterday. 'Eight-and-sixpence each, five pounds and two shillings the dozen. . .the figures will go to the grave with me!' They had their own sheep and would wash the wool and scour it and then carry it down to the harbour in sacks to be shipped over to Galway for carding. Then they spun it and dyed it with bought dyes: red, yellow, green, black and royal blue, before finally setting up the long warp threads and deftly weaving the narrow belts. She also made 'bobailín' caps and knit sweaters for The Country Shop and when an order was ready she would parcel it all up with paper and twine and post it off to 23 St Stephen's Green, an address she also remembers by heart today.

For Una Dirrane, as for so many others producing for The Country Shop, the real excitement came at Christmas. In 1946 an annual bonus for craftworkers was introduced and in 1947 it was recorded that 'the Christmas bonus had been more popular on Aran than anything that had been done on the island by Country Workers.' The women would watch out for the ships coming in with the mail. There were only two a week, on Wednesdays and

Saturdays, weather permitting, but it could be days before a steamer docked, especially in winter. Once word got around that the mail had arrived – it might be as late as Christmas Eve – the women would walk often five miles and more along the road to Kilronan and stand huddled together for warmth outside the Post Office while Tom Beatty, the postman, called out the names on the letters. If they were lucky, the Country Shop bonus would be there, and 'we would walk home again on air, feeling millionaires even though the cheque might only have been for a couple of pounds.' Others at the far tip of the island, like Mary Tim Hernon in Bun Gowla, would wait for the letter to be delivered. Mary was yet another of Nora Gill's grand-daughters and she can still remember exactly what she was doing when the postman came with the envelope containing her first bonus cheque from Country Workers.

Notes

1. The twenty-eight page article had thirty-four photographs by the author, Robert Cushman Murphy, and by AW Cutler.

2. Brady, Frank. *Citizen Welles*, Hodder and Stoughton, London, 1990, pp. 20–21.

3. Muriel and Livie were lucky: on a stormy day, the crossing could take up to seven or eight hours. Sometimes on arriving at Kilronan pier, the ferry would be unable to dock because of the seas and would turn back for Galway. Minimum crossing time was two-and-a-half hours.

4. The three forts referred to by Muriel are Dún Eochla, Dún Eoghanachta and Dún Aonghasa. In the English spelling they are usually written Dun Oghill, Dun Onacht and Dun Aengus.

5. Margaret Barrington, a writer, was married to the Professor of History at TCD, Edmund Curtis. In 1926, having obtained a divorce, she married the famous Inis Mór-born novelist and short story writer Liam O'Flaherty and their daughter, Pegeen, was born soon after. Liam O'Flaherty was born in 1896 – hardly 'just a little boy' in 1931!

6. Indigo was still widely used to dye the raw wool which would then be carded, spun and brought to the weavers' – the Gillans – to be woven for the men's clothes, along with the grey-brown wool from the 'black' sheep. Dyeing the wool with indigo involved a lengthy and smelly process (urine was used as a fixative) when the pot of dye was kept in a warm place by the kitchen fireside for up to a week. Indigo was not used to dye the ganseys. The dark blue ganseys were first knit in white wool because it was easier on the eyes and then dyed by the simpler and quicker process of a chemical dye. 'Colour-me-quick' is a trade name that is still remembered.

7. From an unpublished manuscript by Elizabeth Rivers.

8. Vyvyan, C C. *On Timeless Shores*, Peter Owen Ltd, London, 1957, p 133.

9. Quoted by Muriel in the Country Workers Ltd annual report, 3 December 1968.

10. First prize was ten pounds, second was five pounds and third three pounds. This would be approximately £200, £100 and £60 in today's money. The first prize for the under-sixteens was two pounds. Celtic brooches made by Nan Holland were also awarded.

11. Ó hEithir, B. *Irish Life* Gmelch S (ed), The O'Brien Press, Dublin, 1979, p 138.

12. This was done through the intermediary of the local schoolteacher, Joe Flanagan, and James Johnston from Kilmurvey House, who called on Mary Villa asking her if she would like to take part in the film. Shocked at the idea, she refused without hesitation and they went instead up the road to Maggie Dirrane who accepted and whose name became famous as the wife of *Man of Aran*.

'There Was Something You Had to Like About The Country Shop...'

Muriel's first and last enthusiasm was for the aims laid down by Country Workers Ltd and she was never happier than when out on the road pursuing them. After all, it had been Lucy Franks' idea, not hers, to open a restaurant in The Country Shop. Muriel once went so far as to make the heretical statement that she 'wasn't interested in the restaurant at all, it was just there to pay for any expenses we had to pay our craftsmen'. This was true of course. The restaurant and craft shop were the means to a well-defined end and the staff of The Country Shop were only too aware of it. But while Muriel may not have been interested in the daily running of the restaurant – she was blessed with a devoted and highly efficient staff – there is no doubt that The Country Shop was as dear to her as home. In many ways The Country Shop *was* her home since, when in Dublin, she did all but sleep there.

In 1938 Muriel's parents moved from Leinster Road to a large old house in Shankill called St Brendan's, big enough to fit Teddy's two sons, John and Michael, who had been sent home from Africa to school. Muriel also moved with them. During the war years, when the boys' mother, Vera, moved to Ireland, Muriel and she rented Cherry Tree Lodge, a small cottage on the grounds of Laragh House in Co. Wicklow. They rented it from Joyce Somerville-Large, wife of the third Somerville-Large brother, Coll. While her husband was away at the war, Joyce ran Laragh House as a hotel, but lived in another cottage on the estate. This allowed Muriel, Vera and the boys a place to escape to at weekends and space and independence from the older generation. But Muriel's base would always remain with her parents. When Teddy left Africa for good in 1952 he moved into St Brendan's and Muriel and her parents moved into the gate lodge, Carrigfern, where she stayed after her parents' deaths, sharing it in later years with Teddy and Vera.

Muriel was fiercely and justly proud that she had created and ran The Country Shop. At least until 1964, when the ICA moved into its own separate premises in Ballsbridge, and arguably until its closure in 1978 The Country Shop was the hub of a vast and ever-expanding nexus of complexly interconnected activities and for as many years there is no doubt but that Muriel Gahan dominated it.

Close to government ministries and the Dáil, a stone's throw from the National Library and Museum and equidistant from Dublin's two universities, The Country Shop was a haven for office workers and shoppers alike, for actors, students, politicians, civil servants and Merrion Square-based architects and doctors. Paddy Kavanagh, the poet, was an irregular regular there. There can be few Dubliners over the age of forty who do not have a Country Shop story to tell. For some a visit there was the last treat before going back to school, or where they got their first ever whiff of fresh coffee. Others practically lived there. There were whist drives, teenage 'hops' in the evenings, wedding receptions on Saturdays. There was even a funeral party once. Over the years countless associations and clubs hired rooms for meetings there, from the Gramophone Society and the Legion of Mary to the Hellenic Society and Friends of the Harp. When Alcoholics Anonymous chose to set up their first European group in Dublin in 1946 they met in The Country Shop and continued to do so until it closed.

When people evoke memories of The Country Shop they tend to use words like 'homely', 'friendly', 'warm', or 'cosy', even when the detail of their picture is vague. For journalist Maev Kennedy it was the súgán chair in front of a turf fire that she remembered, as well as 'the top-lit studio room, with its walls full of rush baskets and scythes and slanes and a gallery-worth of Irish drawings and paintings.' The waitresses could strike terror in a child, though. 'My father once instructed me and a school friend to wait there to be taken to the Grafton Cinema and he'd settle the bill when he came from work. We were so frightened of being thrown out that we kept re-ordering and by the time he arrived the bill had soared past the half-crown Country Tea to something terrifyingly close to ten bob.'[1] Others remember the kindness of the staff under a fearsome exterior. Impoverished office workers unable to afford more than a small soup at lunchtime would watch as a poker-faced waitress served them a large one for the same price. For many women it was a place where they felt secure. One elderly woman, a lonely person who lived in a hotel on Harcourt Street, came every afternoon and would sit at the small red table directly under the red wooden clock at the back of the basement restaurant. As closing time approached and she was sure no waitress was looking she would use the crook of her walking stick to drag the minute-hand back and thus put off the moment when she would have to leave.

Though 'cosy' and 'homely' it may have felt and despite the miniature thatched cottage it displayed in the street, The Country Shop never played on a nostalgic version of the country. It was no accident that it became a meeting place for artists and intellectuals. The White Stag Group, a small but influential group of London-based avant-garde artists who had moved to Ireland during World War II, would gather there every Saturday morning, joined by Dublin's more progressive Irish artists, such as Mainie Jellett, Patrick Scott and Norah McGuinness. The table reserved each lunchtime for a group of architects has been likened, admittedly somewhat exaggeratedly, to the Algonquin Round Table in New York. In terms of decoration it was, in the words of Paul Hogan, former design manager of the Irish Export Board, 'an oasis in an uncaring desert'. Patrick Scott remembers his delight at finding stacking stools in bent birch plywood by the Finnish designer Alvar Aalto when he started frequenting The Country Shop as an architecture student and artist in 1940. Muriel's superb sense of colour and design pervaded the place.

It was fortunate for The Country Shop that as business grew, which it did steadily over the years, it was possible to expand upwards into the building. At first there was just the basement with its entrance area (housing the shop, known as the Cottage), two main rooms and extensive kitchen area out the back of the house. In the beginning only one room was used as a public restaurant, the other being the Club Room where members, 'for an annual subscription of one guinea, will have books, papers and notepaper. It is hoped to be of special use to country members as a place where they can leave parcels, telephone, make appointments etc.' The 'club' idea was central to the founding of

Muriel (*extreme left*) entertains The Country Shop staff at her parents' house, St Brendan's.

Rush-cutting on the River Anner. Once they had been cut the rushes were made into rafts which Muriel *(front right)* and her friends would race down the river.

Summer School 1932. Miss Stops *(centre)* introduces lumra work to the United Irishwomen.

Muriel's understanding of the crafts can be seen in the elegance of the exhibition she organised in The Country Shop in 1933. Lucy Franks is the right-hand figure, talking to a friend.

When Muriel went to the Aran Islands in 1931 traditional crafts were still central to the islanders' way of life.

Elizabeth Rivers, a close friend of Muriel's was much loved by her island neighbours. She was denounced from the pulpit for wearing trousers.

Elizabeth Rivers spent much of her time sketching her island friends. Here Patch Ruadh Mullen makes a creel while his wife, Naneen, weaves a crios.

Joseph Hughes of Armagh holds an audience captive at the 1936 Spring Show.

Spring Show 1942. Stout rod baskets were always a favourite with Muriel. Here Joseph Kane from Edgeworthstown, Co. Longford, finishes off a turf basket.

Spring Show 1942. Joseph Greene came of a long tradition of potters from Youghal, Co. Cork.

Spring Show 1942. Peter Mulkerrin, a Connemara weaver, at work. Mainie Jellett's banners decorate the RDS concert hall and member's library.

Women were central to the production of tweed: carding and spinning; preparing the warp and selling the finished product.

The Country Shop and indicated how unsure Muriel and her friends were that the venture would be commercially viable. Shareholders of more than ten pounds became honorary members. Once fifty members had joined new members would be ballotted for. 'Lectures, poetry meetings etc might be arranged. . .and bridge drives to raise funds for the UI Society.' At first club members could have only tea or morning coffee in their room. However, one year after opening, in December 1931, 'it was agreed that lunch should be served in the Club Room for club members to relieve congestion in the rush hours.'

By 1932 it was obvious that any initial worries had been unfounded. Business thrived and the three back rooms of the ground floor were rented for £175 a year, becoming Miss Tweedy's Snack Bar, the Top Restaurant and the Back Bar or Gallery. Club members had their subscriptions refunded and the club idea was dropped. In 1935 an empty room at the top of the house became vacant and Country Workers took it too. At first this served as an office for Muriel and a place to prepare exhibitions. Then in the autumn of 1937 the ICA were told they could no longer have office space at the Civics Institute in South William Street, where they had moved from Molesworth Street, and they transferred to the top back room at 23 St Stephen's Green, sharing it with Muriel and *An Cumann Sniomhachain*, the Irish Homespun Society. This was not without its problems. The Homespun Society and Muriel were forever preparing exhibitions and had to be reminded that the room was shared with another society 'and therefore should be kept reasonably tidy'. The ICA was warned that 'Miss Gahan's desk should not be used by them in any way'. In 1941 a solicitor left his rooms on the first floor and offered his lease to Country Workers for £90 a year. There were three rooms: two small storage rooms and a larger one, to become the famous 'boardroom', Muriel's office and sanctum where the chosen few could join her for lunch. It was decided to decorate this room 'comfortably'. This was done at some cost, but by the end of 1942 the boardroom had already 'paid its way in lunches.' In 1944 two more rooms at the top of the house, front rooms this time, were taken and handed over to the ICA. In 1946 the possibility of renting the whole building arose but it came to nothing.

The miniature thatched cottage hanging over the front area of 23 St Stephen's Green was how Dubliners recognised The Country Shop. Over the years the little cottage would disappear and have to be replaced, as a favourite student prank was stealing the house from its perch. Even when eating space and meeting rooms had spread upwards through the building, entry remained down the steps from the street and in through the basement. Except for a very select few who had a key to the hall door, that is, and for the kitchen staff. The latter would be the first to arrive at seven in the morning, entering through a lane that ran along the side of the building. 'I'd have to open up the gate and come down the dark lane', Sadie Quigley, cake cook for forty-one years, remembers, 'I was terrified. You could be murdered, anybody could be in there.' Sadie's sister Lily had been the first of the family to work in The Country Shop, starting at fifteen, and then three more of her sisters as well as neighbours Kathleen Muldowney and Kathy Coates, all from Ringsend, spent many years working in the kitchens too.

The kitchen staff were the most long-suffering and hard-working but possibly also the happiest of all Country Shop workers. With the exception of white bakery bread for sandwiches, all bread, cakes, pies and pastries, both for consumption in the restaurant and for sale in the shop, as well as for outside catering, were made daily on the premises. Kathleen Muldowney was in charge of bread. When she finally retired Muriel praised her work saying that 'her skill, like any other craftsman's, was the result of loving, intelligent handling of her material.' At Christmas time, when The Country Shop took orders for cakes and mince pies, staff from the cake kitchen would work weekends from early morning until late at night producing up to seventy-two cakes in a day and then coming back on succeeding Saturdays and Sundays to make the almond paste and then ice them. During the Emergency, as World War II was known in neutral Ireland, Kathleen Muldowney, Sadie Quigley and another member of the kitchen staff, Doreen Ryan, all slept on camp beds in Muriel's office in order to catch 'the glimmer' or rationed gas supply when it came on at five in the morning. 'I'd sleep in the middle bed because I was afraid of my life,' Sadie remembers. All the cakes, scones and brown and white breads would be out of the ovens by eight.

But they had fun too. At Christmas time Sadie would collect money from the other kitchen staff and as her sister Lily Harte remembered, 'we'd buy a drop of drink and we'd buy meat and potatoes and we'd have a big dinner in the kitchen at the big table with paper cloths and we'd have a great old time. Miss Gahan allowed all that. We'd have a sing-song when we'd had a drop of drink.' In the very early years of The Country Shop, when she was still in her teens, Lily ('Little Lily' to distinguish her from Lillie Curtin, the cook, who was both older and larger) remembered staff dances. The girls would wear long dresses and dinner would be in the downstairs restaurant. There would be a band in one of the big rooms upstairs afterwards. On another evening the waitresses would have their own separate party.

Country Shop staff was a mixture of 'lifers', women who had joined shortly after the restaurant and shop opened, and short-term staff, often offered a job by Muriel to tide them over. Amongst the long-term staff there was terrific loyalty, many women staying, in spite of low pay, long past retirement age or until the shop closed. Quite early on Muriel had introduced a 'ten year award' for staff. This was a specially commissioned Nan Holland brooch, inscribed on the back with the person's name and length of service. The loyalty worked both ways and Muriel was as good to her staff as they were to The Country Shop. She was always generous and considerate to staff in times of illness or bereavement not only giving them money and time off, but also finding time to visit them in hospital, worrying about their health and helping to sort out their housing problems.

The second category of staff, mostly waitresses, would work temporarily until something better turned up, or until they married or emigrated, or in the case of students until they left college. Muriel liked to think of The Country Shop as a 'passing through' place offering young women the possibility of a stop-gap job while they worked out their lives. Breda Garrivan, who now lives in Westport where she is involved in the Country Market, remembers such an offer from Muriel, though in her case she turned it down. In the 'fifties, when she felt she had got as far as she could in her telephone exchange job in Dublin, Breda decided to try her luck in America. She regularly had her lunch in The Country Shop and when Muriel heard she wanted to leave the country she took her aside and offered to find space for her as a waitress, calling on Breda's sense of patriotism and pleading with her not to emigrate.

Many Country Shop employees were girls 'of good family', expected to hang around until a suitable husband materialised. Georgie Hamilton's first contact with The Country Shop was typical. 'I was bored to distraction, with nothing to do and just small pocket money from my father who was a doctor and thought that girls were girls and should be left there until they found a husband.' Then, through a common interest in sport, her family met Muriel. Suddenly the chance of going into The Country Shop as a part time waitress appeared, a blissful alternative to boredom. 'To me it was absolutely wonderful,' Georgie remembered, 'this lovely place. . .!' Georgie was in and out of The Country Shop as a waitress until she married, returning much later when her children were almost grown up.

The very first waitresses to work with Muriel were her friends Joan Stoker and Nora Ringwood. Joan, a close friend, who had been made manager of The Country Shop in October 1938, died unexpectedly in 1942. Nora will forever be remembered in Country Shop lore as the first waitress to get the sack. The cause, again according to legend, was her bad language and being seen combing her hair and powdering her face within view of the customers. (This did not prevent Nora's daughter, Blanaid Reddin, from being employed as a waitress years later and becoming a champion of the crafts alongside Muriel, both through Bord Fáilte and through the Crafts Council of Ireland.) Lillie Curtin joined the staff in 1931. Over the years she and Muriel became good friends, Lillie becoming part of the Gahan family. They would travel together on their holidays and in 1955 they bought a cottage in Roundstone. Lillie was made a shareholder in the Company in 1942 and a director in 1956 and her skill not only as a cook but as a manager and organiser, as well as her great loyalty to the establishment, made her one of its indisputable pillars. Just as for Muriel, only more poignantly, The Country Shop became a surrogate family for Lillie Curtin. She gave it everything. When she first arrived, she had led people to believe that she was an orphan or that her family had all emigrated to Australia leaving her behind and it was not until her death in 1985 that it was discovered that she did have relatives in Ireland after all and that she had been in touch with them all along. Muriel was deeply upset and mystified that her friend could have concealed this from her.

Lillie Curtin and Sadie Quigley ran the kitchens, Lillie being in charge of overall catering and restaurant management. Angela Kehoe, the other pillar of The Country Shop, a sister of Muriel Kehoe, one of the ICA's very first craft organisers, started working there in 1940 and became official company secretary in 1959 a post she still fulfilled tirelessly, along with Country Markets accounts, until The Country Shop closed in 1978. Marion

Tweedy joined in 1932, Dorothy Moore in 1938, Deirdre Ennis in 1939 and Betty Irwin in 1945 and all gave long and loyal service in positions of responsibility. Muriel Gahan was the overall figure of authority, the linchpin of the business and the ultimate arbitrator. She endlessly reiterated her debt to the loyal and unstinting staff.

If Muriel was in town, her arrival in the morning never went unnoticed. Whoever first spotted her coming down the steps would quickly put the word about that 'Miss Gahan' was on her way. Although the staff were fond of her and recognised her warmth and generosity, their respect for her bordered on fear. 'We were in awe of her, we were in respect of her, *and* we were very fond of her,' said Eileen Neary, a waitress in The Country Shop from 1944 until it closed. What they most liked about her was that, as Georgie Hamilton remembered, 'we were all treated as one'. Muriel made no distinction between people, treating an admiral or a bishop in exactly the same way as the man who cleaned the traffic lights on St Stephen's Green and who used to come in for a cup of coffee. She would never ask anyone to do anything she was not prepared to do herself and if staff were short, she would roll up her sleeves and wash up or set tables. But Muriel was human too, and Country Shop staff learnt to tell her mood by how she descended those steps to the yard and entered the Cottage. If she was overheard to be humming ('Moya, my girl' was the most dangerous tune), you looked busy or kept out of her way. If on the other hand she was singing or breezed in with a 'Hello girls!' you could relax. As she swept into the Cottage and through the dining area, although she seemed to look neither to right nor left, nothing would escape her attention.

When the waitresses arrived in the morning, two hours after the kitchen staff, the first thing they smelled was hot scones. The turf fires would be got going and the waitresses would warm up and have some breakfast – often the hot fresh crusts off the bakery bread – before The Country Shop opened to customers. But then it was down to work: butter pats had to be prepared, salt and pepper pots filled, the decorative brass jugs polished and coffee prepared for the first customers. In the Cottage the deal table on which fresh produce was displayed for sale had to be scrubbed each day with a hard brush and hot soapy water. Then the fresh brown loaves, sultana bread and brown and white scones would be laid on it, along with a basketful of country eggs, country butter and pots of jam. The cakes were displayed separately in a glass fronted case in the restaurant. By the time the first customers came in the smells had become a delicious mix of fresh baking, scrubbed wood and the faint whiff of turf smoke. Jams and fudge were made by Marion Tweedy in her own little kitchen upstairs. Known as 'Tweedy' by the rest of the staff, Marion Tweedy was also in charge of flower arrangements.[2] Eileen Neary remembered her disbelief when she first saw these. Eileen was a country person from Co. Louth. As far as she could see the arrangements were made up of weeds, 'the sort of things my father would go along the road or through the garden whacking with a stick and cursing them.' These 'weeds', collected by Marion Tweedy from the fields and lanes around her Co. Wicklow cottage and brought into town in her van every Monday morning, added to The Country Shop's unique atmosphere.

The basement restaurant, the original 1930 area, remained virtually unchanged over the forty-eight years of The Country Shop's existence: the same red and green painted tables and chairs, the white walls and the stone floor. Only the open fires were replaced by gas towards the end, though the open fireplaces were preserved. The flagged floor had to be scrubbed. Margaret Milne, who for more than forty years did 'essential tedious jobs all day long', was paid an extra 2/6d a week to get down on her knees and scrub the cold flags. According to Muriel's calculations, by 1957 she had given the downstairs restaurant 1,300 scrubbings, 'reckoning at only one a week and there were many more.'

A narrow flight of stairs at the back of the basement led up to the ground floor and 'Miss Tweedy's Snack Bar'. A favourite with students, this (for its day) ultra-modern bar, all scarlet and black gloss paint and yellow walls, served tea and coffee in red and white striped mugs as well as soups and pies and toasted sandwiches. It was doubtless here that Marion Tweedy, kind behind a gruff facade, sized up the hungry office girls and served up large soups to those she deemed deserving. On through the bar was the more staid 'Top Restaurant', a carpeted room with round tables and comfortable chairs with Avoca tweed-covered seats and backs, originally sewn by fifteen-year-old Lily Harte when she came to work in The Country Shop. Here the staff would have a three-course lunch before the restaurant opened to the public.

The Top Restaurant was where those regulars who were not part of Muriel's inner circle had their tables. When the Bonne Bouche restaurant in Dawson Street closed down in the early 'thirties, a group of businessmen transferred to The Country Shop for lunch. One of them was a vegetarian and it was because of him that The Country Shop always had a vegetarian dish on its menu. The 'architects' table' was the best remembered one, a large round table looked after by Dorothy Moore, where such people as Dem FitzGerald, Alan and Mairin Hope, Gerald McNicholl, Ken Kiersey, Dermot O'Toole, Percy Le Clerc and Raymond McGrath regularly lunched. A core of five to seven people came every day at 12.30, often joined by Paddy Kavanagh. The waitresses would watch him arrive with trepidation, trying to gauge his condition. He was not, according to them, always welcome at the table, with his hawking cough. 'He would have eaten anything put in front of him, he'd be talking so much.' Kavanagh himself is reputed to have declared of Country Shop food ' 'tis cheap and 'tis dainty'. The Country Shop became like the centre of Dublin itself, a place where you expected to bump into your friends or recognise well-known faces. Regulars would eventually be given nicknames by the staff. 'Crumbs', 'Turnips', 'Fish', and 'Danny Kaye' were some of these. There was even an underwear salesman known amongst the waitresses as 'Ballybra' and a solicitor they called 'Huggy Bear'.

Along a small passage from the Top Restaurant was the Gallery or Back Bar, a magnificent room, tall and airy with a tremendous feeling of light and space. It had a bare pale wooden floor and it was for this room that Muriel had bought Alvar Aalto stools in 1939. It was here too that exhibitions were held, both of crafts and paintings – Belfast artist Gerard Dillon had his first exhibition here in 1942, for example, opened by Mainie Jellett – and where the Country Workers collection of crafts was on permanent display: woodwork, basketry, ironwork and pottery as well as a series of drawings of the traditional Irish crafts specially commissioned by the directors of Country Workers from Elizabeth Rivers in 1943.[3] These now hang at An Grianán, having been donated to the ICA's adult education college at Muriel's suggestion when The Country Shop was closing. Also hanging permanently in the Gallery were paintings by Mainie Jellett and Evie Hone.

Up another narrow flight of stairs was Muriel Gahan's room, the boardroom. For twenty-four years Georgie Hamilton balanced heavy trays of food up the windy stairs from the basement kitchens to this room. This was the holy of holies where Muriel's close friends and chosen visitors would lunch or join her for a cup of tea or coffee. It was in fact her study, with her desk and books, shared with Angela Kehoe once she had been appointed secretary. But there were also three dining tables, one big one for Muriel and her friends, a smaller one for certain regulars and then a little table that was always kept for Muriel if she was out and wanted to bring someone back to lunch. Georgie Hamilton's job was a delicate one. She had to see who was waiting in the queues downstairs and discreetly approach those she thought worthy of bringing upstairs. 'It was very select and I had to be very careful because there were huge queues. It was a very holy place!'. Once the choice had been made, Georgie would lead the elect through a private door on the ground floor which led directly to Muriel's room.

Right up to the time of its closure in September 1978 it would not have occurred to Country Shop regulars that the primary aim of the eating place was anything but their own comfort and enjoyment. It would have been like discovering that their mother had more favoured children elsewhere. Whenever the price of lunch or of the Country Tea had to be increased they would 'give out yards' to the waitresses. But then even the staff, that amazingly devoted and hard-working regiment of women, who *did* know that the restaurant had a higher purpose, were not always well-pleased with the idea either. 'Just when you'd think things were going well and there'd be a nice fat bonus at Christmas, wouldn't we hear that "poor" so-and-so's cow had died or that some "poor" weaver needed a new loom, and that was our bonus out the window.' But the grudge was short-lived. 'There was something you had to like about The Country Shop', former staff agree, 'Miss Gahan just kept a very, very happy place.'

Notes

1. From an article by Maev Kennedy in *The Sunday Tribune*, 6 November, 1994.

2. Marion Tweedy had trained at the Munster Institute. With her friend Eithne Dalton, she set up the first Oxfam shop in Ireland and was an active fundraiser for the Royal United Kingdom Beneficent Association (RUKBA).

3. 'It was agreed that Miss Rivers should be asked to do a complete set of drawings of craftworkers at £5 5s each.' Minutes of Directors' Meeting, 26 February 1943.

— 9 —

Saving Ireland's Homespuns

The Country Shop did not take up all Muriel's time. In 1935 she hatched a new scheme: the Irish Homespun Society or *An Cumann Sniomhachain*. Muriel had grown up with homespuns. The clothes her mother made for her as a child must often have been scratchy and uncomfortable, but they did not prevent her from dressing in hard-wearing tweeds, as far as possible homespun, for the rest of her life. Much of her father's work had been to do with preserving and promoting the tweed industry and, in her mind, her home town of Castlebar was closely bound up with homespuns through Lady Lucan's work to revive production there in the 1890s. One of Muriel's favourite smells was the 'never-to-be-forgotten rich homespun smell' of the crottle dye.

When Muriel was on her weaver hunt in Mayo one of her most memorable encounters, as well as that with Patrick Madden, was with a spinner in the mountains behind Newport. She always told the story with real affection and admiration for Mrs Margaret Murray of Shramore who used to bring her beautifully dyed wool (indigo and crottle flecks were her speciality[1]) to Mr Mulchrone to weave. Muriel stayed in contact with Margaret Murray for many years, buying homespuns woven from her wool and visiting her whenever she was in Mayo. She even kept her supplied with yeast during the war, though she knew it was more likely to be used for making poitín than bread. When she spoke of spinners Muriel did not see exploitation or drudgery, even though she had no illusions about the fiercely hard physical effort involved in breaking and carding wool, nor a craft subsidiary and therefore somehow inferior to weaving (almost entirely done by men), but instead she saw the skill, pride and independent spirit of the diminutive woman she had met in that autumn of 1929. Margaret Murray was washing wool in a mountain stream when Muriel and her sister Grania finally tracked her down:

> Some of it (the wool) was spread out to dry on the whins[2], like a great ragged sheep caught in the bushes. . .Her face, rosy red, was seamed with a thousand wrinkles, and smiles ran out of her eyes and round her mouth. When she spoke, her deep voice echoed round the valley. She was not five feet high. She brought us back to her cottage, and bare-footed, she danced rather than walked along beside us, telling us about her flock of lovely white Cheviots, and the soft wool she got from them to spin her yarn. The indigo was hard to come by now, she said, but not long since she had found a lump of it in her roof, and it had stood by her till now. Looking up at the roof, shining black as ebony through the mysterious wreathing blue of the turf smoke, we would have felt no surprise at anything coming out of it. . .On the fire a black three-legged pot was boiling. It was wool being dyed with the moss. The house was filled with the smell of it. . .[She] took down from a beam a huge ball of yarn she had just spun. It was beautifully fine and strong. . .It was being sent off the next day to the weaver four miles over the mountain. . .We understood the important part women take in making a piece of homespun. Nine tenths of the work is theirs. There is of course good weaving and bad weaving, but it is the dyeing and spinning that makes the real difference between a good and a bad homespun.

It was with spinners like Margaret Murray and weavers such as Patrick Madden in mind that the idea of an organisation specifically designed to save Ireland's homespun tradition slowly took shape in Muriel's imagination. Exterior events nudged the idea along towards realisation and one can only speculate about the part Muriel's father, aged sixty-nine in 1935, must have played in working out the aims and make-up of such a body. The seed itself was nurtured by Muriel's real personal affection and respect for individual producers.

The idea grew slowly. When in July 1932 the Country Workers directors unanimously decided to take over more space on the ground floor of 23 St Stephen's Green they opened up a whole new range of possibilities, the significance of which would slowly dawn on them once expensive alterations had been carried out and the attendant headaches had faded. In January 1933 they realised that the 'end room' at the back of the ground floor would be very suitable for lunch parties, whist drives, meetings and such like. Most of all, with its tall ceiling and high windows it was going to be perfect for 'exhibitions of all kinds'. It would not be long before the 'end room' became the 'Gallery'. The first exhibition to be held there, a display of traditional crafts, was staged by Muriel for Country Workers in October 1933. It was opened by the Countess of Fingall, president of the UI. With the excitement of seeing it still fresh in her mind, Livie Hughes wrote about it in the train as she travelled home to Fethard:

> I have come from an exhibition of country industries at The Country Shop, and it is my wish that everyone interested in country industries will visit the show without delay so that they may feel hopeful and proud and ambitious. It is not like an ordinary exhibition, still less like a bazaar. You get in free and no-one seems to want to sell you anything. There is no dreary impression of heaped up objects, but light, colour, agreeable broken outlines, comedy, homeliness, good design, usefulness and simplicity. As a country woman I do not like things called country industries which are made in Dublin factories, but there are none of these things here. Where the exhibits come from is written beside them, also who made them, and sometimes the maker's account of their own industry. Much of the work has been done or collected by different branches of the United Irishwomen and, as a member of the UI, I am proud of what we are doing to build up home industries.
>
> Almost all the exhibits are made from home-grown materials such as willows and rushes and wool, and the pottery is made of rich clay. The first impression of the exhibition is of profusion of colour. There is a gorgeous old quilt from Sligo, orange and green and red. Then there is the black glaze of the Coalisland jars, the creamy yellow of the big cheeses, the glowing richness of tweeds and rugs, the soft green of rushes and the gaiety of toys. The next impression is the interest of design, which is also clearly shown in the arrangement of the exhibits. There are distinguished and austere futurist rugs and modern furniture. There are flowery designs, flamboyant designs, comic designs, dainty designs. . . nothing heartless, or automatic or 'stuck on'.

Livie goes on to list in detail all the crafts on display: lace, sycamore bowls, rushwork, toys, gloves, tweeds, ironwork, including a 'beautiful curly bread iron from Donegal', and a rich variety of objects from the Aran Islands. She also describes the 'vegetable dyes with their accompanying "vegetables", such as birch bark and walnut, elderberry and wild mignonette and lichen', and a display of herbal cures 'with rather comic notes on their uses sent by the gatherer in the mountains of Mayo' who turned out to be Muriel's friend, Margaret Murray. There was also 'a splendid collection' of jams, pickles and bottled and crystallised fruits. Both Mrs Faherty from Inis Mór and Patrick Madden won awards, the former for her knitting, the latter for a homespun rug.

There had been no major UI exhibit at the RDS Spring Show since 1930. Yet Muriel's mind went back to the excitement of the two Spring Shows she had helped at. She remembered the look of child-like delight on visitors' faces as, spellbound, they watched the different craftworkers demonstrate. When, in September 1934, it was decided that it would be too disruptive to hold an exhibition on the scale of the 1933 one in The Country Shop every year, as had at first been envisaged, surprisingly Muriel did not object. She had been in London during the summer where Heal's, the department store, had staged a magnificent exhibition of traditional country crafts. This had so impressed her that she started thinking of the Spring Show again. There was nowhere else that the crafts would be exposed to that sheer volume of visitors from all over Ireland. However hard she worked, however impressive the display of crafts she mounted in The Country Shop, she could never hope to see the same numbers file through the Gallery as through the halls of the two-hundred-year-old RDS in Ballsbridge.

Muriel got to work. Early in 1935 she sat down to write to the director of the RDS, Edward Bohane, on behalf of Country Workers Ltd, asking for a grant to mount an exhibition of crafts at the 1935 Spring Show. Her request was turned down. But Professor Felix Hackett, who had recently been made an honorary secretary of the RDS and who was a keen supporter of the crafts, came to The Country Shop to see her and discuss the reasons behind the refusal. Felix Hackett, a Derry man, was Professor of Physics in UCD and would later become President of the RDS (1953–56). He already knew about Muriel and her energy. He and his wife had been introduced to the Gahans on their return from Castlebar by a mutual friend. Then, in May 1931, he had chaired the founding meeting of An Óige, the Irish Youth Hostel

Association, held in UCD. Muriel was there too and in her inimitable way had immediately stood up and offered The Country Shop as a meeting place for the fledgling movement. From June to October 1931 weekly meetings of An Óige took place at 23 St Stephen's Green. Felix Hackett also remembered how freely Muriel had offered her skills as a decorator, spending a weekend in July 1931 with Marion Tweedy, who was on An Óige's committee, making the Steward's Lodge in Laragh, recently acquired as a women's hostel, habitable.[3]

Felix Hackett explained to Muriel that the RDS was not in a position to give money to a private business like The Country Shop, albeit non profit making, 'but if some kind of a representative Association could be formed, of people interested in helping country industries, the Society would then consider, another year, giving a grant to such a body.' Muriel at once saw the advantages of such a voluntary body in terms of being eligible not just for RDS grants but possibly for government support as well. It was also an opportunity for her to be involved in an organisation which was *purely* concerned with the traditional crafts. Her mind returned once again to wool, one of Ireland's most abundant raw materials and a source of rural employment and development. She knew it was also an area where women had a huge role to play. And homespun happened to be the craft most seriously in danger of extinction, 'the most important and the most in need of help'. By 1935, genuine homespun was being produced only in northwest Donegal and in a few small districts in Mayo and Kerry and then in very small quantities.

While touring Donegal late in 1934, visiting her old spinning and weaving friends and making new ones, Muriel had heard of the work of a 'Donegal Trust' which since 1931 had been financing apprenticeships in spinning and weaving in the Gweedore and Cloghaneely districts of northwest Donegal. Evelyn Gleeson, founder of the Dun Emer Guild and an important figure in the Irish Arts and Crafts Movement, was involved with its work and so was her niece, Kitty MacCormack. The more Muriel found out about it the clearer it became that the purpose of the John Conor Magee Trust, for that was its full name, and her own aims to promote and preserve the traditional crafts coincided closely.

John Conor Magee had died in 1924 and his will had been the subject of a long and complex legal saga. Born in Co. Derry, Magee had emigrated to America where he became a private detective and amassed a certain amount of wealth. In 1914, by now a widower whose only son had settled in California he retired and came back to Ireland. He made his base in Skerries, north of Dublin and described as 'a man of very eccentric manner and habits [who] did not exhibit any outward sign of financial prosperity', he proceeded to travel around the country contacting prominent people and discussing with them 'schemes for national development and improvement'. In 1915 he chose a solicitor in Dublin and for over a year visited him nearly every day, sometimes spending the whole day in his office, endlessly amending his will. Then without warning he left again for America at the end of 1916. Nothing more was ever heard of him until news of his death reached Ireland in 1924.

Apart from sums of money for his only son, for relatives in Co. Derry and an annual prize towards the promotion of temperance, the main object of the will was the 'improvement and development of manufacturing industries in Ireland, especially in those parts of Ireland where the Irish language is generally spoken as a home language, such improvement and development to be carried out by the provision of instructors, organisers, lecturers, teachers, the payment of premiums, the payment of money to Societies existing at the date of my death directed in whole or in part to the promotion of like objects. . .' A trust was to be set up and known as the John Conor Magee Trust. His chosen trustees were 'Dr Douglas Hyde, Miss Agnes O'Farrelly, Dr Timothy Corcoran, SJ, all at present of the University College Dublin, Colonel Sir Nugent T Everard Bart HML of Randalstown Navan in the county of Meath, W E Shackelton of Cannonbrook Lucan in the County of Dublin and Mr E J Riordan at present Secretary of the Irish Industrial Development Association at 102 and 103 Grafton Street in the City of Dublin.'

By early May 1935, when Muriel gathered together a dozen interested people in The Country Shop for an exploratory meeting, the active trustees of the trust were Agnes O'Farrelly, Professor of Modern Irish Poetry at UCD, Seán Ó hUadhaigh, solicitor for the Gaelic League and well-known nationalist figure and William Shackleton, Quaker flour miller and pioneer of Ireland's industrial revival, a second cousin of the Antarctic explorer, Ernest Shackleton. Douglas Hyde, soon to become Ireland's first national president, had dropped out since he moved back to Frenchpark, Co. Roscommon in 1932. The other names had never been much more than figureheads. The trust's activities at this time were described thus by Seán Ó hUadhaigh:[4]

The three of us are in the habit of going down [to the Donegal Gaeltacht] every year and seeing how the scheme is working out. The present scheme is that Miss Gleeson of Dun Emer goes down once a year and selects the likeliest looking girls and boys in the District whose Irish is passed as being OK by Mr. McAnaspie, the Principal Teacher in Gortahork Bilingual National School, and by Canon McDwyer, the Parish Priest there, and they are then apprenticed by us, the girls to spinners and the boys to weavers. . .The spinning is of course the more important end of the matter as it takes from 10 to 15 women spinning to keep a weaver fully occupied. You can see how this works out in terms of employment. My own idea would be to have a Depot in Dublin where the stuff would be very carefully examined and remorselessly rejected if it was not up to the standard in every respect, and every yard of the stuff would then be stamped on the selvage with a special mark which would be the property of a small company to be formed by us, and which would be a guarantee that the stuff was home spun and home woven and quite possibly, if we find it practicable, home dyed also.

Muriel was delighted. Her new association had fallen ready-made into her lap, complete with known 'names' such as Agnes O'Farrelly and Evelyn Gleeson. There was also Mary McGeehin of the Women's Industrial Development Association (WIDA)[5] and Dulcibella (Daa) Barton, sister of Robert Childers Barton, who had been a signatory of the 1921 Anglo-Irish Treaty. Daa Barton was a member of the Gaelic League and an early member of the UI. There was also the potential financial backing of the John Conor Magee Trust (when the law case was settled they had £5000, more than £150,000 in today's money, lodged in the bank), an aspect not to be sneezed at. For her part, Muriel brought in Felix Hackett, Robert and Fania Stoney of Rosturk Castle in Co. Mayo, both Country Workers shareholders, and two indefatigable ICA workers, Mairin McDonald and Joyce Nicholson. Amongst artists whose advice was sought from time to time were Stella Frost, Gladys Wynne, a cousin of the Wynne sisters in Avoca, and Lillias Mitchell, whose expertise was sought both as an artist and as a teacher of spinning, weaving and dyeing. On several occasions Mainie Jellett and Elizabeth Rivers helped with designs for shows. Gerald Elliot, of the well-known poplin weaving establishment, S C Hughes of Cottage Industries, and Seamus O'Farrell of the NAIDA were all invited to contribute their knowledge to the new society. Kevin Danaher, the folklorist, was co-opted on to the committee in the 'forties. Two other subscribers to the Homespun Society who were to prove important allies for Muriel later on were Tomás O Deirg[6], minister for education from 1932 to 1948, and P J Little, minister for posts and telegraphs from 1939–48 and who in 1951 was appointed first director of the Arts Council to which he nominated Muriel. The Homespun Society worked closely with Seamus Delargy and other members of the Irish Folklore Commission which like the former had been set up in 1935.

By the time the second meeting of the not yet christened Irish Homespun Society was held, on 29 May, Muriel had drawn up an exhaustive and somewhat exhausting plan of action. Her enthusiasm is palpable in the scheme she presented:

1. To form an association having as wide a membership as possible, with an annual subscription of 5/-, donations invited. An executive committee to be elected to draw up a constitution, and conduct the business of the society, and a Trade Mark to be taken out. This mark to be used as a guarantee of quality. The association to carry on as such for one year, when in the light of knowledge gained, the position will be reviewed, and if thought desirable, steps taken to form a Friendly Society, or a limited company.

2. To enlist the co-operation of the Dept. of Lands and Fisheries, Gaeltacht Services, and technical education, and their practical help in whatever way it may be forthcoming, but not to apply for any grants or loans of money.

3. To hold a public meeting at the end of June for the purposes of publicity and to get annual subscribers. Notices of this meeting to be sent to all those who might be interested, and to the press.

4. To hold an all-Ireland Homespun competition and Exhibition in Dublin early in October, with substantial money prizes. All the tweeds of lengths of 15 to 30 yards, divided into two classes, light and heavy, to be examined by competent judges, and stamped with the society's mark. The Exhibition to last for one week. The first day to be a private view and sale to the trade only. The buyers to be invited to a conference to give their views, and lend their co-operation.

The rest of the week, the exhibition to be open to the public, admission to be charged. Orders of lengths of tweed to be booked through the firms who have bought the rolls, and through the society. By way of interest, demonstrations of carding and spinning, vegetable dye exhibit. Exhibits of made up goods using homespun, curtains, chair covers, cushions, rugs, coats, skirts, suits and the sellers dressed in homespun. Homespun wool to go with the tweeds, and stockings, gloves and jerseys knitted from it.

5. If practical, to send an exhibit of homespuns to the London Exhibition of Homespuns and Vegetable Dyes, on October 10th. Patterns to be brought round London wholesalers.

6. After the Dublin Exhibition, to approach the Royal Dublin Society, with a view to securing their interest and help in staging a comprehensive exhibition of country industries at next year's Spring Show.

- In the Autumn to procure a salesman working on commission to bring round samples of any tweeds the Society may have in stock after the exhibition, and to secure fresh orders.

- Agents in other towns in Ireland and in other countries to be looked for.

- Managers of hotels and shops in tourist centres to be asked to co-operate.

- Organisers of country Feis to be asked to stage homespun exhibits, the Society to offer prizes.

- All members of the Society to give as much publicity as possible to the uses of homespun, by using it in their homes, by wearing it when suitable, and by recommending it to their friends.

- The Society must try by every means possible to raise the standard of the homespun produced, and only to sell under their mark the very best.

The Society was formally launched in June. Although she was not elected to the chair until 1941 when Daa Barton resigned on a point of order, Muriel was extremely active from the start. Organisation of the exhibition went ahead, Muriel persuading her fellow directors of Country Workers that 'as its contribution to the Society, The Country Shop should give the Gallery free and undertake the staging and running of the exhibition.' She said she thought it would cost them between thirty and forty pounds. Muriel went into top gear to prepare the exhibition. It was principally she, of course, who would be 'staging and running it'.

The exhibition – 'From Fleece to Finished Garments' – was a success in every way. Many orders were taken for homespuns and £230 was sent to the country in sales and prizes, the Homespun Society having first deducted a ten per cent commission, its other source of income apart from annual subscriptions. Equally good results could be seen in the list of names of those who had come to the exhibition: 'Mr Connolly, Minister for Lands, Mr Moran, director of Gaeltacht Services, Mr Ingram, Head of the Technical Education Dept. and Mr Bohane, Director of the RDS. As a result of these visits, the society had been invited to send a memorandum to the Government on the homespun industry, Mr Ingram had offered to help in any way he could, and Mr Bohane held out prospects of an exhibition of Country Crafts at the next Spring Show.' It was an excellent catch. By February 1936 'the Vocational authorities had taken up the improvement of the industry in different parts of the country and were appointing instructresses in spinning and dyeing in various centres in the country.' Bohane confirmed his offer to stage 'an exhibition of country crafts at the forthcoming Spring Show, to be arranged by the Homespun Society.'

With the exception of three years, the Irish Homespun Society's presence at the RDS was to become a regular and eagerly anticipated event from 1936 until 1946. Foot and mouth disease in 1941, a shortage of crafts to display in 1943 and wartime transport restrictions in 1944 were the causes of their non-appearance. In 1944 it was the whole Spring Show, not just the Society's part in it, which was cancelled. In the early days of the Society Muriel did a lot of the footwork for the exhibitions herself, but she was soon obliged to delegate as wanting to do so much left her exhausted. On her doctor's advice she took a long holiday at the end of 1937, spending from December until July of the following year in Kenya with her brother. Delegation also became a necessity for the efficiency of her schemes as these multiplied.

In the Spring of 1936, however, she personally travelled to the four corners of Ireland to arrange for demonstrators to come to the Show in May. From Mayo she brought Andrew Dever of Glenhest to weave and Kate McNea of Newport to demonstrate spinning on the big wheel. Nancy Ferry agreed to travel all the way from Dunlewey to demonstrate on the smaller flax wheel used in Donegal. Naneen Mullen came from Inis Mór to show how crioses were woven, also bringing some knitting to display. Muriel was always very keen on traditional Irish dress and had insisted that Naneen wear the traditional Aran woman's clothes to the Show, which she obediently did. 'She was a tall woman and she looked beautiful in her long crimson skirt with its black bands and the dark top and the shawl', Muriel remembered. 'I invited her to come to The Country Shop to have lunch with me and I asked her while she was there would she like to go to Woolworths. The Aran women take these great striding steps in their lovely full skirts and as we walked along the Green of course everybody turned to look at her and she turned to me most sadly and said over and over, "We had coats at home!".' Her other demonstrators included Joseph Greene, the potter, from Youghal, a súgán chairmaker from Ennis, and Joseph Hughes from Armagh, one of the three remaining woodturners still to use a pole-lathe to make his sycamore dishes, 'turned out of solid sycamore blocks, one dish taken out of another'. There were also demonstrations in lacemaking, toymaking, rush and willow basketry, lumra rugs and wrought ironwork.

Sales figures were over £500. Unfortunately, despite RDS support, the show cost Country Workers over £50 in expenses, more than Muriel had foreseen. When she pleaded the case for Country Workers' support for the next Homespun Society exhibition, Livie Hughes was not impressed. 'Should the RDS require their assistance another year they should pay for it', she said, adding that they had 'got a splendid show at practically no expense to themselves.' Livie always took a tougher line than Muriel on such matters and, where money was concerned, her feet were more firmly on the ground having, unlike Muriel, a household and farm to run. Muriel, on the other hand, was incapable of feeling detachment from any of the associations she was involved with. For her, as long as the RDS understood her aims and was helping to forward rather than hinder them, she felt part of it and did not greatly mind where the money came from in the end. Country Workers had money, why couldn't they pay? From 1937 on, however, an annual grant of £160 was provided by the RDS and this fully covered fees to demonstrators, their travel expenses, board and lodging.

The Homespun Society's display filled the members' hall and library, today the RDS concert hall. The 1937 programme notes, prepared by Muriel, were to serve as the basis for subsequent years, any additional achievements of the Society being added on to the original text. Muriel's voice can be clearly heard through it:

> That our Irish country people are born craftsmen there is no doubt, and in the old days, there were none to surpass them in skill, but they have been left so long without any interest being taken in their work, that they have come near to losing interest in it themselves, an attitude of mind which is the end of all creative effort. . .If they are to survive, our craft workers must have appreciation and encouragement from the rest of the community. . .In this exhibition the Homespun Society has aimed at showing *each craft in detail*, so that it may be better understood by the public, and in particular by people living in the country, to enable them to help the craftsmen in their own districts. If, in addition, the educational authorities would see that young people in the country were taught the appreciation and the use of the natural products growing around them, a tradition of craftsmanship would again be built up in Ireland and the enrichment of our national life.

The war years were difficult and each time a show was cancelled, often at the very last minute after months of arduous preparations, it caused huge disappointment amongst those craftworkers who were to demonstrate. In 1944 the theme chosen by Muriel was to be 'Women and Wool' with weaving, spinning, quilting, dyeing, crios- and rug-making as well as knitting from the Aran Islands and Fairisle knitting from Cruit Island, Co. Donegal – all done by women. There was also to have been an all-Ireland spinning competition with a spinner representing each of the thirty-two counties. Just two weeks before the Show was due to open, the cancellation was announced. The programme, a real affirmation of women's role in the crafts, was successfully staged in 1945.

That autumn the RDS wrote offering the Pembroke Hall and the Horse Show for the Homespun Society's 1946 exhibition. RDS members had been muttering for some years about the fact that they were unable to avail of their library during Spring Show week because it was occupied by the Homespun Society's exhibit. 'Owing to the circumstances of the war,' it was explained, 'considerations of the various objections had been deferred, but the time has now come when the Committee must deal with the matter.' Since there was no alternative space available for them at the Spring Show, the Homespun Society had no choice but to look into the Horse Show option. Muriel took Elizabeth Rivers with her to examine the long, narrow hall to see how best it could be used. 'The hall, after occupation by the military, is looking its worst', Muriel reported back to the Society, clearly appalled by the impossible proportions of the place. 'The impression on entering the hall is one of enormous length. If exhibits and demonstrators are not to be completely dwarfed, it will be essential to break this length and introduce some incident into the scheme of decoration. Above all the hall cries out for colour.'

Elizabeth Rivers submitted her suggestions for the re-decoration of the Hall but unfortunately the RDS did not accept her design. Preparations went ahead all the same. Two new members were 'invited' on to the committee, Winifred Drury and Lillias Mitchell. Win Drury was given the task of organising the basket exhibits, while Lillias Mitchell, recently returned from teaching spinning and weaving in Wales, was put in charge of everything to do with wool. She travelled up to Dunlewey with Muriel in April and had her first introduction to the spinners and weavers there and the great warmth of their welcome for 'Miss Gahan'.

Memories of that 1946 Horse Show remained engraved in Muriel's memory:

> Two pictures of the exhibition are conjured up. The first, a pre-Exhibition one of Win Drury saving her aching feet by bicycling up and down the Hall (it is 288 feet long) with her exhibits for the basket stand; festooned in rushes one time, rods and baskets another. We all envied her foresight. The other picture, a more sober one, is during the Exhibition, of Dr Seamus Delargy, Director of the Folklore Commission, standing in the Hall looking round him at the traditional crafts of every kind, at spinners and weavers at their looms and wheels, at basketmakers, the blacksmith, the chair maker, the stone carver, all part of that material Folk Culture almost as dear to him as the Folk Lore to which he has given his life – and saying as he looked 'Everyone should know about this.'

Notes

1.   There is a piece of Margaret Murray's indigo and white homespun with a crottle fleck in the National Museum's folklife collection, presented by Muriel Gahan in 1951.

2. 'Whin' is another name for furze or gorse, 'an evergreen shrub which has yellow flowers and thick green spines instead of leaves.'

3. Trench, Terry. *Fifty Years Young – The Story of An Óige*, Dublin, 1981, pp 10–14 and conversations with the author.

4. From a letter to the minister for lands and forestry, Senator Joe Connolly, dated 2 May 1935, the day of the first Homespun Society preparatory meeting.

5. 'The Women's Industrial Development Association is a society whose members purchase exclusively Irish goods, in so far as they are obtainable, and they endeavour to encourage the use of Irish goods by all citizens of Eire. It has no political affiliations and works mainly to encourage the idea of purchasing Irish goods and so helping brother workers and manufacturers and adding to the wealth and stability of our State. The WIDA was brought into being in 1932 by the late Miss Somers, Secretary of the National Agricultural and Industrial Development Association and has had an autonomous existence since 1933. By propaganda, dress parades and other activities it has materially fostered the demand for Irish goods.' Programme note, Royal Dublin Society Spring Show, 1938.

6. Basketmaker Pat O'Connor remembers Tomás O Deirg, Mayo-born founder member of Fianna Fáil and minister for education from 1932–48, sitting for hours beside him at the 1931 Spring Show watching him make baskets.

— 10 —

Spreading the Word

In the thirty years it existed (it was finally wound up in 1965 after six years' inactivity), the Irish Homespun Society, while ultimately defeated in its fundamental aim – not least by World War II – nevertheless achieved impressive gains for Irish traditional crafts. In its early years the ambitious Spring Show exhibits with demonstrators, as well as regular sales of homespun in Dublin at other times of the year, brought wide publicity for the crafts, provided a strong incentive for workers not to give up and generated a vital income for homespun producers and other craftworkers. After 1946 RDS support was transferred to Country Markets Ltd, the co-operative company formed jointly that year by the Homespun Society and the ICA. The RDS grant would go towards financing shows and competitions at local, as opposed to national, level. Country Markets also took over the marketing of homespuns and other crafts from the Homespun Society which was then free to switch its efforts to education and training. In 1945 Muriel had become a member of the RDS and was appointed to their panel of extension lecturers, travelling to seven different small country towns between September and November alone, laden down with sample exhibits, to speak about 'Irish Country Crafts' and 'Irish Handweaving'.[1] With Muriel in the forefront, the Homespun Society began persistently to lobby government departments for the introduction of craft instruction, particularly of spinning and weaving, into the education system.

Throughout her life, one of Muriel's hobby-horses was Ireland's lack of a folk museum. In the programme to the Homespun Society's 1937 Spring Show exhibit she wrote, 'Other countries have their Folk Museums where the hand work of the people is proudly displayed. Ireland has no Folk Museum, and few people even realise that our traditional country crafts are something to be proud of.' In her ten years of overseeing and participating in the preparation of shows and exhibitions for the Homespun Society, a considerable number of artefacts of historic interest accumulated, especially after an 'historical exhibit' had been planned and then abandoned in 1940. A problem of storage arose. It occurred to Muriel to offer such material to the National Museum. In March 1941 she offered to lend whatever items in the Homespun Society's possession interested them. By June she had co-opted Michael Duignan, who worked in the Antiquities Division of the National Museum of Ireland, on to the Homespun Society's executive committee and asked him to draw up a list of objects the museum would like to acquire. The Homespun Society set up a fund (worth £57 10s at the end of 1941) 'for the purchase of old farm, craft and domestic implements to be presented to the National Museum Folk Collection' in the hope 'that this may help to form the nucleus of a Folk Museum.'[2]

Muriel continued to donate both artefacts and information to the National Museum over the years, earning the high esteem of Dr A T Lucas who on joining the staff in 1947 became the first person to be given specific responsibility for the Folklife Collection, hitherto lumped together with the Irish Antiquities division. Lucas, who would later become the Museum's director, wrote to Muriel in January 1951 thanking her for a donation of homespun tweeds and knitting from the Aran Islands she had just made. 'This institution already stands heavily indebted to your kindness for magnificent and unstinted help in the past,' he wrote. 'No-one knows better than yourself how much the Folk Life department of the museum needs help and no-one has come forward so willingly and for so long to afford it that help. Our collection of textiles of all kinds is disgracefully bad, but this latest consignment from Country Workers Ltd will go far to remedy that unfortunate state of affairs.' Two years later Muriel had offered the services of the ICA to collect material for the Museum from all around the country. At the end of an irate memo to his then superior, Dr Joseph Raftery, who had queried the nature of Muriel's proposed scheme, Lucas wrote, 'As the whole debt of obligation in the proposal rests upon the museum and as Miss Gahan has most generously absolved us from the smallest commitment to take any of the material collected it will be agreed that it might be construed as churlish and obstructive were we to enquire for details of how she proposes to operate her completely altruistic scheme.'

As early as 1937 Muriel had had the vision to foresee the growth in the Irish tourist trade and the accompanying demand for crafts of quality. In a letter to John Ingram of the technical education branch of the department of education and author of the 1930 Vocational Education Act, she wrote:

> In case there is any doubt in your mind as to the ultimate value to the country of the fostering of the homespun industry, we would like to say that it is impressed upon us more and more that there is a genuine world wide demand for Irish homespun, and we believe that this demand, as for other hand work, will increase rather than lessen in the future. Ireland is now the only country producing homespun as we know it in any quantity. Within the last year we have been asked to send tweed to England, Scotland, Sweden, Australia, Canada, New Zealand, Japan, and above all to the United States, but we have been unable to do so, because we have not had a supply of good homespun to send. . .The tourist industry should hold out great possibilities of sales of homespun, and here again, the demand is increasing each year with the ever increasing number of people who bring over their cars, and explore the remote corners of the mountains where tweed is made. What happens too often at present is that the tourist is palmed off with a piece of inferior factory spun tweed, because there is not the genuine homespun available.'

After the war, there was even less 'genuine homespun' to be found and the Homespun Society had to devise a new strategy for its survival. It was as if all their efforts had to be started again only differently this time. There was the growing sense that Dublin-based exhibitions of crafts, though useful in the short term and encouraging to individual craftworkers, were not achieving the longer term goal of reviving rural industry in a permanent and economically viable way. Muriel's experience as an extension lecturer had been a sobering one. Until she began to lecture in 1945 her travels around the country had mainly brought her into direct contact with craftworkers, or with ICA guilds where the crafts were always present. Now she was addressing the 'ordinary' country people in small country towns.

Lecturing in a village in Co. Westmeath in 1946 she reported that 'For such a completely rural district, it was a matter of interest that the subject of the lecture (Irish Country Crafts) was one of which the audience had no knowledge whatsoever, nor any knowledge of the existence of any craftsmen in their neighbourhood. They were like a people cut off from the rest of the country, shut in on themselves.' Yet wherever she went the turnout was high – from fifty to over a hundred people – and interest was clearly high too. In Tipperary Town on 28 January 1947, 'About 60 people were at the lecture – all women – and again it was noticeable what an interest the audience took in the crafts, and how little they knew about them. The almost unnatural earnestness with which everyone listened to the lecture brought home how much Ireland's small towns are in need of something more than the usual round of bridge, the pictures and greyhounds. This was their only lecture in the year, they told me afterwards.' The week before, lecturing in Wexford Town, Muriel had found that 'not one member of the audience knew of even the Wexford crafts carried on less than ten miles from the town, nor did anyone seem to have considered craftwork except as the making of some more or less unnecessary object as quickly and with as little study as possible.'

The work the Homespun Society had done to strengthen the homespun industry in the years leading up to the war, and in the early war years – 'giving advice on design, colour and quality of material considered marketable, sending patterns and giving practical instruction in dyeing' – had proved ephemeral since the established spinners and weavers thus targeted were lured away from producing genuine, high quality homespuns by the increased demand for tweed of just about any quality as a result of wartime shortages. 'At the beginning of the war,' Muriel wrote on the Homespun Society's behalf in a strongly worded memorandum to the Gaeltacht Services in April 1946, 'the high standard of craftsmanship evident in North Donegal and Mayo was witness to the lasting value of help and encouragement given by individuals and voluntary organisations, and to self-help and local initiative. Up to the time of control no government aid was sought or received in these districts. South Donegal on the other hand, where for the last sixty years government assistance has been in constant demand, was melancholy testimony to the effects of outside aid without corresponding local effort and of a policy of large scale production with emphasis on quantity rather than quality.'

In 1943 Gaeltarra's control of the homespun market had been extended to North Donegal and in particular to the community of spinners and weavers in Dunlewey, with the result that spinners' skills and their control over quality were largely by-passed and the tweeds produced were, in Muriel's words, of 'distressingly low standard'. Gaeltarra offered the same price for real homespun as for handwoven tweed using millspun warp thread, giving spinners no incentive to do the extra work of spinning the warp themselves. As for the weft, spinners were provided with machine carded rolls of wool by Gaeltarra, a huge saving in labour for them, but cutting out the skillful proccess of selecting from their own fleeces which, for Muriel, represented an essential part of the craft. 'We have proof from all parts of Ireland that where homespun organisation has remained in the hands of the spinners and the weavers themselves, it has remained a home craft', wrote Muriel. 'Where the organisation has been taken out of their hands, and in particular out of the spinners' hands, no matter how efficient the organisation, the craft has dwindled and eventually died out. Just as nine-tenths of the work of making a piece of homespun is the spinner's, so it is her initiative that keeps the organisation going.'

The absurd situation was reached where Dunlewey spinners and weavers were producing genuine, good quality homespun *only* for RDS competitions and in particular the Robert Stoney Cup which was donated to the Homespun Society after Stoney's death in 1944 by his widow, Fania Stoney, and which brought a ten pound prize. An indication of just what sort of quantities of tweed Gaeltarra Eireann were buying up can be had from the following brief news item in *The Irish Times* in August 1946: 'A Danish aircraft which had come over from Copenhagen the previous day took three miles of Donegal tweeds from Dublin on Thursday, the first of several consignments to go to Denmark. Big orders have also been received from Belgium, Norway, Iceland, Canada, USA and Iraq.'

Time and effort would be more valuably spent building up crafts and finding a market for them, it was decided, and the only way to do this was through education and, in the case of Donegal, by persuading the homespun producers there, once Gaeltarra lifted their control, to reorganise by forming co-operatives and taking charge of their own production and sales. Much of Muriel's energy in the post-war years went into these crusades. She knew that producing homespun, home-dyed yarn was an arduous, labour-intensive task and wanted the spinners' work to receive a correspondingly adequate financial reward. 'There will always be a market for good homespun', Agnes O'Farrelly had argued on behalf of the Homespun Society in a letter to the *Irish Independent* in 1939, but 'it can never be a mass produced article, the price can never be low.'

Many of Muriel's arguments when pleading with the various government departments still ring true today: 'In a small country such as ours,' she wrote in 1946, 'it is only by concentrating on quality and originality that our products can hope to find a place in the world market.' Referring specifically to tweeds she said, 'Everything is in favour of making both handwoven *and* homespun rural crafts of outstanding worth, if only we recognise and develop their essential qualities and differences. Each has infinite possibilities, each must stand on its own merits.' It was more than just giving the producers fair pay, though this was vital, too. Their skill was precious. In a memorandum to the department of education also drafted by Muriel in 1946 she said, 'The value of our crafts cannot be reckoned in money. They are like the language, part of our national tradition handed down to us through the generations. The voluntary organisations are doing their best to do their part, and they look to the State to do its part in its own sphere – education.'

Through Country Workers and the ICA, Muriel had for some years worked in close co-operation with sympathetic individuals within the Vocational Education department, often the county Chief Executive Officer (CEO). As early as 1937 classes in spinning had been set up in counties Galway, Leitrim, Clare and Mayo. But, as she stated in her 1946 memo to the department of lands, 'plans for instruction on a large scale had to be abandoned in 1939 due to the war.' It is difficult to gauge whether Muriel's hopes for such 'large scale' plans were based in reality or were simply a sign of her irrepressible optimism. Certainly Gerald Bruen, a professional artist who became the department of education's art inspector in 1944, a post he was to hold until 1973, remembered resistance from within the department, especially from the domestic science sector, to implementing Muriel's demands for increased craft instruction in vocational schools.

Notes

1. The system of extension lectures had been started by the RDS in the late 1930s. In 1937 ten such lectures were given in venues outside

Dublin; by 1946 the number had grown to 121, lecturers being chosen by local Vocational Education Committees from a panel of 23 established by the RDS.

2. One of the Irish Homespun Society's first donations to the Museum was when a damask loom ('cost approximately £20 including setting up') was presented in June 1942.

— 11 —

Putting Crafts on the Map

B ut Muriel always stuck to what she passionately believed in.
Her decision after the war to concentrate on a radical
demand for the widespread teaching of art and the crafts
from primary school right up to the College of Art, in vocational
schools and in the Gaeltacht, was strengthened by an increasingly
informed appraisal of the state of the crafts in Ireland. As early as
1939 it had been felt that 'a member should go round finding out
other craftworkers through the country – the Society providing
expenses and salary.' Eventually the right person turned up. Muriel
was always quick to recognise in others the qualities she had in
abundance herself – resilience, perseverance and a passion for rural
Ireland. When she could, she would foster and encourage them.
At the 1942 ICA Summer School in Bray, Co. Wicklow, she met
a young woman from the Co. Tipperary guild of Dualla called
Chrissie O'Gorman. 'A vivid impression of Miss O'Gorman's gifts
of observation, initiative and feeling for country life remained with
me after the school', Muriel was to write later. Just like Miranda
Scally whom Muriel would hire as organiser for Country Workers
Ltd in 1946, Chrissie was 'on' for anything and the idea of
travelling the length and breadth of Ireland in the pursuit of crafts
with only her bicycle for company did not bother her. At a
Homespun Society meeting in January 1943 'the difficulty of
getting in touch with rural craftworkers was discussed, and, on the
suggestion of Miss Gahan, it was decided to try a three months'
organising experiment beginning in some county like Carlow. Miss
O'Gorman to be asked if she would undertake it and offered £5 a
month and expenses for March, April, May.' That three months'
'experiment' grew into a major survey of the crafts in Ireland
which lasted close on four years.

Chrissie O'Gorman was in her early thirties and a fluent Irish speaker. Between March 1943 and November 1947 she carried out a meticulously documented county by county survey, reporting back almost daily either to Muriel herself or to Mairin McDonald or Joyce Nicholson. She visited the twenty-six counties and was eager to continue until all thirty-two had been covered since it had always been Homespun Society policy – as it would always be Muriel's policy on the crafts – to include the whole of Ireland in their work. By 1954 the six counties of Northern Ireland had still not been documented and Chrissie wrote 'I hope we won't have to wait until the border is shifted.' Her time on the survey was interspersed with time spent learning crafts herself and teaching at ICA summer schools. In 1944 Muriel arranged for her to spend three months learning to weave with Peter Mulkerrin in Carna, Co. Galway, who had demonstrated at the 1942 Spring Show; in the Spring of 1945 she learnt about colour and design with Emily Wynne in Avoca; and a year later she took a course on vegetable dyes with Lillias Mitchell. In 1950, as a result of the skills and experience she had acquired, and thanks to Muriel's constant encouragement, she travelled to Sweden with Miranda Scally for a six week course in weaving.

Chrissie's survey began in Carlow and for the rest of 1943 she travelled through the counties Kilkenny, Waterford, Cork, Kerry, Limerick and Clare, ending in November. When she took up the survey again in 1944 she returned to Clare to finish her investigations there and then moved on to Galway, Sligo, Mayo and Donegal. In 1945 she was in Mayo once more and then, after her course in Avoca, she travelled to Leitrim, Roscommon and Longford. In 1946 she travelled through Cavan, Louth, Meath, Monaghan, Westmeath and her home county of Tipperary. Between April and November of 1947 she visited Wexford, Wicklow, Kildare, Laois and Offaly.

In May 1943 Chrissie reported that 'notwithstanding all the disappointments I meet with on the whole I seem to enjoy it. I must say all the craftworkers I have interviewed are very kind, and even though some of them appear to be very suspicious of me at first, I part with them on the best of terms.' Her reports and letters cover more than just the crafts. They include descriptions of evenings of traditional music in people's homes, lists of herbal cures, amusing anecdotes and incidents that happened to her along the way. Sometimes everything seemed to go against her. From Sligo she wrote: 'Well I seem to have nothing but ill luck since I came to Sligo. To begin with I found it very hard to find a place to stay – seemingly they were all afraid of me! So far I have failed to contact anyone that would be a help to me, and the CEO whom I was to see is away. I cycled out to Mrs Creighton, Beltra ICA, who lives ten miles from here but if I did I paid for it coming back with storm, rain and lightening, and to make matters worse it got dark. . .I can't see anything but failure before me in Sligo, as I feel I won't get on there atal (sic).'

All along the way Chrissie would parcel up items of crafts and post them to Muriel in Dublin. From Rossinver in Co. Leitrim, for example, she sent a shoeing hammer in October 1945. The next month she sent Muriel a donkey's collar of rye straw made by a man in Ballaghadereen, Co. Roscommon. 'It is the only place I know where they are made,' she told Muriel, 'so I thought it would be worthwhile to send you one as Mr Duignan may like to have it for the museum.' In November 1946 she wrote from the Central Hotel Roscrea saying, 'Here is a mug given to me by Thomas Loftus, The Square, Borrisokane, made by his father - now dead - who was the dishturner who owned the pole-lathe now in the museum. Himself never took on the craft - still what he doesn't know about it isn't worth knowing.' The letter ends with 'the full of the mug of good wishes' to Muriel.

Chrissie, while full of admiration for Muriel – in 1950 she called her the 'friend of all craftworkers' and stated that 'there is no-one who has done more for country crafts than she has' – did not share Muriel's unshakeable optimism and must have served as a useful foil to her. On several occasions while travelling around the country Chrissie speaks of a time in the future when all crafts will have disappeared. Telling of a man who made cards (for carding wool) but who would not take on an apprentice she wrote, 'so in time to come there will be no-one left in Ireland who will be able to make cards. But I'm thinking there'll hardly be any need for them then either.'

Muriel was not prepared to give up the fight so easily. In the summer of 1944 she wrote, 'There is no foretelling how our homepsun and other traditional country crafts will fare in the years to come, but it is certain that their only hope of surviving post-war competition is the country wide employment of trained handcraft teachers and a comprehensive programme of craft instruction ranging from the primary school to the National College of Art.' Chrissie, for all her relative pessimism, did not give up either and taught craftwork under the Galway VEC as well

Without the determination and vision of Lucy Franks, photographed here in 1946, little would have been achieved for rural women in Ireland after the political upheavals of the 1920s.

1946. Phyllis O'Connell is on four wheels at last thanks to an 'anonymous' gift from Mrs Beatrice Hamilton.

1947. Fethard was a pioneer when it opened its Country Market against all odds. Livie Hughes *(extreme left)* was its chief inspiration, seen here with *(left to right)* Phyllis O'Connell, Dolly O'Keefe and Peggy Moore.

1948. A rare photograph of weaver Patrick Madden and his family taken by Muriel at their new home in Charlestown, Co. Mayo.

1995. The boy in arms *(previous photo)*, Michael Madden, has kept up the family craft. He still uses his father's old loom on which prizes won at the Irish Homespun Society are displayed.

1949. Many of the ICA's key players gathered at the Summer Schools and College in Sligo. *Back row (left to right):* Alice Ryan, Bea Trench, Miranda Scally, Chrissie O'Gorman, Joyce Nicholson, Sarah Ryan, Muriel Kehoe, May Quinlan. *Front row:* Josephine MacNeill, Muriel Gahan, Lucy Franks and a visiting speaker.

1951. At a specially convened weekend conference at the Grand Hotel Tramore, ICA executive and federation presidents gathered to discuss the urgent need for a permanent residential training college. Sarah Ryan, Muriel Gahan and Livie Hughes can be seen centre front.

1951. No-one escaped the washing-up at the handcraft school in Annamoe, Co. Wicklow. *Left to right:* Phyllis O'Connell, Olive Rowe, Muriel Gahan, Muriel Kehoe and Miranda Scally.

On the road in the early 1950s. Molly Craig, Lillie Curtin and Muriel stop for a quick break.

Spring Show 1951. John Surlis makes one of his Leitrim chairs which were to become famous. Lettering on the stand is by Michael Biggs, then a novice calligrapher.

1952. The 'Good Work Exhibition', a travelling show of the best of ICA members' work.

The first meeting of The Arts Council, 25 January 1952. *Seated left to right:* Thomas McGreevy, Monsignor Patrick Browne, Eamon de Valera (Taoiseach), P J Little (Director), John A Costello (Leader of Fine Gael), The Earl of Rosse, Muriel Gahan. *Standing:* John Maher, Prof Seamus Delargy, Dr R J Hayes, Senator E A McGuire, Prof Daniel Corkery, M Moynihan (Government Secretary), Dr Liam O'Sullivan (Secretary of Arts Council).

as at An Grianán until her death in the 1970s. Her minutely and lovingly detailed reports on the state of the crafts, county by county, gave Muriel the sort of comprehensive picture she had been lacking. It filled her with a sense of urgency and refuelled her determination to do all in her power to preserve from oblivion the great wealth and beauty of Ireland's traditional crafts. Muriel shared the concern of such people as Gerald Bruen and Thomas Bodkin, whose lecture in TCD in 1935[1], while still director of the National Gallery, and subsequent *Report on the Arts in Ireland* (1949)[2] reflected Muriel's deep worries about the lack of basic artistic training in and appreciation of the creative arts, from which she refused to exclude crafts. In the memorandum she drafted to the department of education in January 1946 she said:

> Education in handcrafts is in its infancy in Ireland, and it is to our Vocational Schools we must look for the progressive handling of the problem. An earnest plea would also be made for the inclusion of some form of hand work in our primary schools, and the early re-instalment of drawing in the school programme. An inability even to hold a pencil correctly is the severe handicap to practical work of any kind now placed on our young people on leaving their primary school. We have no big training colleges in our cities as they have in other countries for the study and practice of handcrafts. Our National College of Art has been able to do no more than touch the fringe of the problem.
>
> The present position of handiwork in our rural Vocational Schools is that expert instruction is given to boys in woodwork and metal work and to girls in cookery and housewifery and kindred subjects. No expert teacher is available however to give instruction in such creative arts as handspinning and weaving, embroidery, basket work or pottery and it is over and above all to crafts such as these, taught by experts, that we must look for the re-awakening of Ireland's zeal for craftsmanship, and the raising of the general standard of taste. When Irish craftsmanship was at its zenith we had a system of apprenticeship, the young people learning from the greatest masters of their trade. It is a worthy substitute for that system that we must seek today. . . It is for teachers that we ask. Teachers who will be the best the country can provide with the essential broad approach to craftsmanship. Having as their background a

knowledge of the fundamental principles of art and of the raw materials with which they will be working. Who, while learning from the old will adventure with the new, and in taking what is good from other countries will keep the colour and nature of Ireland always before them. Teachers zealous to rekindle the fires of Irish craftsmanship.

Muriel was acutely aware of public misconceptions where handcrafts were concerned. 'As I see it, Arty-Craftiness is the lion in the path', she wrote to Brigid Ganly of the Royal Hibernian Academy. 'Whatever scheme of training is devised, it must be on the highest possible level, and primarily come within the scope of training in art. Other countries have brought their crafts to a high pitch of artistic perfection, and there is no doubt that we can do the same. We have done it before.'

At the national level Muriel's efforts were in vain, at least as far as immediate results were concerned. In a handwritten note at the end of the memorandum, Muriel wrote: 'Turned down because of cost and doubts as to usefulness of teachers.' Subsequently in 1947 the department of education did agree to an alternative scheme for the training of craft organisers for the western counties but, this time, it was a last minute hitch in the planned training of these organisers that meant the scheme had to be postponed. Fourteen years later a landmark report on *Design in Ireland* published by a team of Scandinavian experts found that drawing and the manipulation of materials were 'a neglected aspect of education in Ireland' and that 'the Irish schoolchild is visually and artistically among the most undereducated in Europe.'[3]

Muriel, beaten but still not defeated, tried a different, more pragmatic tack. In the spring of 1946 she had advertised in the press for a crafts organiser to be attached to Country Workers Ltd and The Country Shop and to take over some of the work she had been doing herself all over the country. On 21 May she noted that 'about twenty-four answers had been received to the advert for a craft organiser, the greater number men. . .The only hopeful sounding applicant was a Miss Miranda Scally at present working in England.' At the beginning of August Muriel interviewed Miranda Scally and she was hired.

Like Chrissie O'Gorman, Miranda Scally was not only an Irish speaker, but had the requisite quantities of enthusiasm and courage. She also had a great sense of fun, another plus in Muriel's eyes. Back in 1929 Muriel had admired in Patrick

Madden the fact that 'there was nothing I asked him that he could not do' and this was frequently the quality she was quick to pick out in other people. Miranda Scally was also artistically gifted, more so than Chrissie. She came of an artistic family and had done a full course in the College of Art in Dublin after education at Louise Gavan Duffy's School in Dublin and Ring College in Waterford. In 1947 she threw herself into her new job, spending six weeks in the Aran Islands organising the knitters after which she accompanied Muriel to Dunlewey and to the Inishowen penninsula. Then she was back in Dunlewey for a month's spinning before spending further time in south Donegal. In July she went on a weaving course in England and then spent the remainder of the year in the top room of 23 St Stephen's Green working on patterns to bring round to spinners.

Early in 1951 it was learned that the John Conor Magee Trust would give £200 a year for use in the Gaeltacht. Since the homespun industry had collapsed they no longer paid out money for apprenticeships. The Homespun Society 'proposed to buy looms for Galway with it and pay for instruction. . .Part also to be used to send Miss Scally to Donegal to teach weaving, pattern drafting, selecting of wool as learned in Sweden. Patrick Madden also to be helped with patterns.' A memorandum outlining a scheme for training in handweaving was submitted to the Co. Galway VEC but was turned down 'as there were very few young people left in any of the districts, not enough to form classes in any centre.' Ring was suggested as an alternative, or perhaps Tourmakeady. Neither was possible and as the whole year had gone by without the money being allocated it was decided to buy three looms anyway and ask for half the expenses of sending Chrissie O'Gorman and Miranda Scally to Sweden in 1950 to be covered retroactively by the promised £200. Then late in 1951 Agnes O'Farrelly died and the future of the Conor Magee funds were thrown into doubt as she was one of the trustees and after her death the trust had to be reconstituted.

Muriel nevertheless forged ahead with the spinning and weaving scheme offering it to the Kerry VEC in January 1952. This time they were in luck and James McDwyer, CEO, responded immediately and positively. Here was yet another person who 'clicked' at once with Muriel and there was nothing he could not or would not do. On 19 January he wrote 'I was very glad to get your letter and Memorandum this morning. I am very interested indeed with what you have to say, and my immediate reaction is that this is a splendid opportunity for us to get a trained teacher, and very useful work started in this county.' Having pointed out all the obstacles in his way, chiefly financial, he concluded, 'however, I, personally, think that the work Miss Scally could do would be of the greatest value in this county, and would be prepared to find the money for it, whatever else might suffer.' James McDwyer, a first cousin of Canon McDyer of Glencolumcille, was a founder member of Macra na Feirme[4] and knew of Muriel's work with the ICA. He shared her approach to education and to the country and went to extraordinary lengths to make possible her scheme. Indeed he became her co-conspirator, coaxing his committee into accepting the idea, making sure Miranda Scally was paid a good salary and even finding a building in which the course could be held. He lost his way one day on his way back from Ballyferriter and passed a disused girls' national school at a place called Murreigh. 'The building is fairly recent – about the 1920s I'd say,' he reported to Muriel, 'and will require fairly considerable repairs. This is one of the snags, because while my committee are perfectly willing to put it into repair they are prohibited from spending money on repairs to any building which is not vested in them. However, I am confident that I will be able to overcome that difficulty.' He did, though not without a fight. On 26 May 1952 he wrote a confidential note to Muriel:

> The primary branch seem to be adopting a dog in the manger attitude. Although neither PP, Bishop, teachers nor local people heard a word of it, they say they have been thinking of repairing this building for use as a school and that they couldn't allow it out of their hands. This, in spite of the fact that it has been going to ruin for 10 or 11 years! Fortunately I had already started repair work before they rang me forbidding me to do so! I say 'fortunately' even though it leaves us open to surcharge by our auditor. However, if they persist in obstructing I think we could raise such a fuss and make them look so ridiculous that they'd be glad to drop it.

The money he spent on repairs at Murreigh never did receive official sanction, but the plans went ahead just the same. In May James McDwyer met Miranda and wrote at once to Muriel:

I was delighted with Miss Scally – a grand girl with lots of courage and initiative. In particular, I liked her attitude of 'tackling in and making the best of things' rather than complaining about conditions and foreseeing difficulties. However you do it, you seem to have been able to keep that fine, courageous spirit right through the whole ICA and Country Workers movement – and it is a greater thing than any amount of mechanical efficiency in work. Nothing becomes a teacher better than a courageous spirit – or, as we say in Donegal – 'spunk'.

In September 1952 nine girls between the ages of fourteen and seventeen and two nuns started Miranda Scally's course, conducted entirely through Irish. It was an example of co-operation, in the loose sense of the term, that must have made Muriel especially happy: 'The County Committee provides accommodation, raw materials and pays Miss Scally's salary; the Society provides looms, acts in an advisory capacity, presents certificates; Country Markets will sell the products; Country Workers are most generously providing looms, van, film strips, lantern.' As for Muriel's role in the whole scheme, 'honorary fairy godmother' is how James McDwyer described it. The girls 'started with design, then weaving and dyeing and spinning. Vegetable dyes were used first, then aniline which they found easier. They loved painting especially. Wool and linen were both used for weaving. . .Cushion covers, aprons, table mats were made.' Between Country Markets, The Country Shop and local outlets all their work was sold.

Sadly, the Kerry Weavers – *Figheadoiri Chiarrai* – did not last. The idea had been that the young women, once they had learnt to weave, would take their looms home and work from there. James McDwyer wrote to Muriel in March 1953:

> The girls do not want to work on their own at home. They appear to want us to establish a work centre for them, run it as an industry, and pay them a weekly wage. Apart from the fact that we have no power to do such a thing, I do not think the work would lend itself to organisation on a factory basis – it is more properly suited to organisation as a home industry. Although this was clearly explained to the students beforehand I can understand their attitiude. It has its roots really in their lack of confidence in their own efforts, and the

only way of tackling it in any fundamental way, is by raising their self confidence and sense of community spirit – in short the very work you do through the ICA. Indeed this has been another useful proof to me of the great need for an organisation like the ICA.

Miranda Scally tried to do this and encouraged six of the young women to try working from home, overseeing their weaving, ordering materials for them, helping with designs, organising sales and boosting morale. With Muriel's help, she even organised an exhibition and sale of their work in Dublin's leading department store, Brown Thomas, in November 1954. But the chance of a steady wage in England or America won them over.

A letter from James McDwyer to Muriel in 1956 when Miranda's work had extended beyond the group of weavers to that of peripatetic teacher throughout the county reflects extraordinarily closely Muriel's own deep conviction in the rightness of what she was aiming for:

Miss Scally is working away very well, though God knows her job is not an easy one. Long journeys to spend winter nights in cold, draughty Parish Halls is no picnic for a girl born and reared in Dublin. I think she is wonderful stuff. There are, I think, only three of the Figheadoiri left now, but I regard the effort as having been well worth while and would jump at the chance of organising the same thing again. Only the *material* fruits have been denied us. The other and more important ones remain – the residuum of skill and knowledge of this craft, which is the starting point from which to build a tradition of handcraft; the stimulation in some measure of an appetite for good handwork; the little accession of courage and confidence in the district; the association of beauty and high quality with the labour of humble hands in humble homes. These things show nothing in terms of £s per week earned in the district, but they mean a great deal to the spirit of the people, and it is the lack of spirit and courageous confidence in themselves and their own efforts that is the greatest and worst handicap to progress in all the West here at present.'

Notes

1.	Bodkin, T. *The Importance of Art in Ireland* Lecture delivered in Trinity College Dublin on 24 June 1935, published by Three Candles, Dublin, 1935.

2.	Bodkin, T. *Report on the Arts in Ireland* Stationery Office, Dublin, 1949.

3.	*Design in Ireland*, Report of the Scandinavian Design Group in Ireland, April 1961.

4.	Macra na Feirme, a young farmers' association, was set up in 1944 as a 'non-sectarian and non-party-political organisation with the aim of promoting and fostering agriculture and rural development.'

— 12 —

A Co-operative Once Again

I t was from an unexpected quarter that Muriel was to find a solution to the government authorities' sluggish response to her appeals for serious education in the crafts. Set up first and foremost as a palliative to post-war market conditions, Country Markets Ltd, the co-operative marketing company created jointly by the Irish Homespun Society and the ICA in August 1946, was to prove a vibrant alternative structure for the training of craft teachers. It was also the means of introducing rigid criteria of standards and design and of promoting traditional Irish crafts country wide. This role was further enhanced when An Grianán was opened for the ICA in 1954, providing Country Markets with a permanent centre for holding bi-annual courses and, from 1968 on, a testing centre for teachers. From the beginning the residential college in Termonfechin was to be 'a centre where seekers after traditional crafts will always find examples and instruction, and provide a spring of inspiration and skill which will keep the crafts alive and renewed.'[1] On a personal level, creating the co-operative company was a hugely enriching experience for Muriel.

One of Muriel's greatest joys was solving problems and putting new projects on the road, 'getting things cracking'. Livie Hughes loved breaking new ground, especially for women. Both revelled in a challenge. 'My joy has been getting hold of [Livie's] ideas, seeing what they can lead up to, in my imagination thinking out how they are going to be carried through,' Muriel told film-maker David Shaw-Smith in 1980. 'That is what I most enjoy in life, carrying things through, and the more complicated they are, the more difficult, the more pleasure I derive.' With the founding of Country Markets the Gahan-Hughes double act came into its own. They were not alone in regretting that the UI's transformation in 1935, involving both a change of name and of constitution, while leading to greater democracy within the organisation, had severed the countrywomen's movement from its co-operative roots.

In the early 1940s Muriel's immediate motivation for re-establishing the co-operative link was the urgency of saving the Donegal homespun industry. Livie, the problems of the local farming community on her doorstep when she woke each morning, was spurred by her anxiety to help farmers' wives make some money in the lean war years by selling surplus produce, especially eggs. As a discussion at an ICA council meeting in 1943 had concluded: 'Women and girls are not unemployed in the country, but they want to see a cash return for their work.' Muriel modestly described herself as 'the missing link' in the evolution of the new co-operative market society. She was certainly ideally placed. As chair of both the ICA executive committee (1941–46) and of the Homespun Society, her headquarters close to the centre of Irish co-operativism, Plunkett House on Merrion Square, she was able to do the arduous spade work required to work out a formula which would satisfy the ICA, the Irish Homespun Society, the IAOS *and* the Registrar of Friendly Societies.

The threat of extinction of the homespun industry in northwest Donegal and in particular in Dunlewey and the Gweedore area upset Muriel all the more that she had grown to love both the place and its people. When Chrissie O'Gorman arrived in Dunlewey on a wild November night in 1944 her mission was more than a mere cataloguing of craftworkers. She was to assess the possibility of mounting a rescue operation. 'The storm and rain were so bad the night I was coming that I couldn't get off the bus at the top of the road so I had to go to Burtonport and remain there until the following day', she wrote to Muriel on 3 December, by which time she had already visited thirty-three spinners 'including those that were and those that weren't on the list'. In Dunlewey she stayed with Nancy Ferry and was accompanied to the homes of forty-nine spinners and nine weavers by Nancy's twenty-one-year-old daughter, Mary, now Mary Roarty, a founder member of Dunlewey's ICA guild. Chrissie told Muriel:

> They seem fairly satisfied under present conditions in so much as they can get rid of anything they make. This is the reason that there are many more people making tweed today than ever did before. They are sure of a market and quick returns even though the price is not all that they desire.

Since they fear that Gaeltarra will discontinue buying even
before the war is over, all would agree to the co-operative
system.[2] I found that they appreciated very much the help
the Homespun Society has been to them in the past and I
felt that they are depending on them now for the future of
the industry.

As a postscript to the letter, the ever-pragmatic Chrissie adds: 'If
co-operative marketing goes ahead where will the market be
found? Does it mean that the tweed will be exported? If so, maybe
the Govt won't allow that, and what will happen then?' She had
written to Muriel just days before she set off for Dunlewey, 'I
think no matter what their system of marketing will be, if the
industry is not profitable from a point of view of the workers it
will surely die.'[3] But the situation in Dunlewey, though critical,
did not seem terminal yet and Muriel was determined to try co-
operative methods to save it.

Since 1943 there had been much discussion within the ICA,
too, about the possibility of re-joining the co-operative
movement. As well as Muriel, Livie Hughes in Fethard and Josie
Mangan in Co. Cork were both very keen. Livie had taken her
own steps to becoming a co-operator by starting up a co-operative
beekeepers' association in Fethard following a talk by IAOS
president Father Coyne at the 1943 Summer School. In August
1943 Josie Mangan called at Plunkett House to inquire about the
ICA's position vis-à-vis co-operation. Josie, like Muriel, had had
her first encounter with the UI at the 1929 Spring Show and had
lost no time in setting up the first Cork UI branch soon after.
Since 1942 there had been an ad hoc summer market scheme
selling vegetables, bread and confectionery in Courtmacsherry,
Co. Cork, and, as a trained poultry instructress, Josie was
particularly anxious to help women find a satisfactory way of
marketing their eggs.

Both she and Livie were outraged by the lack of 'co-operation'
they got from male-run creamery co-ops. They would not handle
eggs and so in summer when eggs were plentiful and the shops
were not buying, the women were obliged to stand on the
roadside waiting for the higgler's cart or the dealer's lorry to turn
up. 'We were told the usual thing,' Livie said many years later,
recalling a confrontation with an IAOS official in Dublin,[4] 'that
every hen died in debt.' Never one to show deference where she
felt it was not merited, especially when faced with a man, Livie

described how she 'said to the fat old fellow who was at the head of it, "I'm sure your hens die in debt because you probably have two eggs for breakfast and two eggs for supper and you don't pay for those. Your wife has to steal the oats to keep the hens going and that's the only way the hen dies in debt!"'

Co-operation became the central preoccupation in 1944, the IAOS Golden Jubilee year. In January and February Muriel and Mairin McDonald had conferred with IAOS officials about the possibility of the ICA reaffiliating. The first meeting was with Harry Norman, one of the pioneers of co-operation in Ireland, at his home on Harcourt Terrace. The second took place in assistant secretary Charles Riddall's office in Plunkett House, the back room on the second floor which had once been AE's office. The curved walls were still papered with AE's paintings. Paddy 'the Cope' Gallagher, famous for his successful early co-operative (referred to locally as 'the cope') in Templecrone, Co. Donegal, had called it 'the queerest room I ever entered; all kinds of queer pictures painted on the walls.'[5]

Margaret Digby, Horace Plunkett's most faithful heir, and director of the Plunkett Foundation in England, was invited to address the ICA's 1944 AGM on 'Women's Part in the Co-operative Movement.' She accepted but was unable to travel to Ireland because of the war. It would not have been her first time as a guest. She was a frequent visitor to Ireland and as early as 1933 had spoken to the then UI on 'Market Stalls and Countrywomen's Enterprise'. By the time the 1944 Summer School came round, held in August at Aravon, Bray, Co. Wicklow, co-operation was on everybody's mind. Just ten days before it opened Muriel paid yet another visit, this time on her own, to Plunkett House. On 9 August two letters written by her from her position as chair of the ICA's executive committee were put to an IAOS committee meeting 'asking that the IAOS Committee should give favourable consideration to an application from the Association for membership.' It was exactly ten years and six months since Lucy Franks had written requesting the reverse.

Muriel saw the post-war situation as presenting 'ideal conditions for co-operation to flourish' and a leaflet on the subject of affiliation with the IAOS was circulated to all Guilds before the Summer School began. At the school Josie Mangan chaired an evening on agricultural co-operation. Both Livie and Muriel were amongst the speakers. The decision was finally taken to register the ICA as an Industrial and Provident Society and re-affiliate with the IAOS. At the next Council meeting, in November, Muriel reported that 'with the help of their solicitor, the IAOS has undertaken to re-draft the rules of the Association to conform with legal requirements. This service is free and when the rules are drafted and approved by the Executive, they will be put before the next Council for ratification.'

It all sounded so simple. Little did Muriel know that her education in co-operation was only just beginning. She was about to spend all that winter, along with Mairin McDonald, secretary of both the ICA and the Homespun Society, in endless consultation in Plunkett House. Charles Riddall, a most punctilious and legalistically-minded man, patiently explained to them the intricacies of the rules governing co-operation. Harry Norman 'spoke gently of the early days of agricultural co-operation, of the founding of the United Irishwomen, and of the meaning of being a Co-operator'.[6] All winter long they tried to draw up a new ICA constitution. Back and forth Muriel and Mairin went between 23 St Stephen's Green and 84 Merrion Square until finally they produced a new set of rules. 'When we brought them back to the Countrywomen they refused to accept them: they were too businesslike', Muriel remembered. 'The ICA was a charity, an educational organisation. To be a co-op you have to be a business organisation.' Josephine MacNeill[7], a prominent member of the Dublin Town Association of the ICA, was then chairman of Council and it was she who was 'one hundred per cent against it. She didn't want to have anything linked to business, we were culture, not business in the ICA.' So back to the drawing board they went. Next it was the turn of the IAOS to object: 'they would not accept us because we had gone too educational, too charity-like.' When at last the IAOS and the ICA agreed, the Registrar turned them down.

At the same time as struggling with the ICA constitution, Muriel was acting on behalf of the Homespun Society, trying to see how best to set up craftworkers' co-operatives. The idea was that 'each district would have its own depot where fleece, dyes and oil could be purchased, where carding could be done by machinery, and for the marketing of tweeds. A sales organisation would operate in Dublin.' In the heart of Donegal weaving, Ardara, where the threat of a post-war slump was as potentially devastating as in Dunlewey, meetings were held in January 1945 to examine the possibility of such a co-operative society.[8] The chosen theme for the Homespun Society's AGM was home weaving in Ireland with special emphasis on the future. And the future, as far as Muriel was concerned, lay in co-operation. Her old ally Felix Hackett was not convinced, as a newspaper report made clear:

> Said Miss Muriel Gahan, 'The co-operative movement had not proved as successful in Ireland as in other countries because the women were not in it.' She was replying to another committee member, Professor Felix Hackett – a sceptic as regards the operation of the system in this country – who asked whether the Society was wise in considering the formation of co-operative societies, as outlined in the secretary's report. 'Where women were brought together as in the guilds organised by the Irish Countrywomen's Association,' Miss Gahan continued, 'much had been achieved.'[9]

Spring 1945 had come and there was gridlock as far as the ICA's re-admission to the co-operative movement was concerned. For all the frustrations of the preceding months, however, Muriel had had an education she would not have missed for anything and which was to prove invaluable for the future, giving her both confidence and authority in co-operative matters. Co-operation had passed from being a somewhat romantic ideal for her – associated with childhood memories of AE's intense figure striding through the streets of Rathmines, or with images of Horace Plunkett so vividly evoked by his cousin and friend Lady Fingall[10] – to a question of economy and ethics, rules and regulations. Those hours spent with Harry Norman, who had been editor of *The Irish Homestead* before AE and a friend of Horace Plunkett and who had addressed one of the first meetings of the UI back in February 1911 on 'women's part in co-operative work', strengthened her vision. Until the end of her life she retained the image of the round room in Plunkett house, the walls covered with AE's paintings[11], and the sound of Norman's voice repeating, 'Persistent goodwill, you need persistent goodwill. . .'[12]

A 'little green book' had been lying on a shelf in the ICA office since 1942. Until she found herself stuck in the impasse of spring 1945, however, Muriel had not bothered to consult it. Or rather she had leafed through it, but without her six months' tuition in Plunkett House it had meant nothing to her. The green book in question was the Women's Institute (WI) guide to setting up market stalls. These had formed part of the English countrywomen's movement since 1932. The WI's markets had grown out of frustrated efforts by ex-servicemen's wives who, having taken to working smallholdings after the First World War, then found huge difficulty in selling, 'wearing out shoe leather taking unwanted produce to the big shops'. At a meeting held in the Albert Hall in 1932 the WI decided to by-pass retail outlets and organise their own marketing system. The Carnegie Trust would only give them the financial backing they needed, however, on condition they did not restrict the stalls to WI members. Old age pensioners and the unemployed were to be allowed to participate in the co-operative scheme as well as women, thus turning the project from a purely commercial into a wider social and educational one. Lucy Franks had visited some of the WI's very early market stalls, in Berkshire, in 1933 and found the women selling 'bottled fruit, cream cheeses, eggs, butter, jam, garden produce and table chickens in cellophane bags.'[13]

Suddenly Muriel saw a way forward. The 'little green book' became as limpid as a child's ABC. 'Instead of trying to turn the Homespun Society into a co-operative and trying to turn the ICA into a co-operative, what we needed was a *separate* market society, founded jointly by the ICA and the Irish Homespun Society, the one interested in produce, the other in crafts', and not something restricted to ICA members or indeed to women. Then in May 1945 Vera Cox, the WI markets organiser who had given Muriel the little green book in the first place, came to Ireland to visit relatives in Co. Waterford. Livie described her as 'a thoroughly sympathetic character with a great love for Ireland.' She was invited to address an ICA rally in Cahir, just ten miles from Fethard. There, telling delegates about the WI market stalls in England, she encouraged her Irish sisters to persist in their co-operative plans. Ill health prevented Muriel from being in Cahir for the rally but she got plenty of help from Vera Cox all the same. In July, presenting the executive committee's report in which she explained to Council that the ICA 'had been found not suitable for registering as a friendly or industrial and provident society', she was able to recommend an alternative: 'that plans were considered for forming a special marketing society to direct and advise local co-operative market societies for the benefit of small producers.' The proposal was agreed to.

Vera Cox had suggested that an advisory committee should be set up comprising three ICA and three Irish Homespun Society members. This was done, Muriel representing the Homespun

Society on the new committee and 'a draft constitution drawn up by Miss Gahan was agreed in general.' The proposal, as put to the Homespun Society by Muriel in October 1945 was as follows:

1) A society along co-operative lines shall be organised jointly by the ICA and the HIS.
2) The object of the society shall be to organise the sale of crafts and produce of small producers through markets and other means.
3) Membership shall be open to craft workers and small producers throughout Ireland, and to such other persons as shall be agreed on.
4) Rules shall be drawn up, and the society shall register as an Industrial and Provident Society, and shall affiliate to the IAOS.
5) A marketing advisory committee shall be formed with representation of the Irish Countrywomen's Association and the Irish Homespun Society, and other persons subsequently admitted to membership.

But re-writing constitutions and setting up co-operatives was not all that was on Muriel's mind. Preparations for the Homespun Society's vast Horse Show exhibit in the Pembroke Hall were in full swing. In May 1946 Muriel had been up to Dunlewey and took the opportunity of sounding out her friends there on the new co-operative idea. She found them still 'interested in the market society, willing to join and form a group.' A leaflet of 'Market propaganda' was prepared for distribution at the Horse Show. Finally during Horse Show week itself on Thursday 16 August 1946, and after a last-minute visit by Muriel to Plunkett House the day before, the first committee meeting of Country Markets Ltd was held at 23 St Stephen's Green. Muriel was elected to the chair, a position she would hold until 8 April 1975, close on twenty-nine years. Also at the meeting were Gerty Grew, Felix Hackett, Win Drury, Ella Walsh and Nora Byrne. Mairin McDonald and Grace Somerville-Large, though not at the inaugural meeting were also part of that early committee. All eight signed the rules of Country Markets Ltd when it was registered under the Industrial and Provident Societies Act (1893) on 11 September 1946. In April 1947 it was affiliated to the IAOS.

Livie Hughes, though not directly involved in building the framework for the co-operative society, was cheering loudly from

Fethard all along and lost no time in taking advantage of the structure once it was there. A great tradition of active involvement in Fethard already existed: in 1915, a year after the UI branch had started there, a milk depot had been set up 'to keep a steady supply of milk available for the poor of Fethard at as reasonable a price as possible.'[14] In the early 'twenties Livie had organised both a public library and a coffee van offering food and hot drinks to farmers on fair days. Once she joined the UI in 1928 the coffee van became a UI activity. As well as providing a much appreciated service, especially in the winter, and reducing drunkenness on fair days, the van was also a profit-making scheme, the proceeds going to charity and towards financing the UI branch and later the ICA guild. A team of seven or so women worked it in relays (only four people could operate inside the van at once) and Livie Hughes organised the rota. As Hannie Leahy, closely involved with the Hughes family and with all Livie's endeavours and who helped on the coffee van in the late 'thirties, humorously put it, 'you had to work on it voluntarily: Mrs Hughes had a rota and you had to go!' According to Hannie Leahy, Livie sold tickets that had to be handed up for tea, coffee or Bovril. 'Bovril was a few pence dearer than the others. Hams were cooked at Annsgift [Livie's home] for the sandwiches. An old woman, Kate McCarthy, boiled the kettles in the town hall and the other helpers served and washed up. The van was stored in the O'Connells yard and the teapots and delph stored in the O'Connell's house across the street.'[15]

Muriel used to refer to the Fethard Country Market as the 'ewe lamb' of the movement. Livie's fellow Fetharder and pioneer ICA organiser, Phyllis O'Connell, called it 'the darling of Mrs Hughes' heart'. The idea of a local market run on co-operative lines and mostly by women (though men were welcome, too, and still are) embodied all that Livie and Muriel strove for: grass roots initiative, 'self-help and mutual help', and above all a means by which country women could generate an income they could call their own. By October 1946 Livie had launched full tilt into the creation of a market in Co. Tipperary. She sent a questionnaire to all the county guilds asking members what they would or could contribute to a market, from time and money to transport and voluntary help on the stalls. She also asked if there were any specialities 'made in your district, or which used to be produced there and might be produced again if the materials were available such as Cashel Rock, grandmothers' recipes, herb ointments, polishes. . .' The slogan of Country Markets appeared for the first time: 'The best at fair prices and money straight to the producer.'

The idea had been to start a market in Clonmel but no suitable venue was found and local support was not strong – opposition from local shopkeepers was something which would dog Country Markets for years – so Fethard ICA guild met and discussed the possibility of starting a stall in their little town instead. 'It can't do us any harm,' was Livie's reasoning, 'it'll probably be a failure but we'll try for a year or so, selling things anyway is a failure as far as we're concerned, so we'll be none the worse for it.'[16] The odds against them were even greater than she had imagined, though. 'We held our last committee meeting about starting a market stall in Fethard on the very day that bread rationing was announced in the papers', Livie Hughes recounted just weeks after the market had been successfully opened. 'I was in the Chair and I felt it was a knock-out blow and that we must postpone the project for some months until there was a possibility of something to sell. We had counted very much on homemade bread and cakes to make the stall attractive.' But the idea had taken root. 'I was quite overcome by the enthusiasm and determination of the prospective suppliers who had all sorts of suggestions as to how we could overcome our difficulties. . .We opened on Friday 17 January and we were sold out in about an hour and a half and had taken £9.' Friday has remained country market day in Fethard ever since. As a fast day a good demand for eggs was guaranteed and being pension day, there were sure to be plenty of people in town.

Fethard market sold garden and farm produce as well as second-hand clothes, books and magazines, cut flowers and shrubs, coffee and buns. More extraordinary than overcoming the bread rationing, the fact that the market survived meteorological conditions was miraculous. The winter of 1946–47 was the worst in living memory. 'It will be a long time before any of us forget the winter of 1947,' Phyllis O'Connell wrote a year later, 'the weeks of snow and ice-bound roads, of bitter cold and deep anxiety about the crops'. At a Dublin TA meeting in March 1947, when the competition was for 'signs of spring worn as a button-hole', Muriel, with typical humour, wore 'a symbolical burst pipe'. The ICA's AGM, scheduled for March, had to be postponed 'owing to the serious condition of the country.' And yet after only six weeks' trading, Livie was calmly stating that although 'the average sale of flowers is surprisingly high for a country town not used to such luxuries. . .I feel we will stand or fall by our dealings in eggs, as eggs are the countrywomen's currency and one penny one way or the other makes a tremendous difference.' Despite unco-operative local co-ops, they stood. After just two years' trading, Fethard's turnover was £1800, £900 derived from eggs alone. Thanks to the combined effort of Muriel and Livie, the goal of getting a cash reward for women had been achieved.

Notes

1. *Farmers' Gazette* 12 December 1953.
2. Paddy 'the Cope' Gallagher had organised a market in Dunlewey for the sale of tweeds just before Gaeltarra Eireann took over and had managed to improve prices for the producers considerably.
3. In a letter written to Muriel from the Lake of Shadows Hotel, Buncrana, on 20 November 1944, just before her visit to Dunlewey, Chrissie wrote: ' 'Tis very hard to solve that homespun problem. I think it's one thing you and I would never agree on.'
4. The 'fat old fellow' was probably Dr Henry Kennedy, chief executive of ICOS at the time and known to have had a mutually antagonistic relationship with Livie.
5. Gallagher, P. *My Story*, Templecrone Co-operative Society, (undated).
6. Gahan, M 'This is How They Happened' ICA *Our Book* Golden Jubilee 1910–60.
7. Josephine MacNeill was the widow of James MacNeill, second Governor-General of the Irish Free State.
8. Two national teachers, Sean Cassidy and Patrick McGill, county councillor Dan Craig and Dan Ward met with IAOS organiser Patrick McGee to examine the situation 'on behalf of the small producers who number hundreds in the Ardara, Kilcar and Glencolumbcille parishes.'
9. *Times Pictorial*, 17 March 1945.
10. Elizabeth, Countess of Fingall (1866–1944) was president of the UI/ICA 1912–42.
11. The wallpaper on which AE had painted has been given to the National Gallery of Ireland by ICOS.
12. Harry Norman died on 31 December 1947. Muriel, by then chair of the successfully formed Country Markets Ltd, told its members that 'the best tribute that could be paid to his memory was to keep the spirit of co-operation always before us.'
13. *Farmers Gazette*, 22 July 1933.
14. *Farmers Gazette*, 22 January 1944.
15. Hannie Leahy worked on the coffee van in the late 'thirties. When Fethard country market started up in 1947 she became the treasurer, earning the praise of the Country Markets management committee in Dublin in 1949 for 'the beautiful way Fethard Market books have been

kept'. She remained treasurer for 31 years until 1978. Hannie Leahy worked closely with Livie Hughes in the ICA and in Country Markets as well as looking after Livie's mother. Quotation from author's personal correspondence with Mrs Leahy.

16. Olivia Hughes in conversation with David Shaw-Smith, 1980.

— 13 —

At the Sign of the Brannra

With yet another structure in her control within which
to organise exhibitions and craft shows it was
becoming difficult to keep track of Muriel's myriad
projects. Between regional field days, handcraft schools, rural
living open days, competitions and travelling loan exhibitions as
well as stands at the Spring and Horse Shows (these continued
until 1992), there seemed never to be a time when she was not
planning yet another display of the best in Irish crafts in yet
another corner of the country. 'I hate permanent things, they're
dead', she had retorted in 1953 to a suggestion that a particularly
successful Country Shop exhibition should be made a permanent
fixture.

For the general public today, however, the words Country
Markets are immediately associated not with crafts but with that
wide network of weekly markets – there are over seventy of them –
where fresh vegetables (often organic), cut flowers and plants,
poultry and eggs, bread, cakes and jams and a small assortment of
crafts can be bought. And yet, with the exception of trailblazing
Fethard, produce markets were slow to take off when Country
Markets Ltd first began. Ten years on, although numerous markets
had opened briefly, there were still only four in steady operation:
Fethard, Naas, Maynooth and Wexford. Margaret Long, an expert
gardener from Balbriggan, had been hired in 1953 as a production
organiser for Country Markets and Country Workers and she did
Trojan work. But she was underpaid and overstretched. Later,
Cerise Parker as honorary secretary of Country Markets put in two
full days a week and Angela Kehoe looked after the Markets' books
on top of all the rest of her work for Country Workers. It was with
Ann Roche that markets began seriously to increase.

Ann Roche, from Cappoquin, Co. Waterford, was one of the first batch of ICA organisers to be brought to Phyllis O'Connell's rescue in 1951 thanks to a long-overdue government grant. Like Margaret Long, she was also a skilled gardener. And she knew what it was like to be a woman in the country with very little money. She had been a Country Market enthusiast ever since she first heard of the idea from Phyllis O'Connell in 1948. Even before she was made production adviser for the whole of Ireland in 1956 she had as a matter of course encouraged ICA guilds to start markets. But she too was underpaid and overstretched and it was not until she was appointed full-time Country Markets organiser in 1965 – Muriel always referred to the post as 'Mr Haughey's present' because it was agriculture minister Charles Haughey who had put up the money[1] – that Muriel's strong crafts bias was effectively balanced out and produce markets grew sharply.

It was not that Muriel was against produce markets. She was always delighted when a new market managed to hold the road and, until the sheer number made it impossible, she made a point of always attending each market's annual meeting. She particularly delighted in the way a 'small' producer, perhaps a person living on their own or who had very little in the way of produce to contribute to a market, could benefit socially as well as financially from belonging to the co-operative group, their life transformed through participation. But it was clear from the start that her obsession remained with the crafts and, given the length of time she was to remain in charge, the crafts were assured pride of place. Just months after Fethard produce market had made its plucky start she defined Country Markets as 'a society to encourage crafts of good standard and help outstanding craftworkers'.

Indeed, the marketing society started out as just that: a sales centre in Dublin for outlying shareholders.[2] Cottages sculpted out of turf, sheepskin rugs, crochet work, knitted shawls and model curraghs were amongst the early items to be passed by the committee and then sold through the shops. Criteria had to be strict. Being a shareholder was not in itself a guarantee of sales and one disappointed producer had to be told that 'articles covered in silver paper were not a country craft'. Once passed for sale, however, the articles were marked with the Country Markets logo, the now familiar Donegal bread iron, stamped in black on a blue label. The 'beautiful curly bread iron', made by a Dunfanaghy blacksmith and collected by Muriel for her 1933 show in The Country Shop, was almost a mascot for the success of the venture.

The *brannra* – 'an upright iron stand on which a cake is baked' – was chosen at the company's second meeting on 4 October 1946 because 'bedded in tradition, its use linking craftsmanship with husbandry, its form beauty with fitness of purpose, it symbolises country craftsmanship at its best.'

Country Markets Ltd quickly became a most dynamic framework for the promotion of good crafts and by 1948 was negotiating export deals for Patrick Madden rugs and Aran ganseys to Holland, South Africa, Australia and England. Once again Muriel skilfully used her position on different committees and bodies and her contacts to the best advantage. On 17 December 1947, for example, two schemes were put forward at a Country Workers directors' meeting attended by Muriel, Lucy Franks and Grace Somerville-Large. One was for 'the appointment of good judges for country shows' and the other to set up 'tests for ICA craftworkers on the lines of the WI Guild of Learners'. These were Muriel's brainchildren. She said that 'bad local judging had a serious effect on the quality of handcrafts. If good judges were available to go to local shows, and if tests were held to qualify people as demonstrators, teachers and judges, this should do much to raise the standards.'[3] It was agreed that 'Country Markets should be asked to sponsor these schemes and that Country Workers would contribute towards their expense.'

Two days later Muriel chaired the Country Markets monthly meeting where it was proposed that the production advisory committee, set up early in 1947 in addition to the committee of management, should be dissolved and re-formed to include a core of two members each from Country Workers, Country Markets and the ICA Competition Committee so that this committee 'could form the nucleus for a panel of judges who could visit and judge at outlying shows'. By April 1948 it was announced through the pages of the *Farmers' Gazette* – that priceless mouthpiece for all ICA-related activities since 1919 – that tests were being introduced for the different crafts. In December Muriel was able to write to Judge Wylie, chairman of the executive committee of the RDS, boasting of Country Markets' achievements and asking for space at the 1949 Spring Show 'on which to stage a small exhibition consisting of two model country markets, one for country crafts, the other for produce'. In 1948 Muriel had been appointed to the Industries, Art and General Purposes Committee of the RDS and her position there further enhanced her effectiveness.

Muriel had by now learnt that a Dublin success did not mean success countrywide. She wrote to Judge Wylie:

> The exhibition would be one suitable for a country agricultural show, and its purpose at the Spring Show would be to attract the notice of show secretaries and other country visitors, in order that they might be encouraged to organise similar exhibitions at their own shows. . .It is of the opinion of all those concerned in this work, that if country crafts are to be preserved and developed, and if the country housewife and young farmer are to grow and use more agricultural produce, more local pride and local effort must be aroused, and more local groups of Country Markets formed. This is the purpose behind the encouragement of exhibitions at local shows.

The emphasis on assisting *local* effort was to remain central to the scheme right into the 1970s, reinforcing the basic commitment which Muriel and her fellow co-operators felt to AE's vision, outlined for the pioneer United Irishwomen in 1911, of building up a rural civilisation through 'the Ireland before your eyes, which you see as you look out your own door in the morning and on which you walk up and down through the day'.[4]

On 1 March 1951, under the combined influence of Felix Hackett and Muriel, a sub-committee was set up by the Industries, Art and General Purposes Committee, of which Muriel now held the chair, rather cumbersomely called the Committee for the Encouragement of Craftsmanship or EC Committee. Perhaps in response to Muriel's irrepressible campaigning zeal, the more moderate Hackett took the opportunity of setting down in writing exactly what the scope of the activities of the RDS was, what it could and what it could not attempt to achieve for the crafts. 'The general policy of the Society,' he began, 'is to promote its objects through activities which the Government or Departments of Government cannot undertake, either because they are too experimental or because they require a greater freedom from regulation than is possible under Government auspices. Though members of the committee may be fully aware of the deficiencies of the system of education in regard to the encouragement of handcrafts in the schools, or to the development of a love of craftsmanship, it is no part of the function of members of the Society to propose reform.'

Hackett, as professor of physics and electrical engineering, lamented just as much as Muriel the lack of early training in art and the crafts in schools. In a paper entitled 'The Pillars of Engineering' he argued that 'the great advances in physical science and engineering spring from the interwoven activity of the hands and minds of the great discoverers and inventors', concluding that 'in our education system the pillars of engineering are scarcely visible. Handcraft is ignored.' One of his favourite phrases – 'the work of hand and eye' – became one of Muriel's favourites too. In 1947 he had lent her *The Aims of Education and other Essays* (1932) by Alfred North Whitehead as a good source of quotations and epigrams, advising her that she need not feel obliged to credit Whitehead when she used them. She should simply incorporate some of the short sentences in her running remarks.[5] It is Whitehead who spoke of 'the co-ordinated action of hand and eye' as the essence of technical education.

What *was* possible from within the RDS was 'to promote craftsmanship in every direction by methods traditional to the Society such as premiums. . .by periodic exhibitions or permanent travelling exhibitions.' Muriel, whose life had already begun to resemble a one-woman crafts roadshow, decided to make even more space in her life for this aspect of promoting the crafts. Her term as vice-president of the ICA was up in March 1951 and she decided to retire from her position as chair of the executive committee at the same time. She also cancelled her RDS extension lectures. By August, after much to-ing and fro-ing between the RDS EC Committee and the monthly Country Markets meetings, a 'Country Craftsmanship Scheme' was ready to go into operation. The aim was for each county in Ireland to have a craft exhibition and competition for local skills at at least one county show in any given year. The RDS would provide financial backing to the tune of an annual grant of £200 to cover the cost of preparation and transport of the loan collection, a demonstrator and the judges' expenses; Country Markets would provide the loan exhibition, the judges and the schedule of craft competitions; and the county show committees would organise entry fees for the different craft competition classes and the prizes.

Muriel wrote a full report on the first year of the scheme, pointing out that those gaining the greatest benefit were the small county shows which without the RDS grant would not have afforded either the judges or the loan exhibition. 'The scheme's most encouraging features,' she went on, 'were the Loan

Exhibition's success in promoting the idea of quality in hand work and its better presentation, and the part of the Championship awards and certificates in giving craftworkers a sense of achievement and pride in their work.' Country Markets judges attended seventeen shows. Altogether there was a team of twelve judges, including Muriel, Chrissie O'Gorman and Miranda Scally, Angela and Muriel Kehoe, Win Drury, Olive Rowe, an expert in woodwork, Lucie Charles of the National College of Art and Sheila Findlater. 'One of the greatest difficulties', Muriel commented, 'was the necessity on occasion to have three lots of judges and three Loan Exhibitions on the road at the same time.' Such work required both dedication and stamina.

Sheila Findlater, for many years heavily involved with the crafts end of Country Markets, remembered it all only too well.[6] 'When we would go to county shows', she recalled, 'MG would insist on filling the car up with samples of good work to display. So when you arrived you had to start by putting up the exhibition, then you had to judge, you escaped for some lunch if you were lucky, and then you had to go back to deal with complaints such as, "My granny didn't get a prize for her socks, why not?" And since the exhibition had to be dismantled and packed back into the car, there was no hope of escaping before the end of the show.' Judges would travel in pairs and be at the mercy of 'hospitality' wherever they arrived. If the show was not within easy distance of Dublin, hospitality meant a bed with an ICA or Country Markets member and the hopes of something to eat. Of course in most cases the welcome they got could not have been warmer, nor the food better. But all the judges had stories to swap of how they worked until late into the evening without food and then were not so much as offered a cup of tea when they were shown to their cold bedroom for the night. There was no such thing as 'mileage' and the judges deemed themselves lucky if they got the price of their petrol back. The annoying thing was that Muriel seemed to take such hardships in her stride. She would very often not even have thought of money for her own petrol and assume that whoever she was travelling with would have money on them.

Noreen O'Boyle, who joined the ICA in 1955 and is still actively involved in Country Markets craft judging, remembers an incident which happened to coincide with Muriel's eightieth birthday in October 1977. There was an RDS-sponsored workshop weekend in, appropriately enough, Ballycroy, Co. Mayo. Muriel and Noreen set off from Dublin each in their own car, Muriel's crammed full of exhibition pieces. They stopped in Kinnegad to pick up Delia Campbell who was to demonstrate sheepskin curing. With six dripping sheepskins fresh from the abattoir loaded on to Muriel's roof rack they continued their journey, Muriel wrapped in a rug, her car heater on full blast and, as usual, singing hymns. 'Hospitality' in this case was an empty fishing lodge some distance from Ballycroy, where the quality of cold was of the sort that only such an unused and draughty place in the west of Ireland can produce. The local organisers of the week could not have been kinder, baking a birthday cake for Muriel and providing home-made wine. But it was cold. Muriel, however, did not turn a hair and insisted on cooking for the whole team of craft teachers, making it seem churlish to complain. In the middle of the night, on her way to the bathroom, Noreen caught a glimpse of Muriel putting her feet through the arms of an old pullover and pulling it up like a pair of tights before disappearing under a mound of blankets and coats.

There were other notorious pitfalls involved in judging county shows which Muriel had not foreseen in her overall scheme of things and which were left to her juniors to sort out. There was no money around in the Ireland of the 'fifties and the cash prizes offered through the Country Shows Scheme made some opportunists feel it worthwhile to do the rounds of different venues. By buying up prize-winning crafts and entering them in several shows under assumed names, you could hope to go home with a good few pounds. But the judges soon got wise. Noreen O'Boyle remembers one particular moment when, driving into a showground with Kay Hogan, another dedicated Country Markets judge, their car had to slow down to let another car out. It was a hot day and all car windows were rolled down. As the cars drew level Noreen and Kay distinctly heard a voice say: 'There's them two bloody bitches from Dublin. We won't get anything today!'

Against the odds, Muriel's scheme nevertheless took off. By 1953, no fewer than thirty-seven categories of crafts were listed by Country Markets for county show competitions and at the end of that year, when the judges attended twenty shows, Muriel was able to report 'improved quality of work in the competitions and a wider understanding of craftsmanship. On the marketing side, as a direct result of the championships and certificates won at Shows, craftsmen have got recognition and sale for work which otherwise would have remained unknown, and the Loan

Exhibition's effective demonstration of "soundness, simplicity and suitability" and the use of home grown materials has spread its influence over the whole field of handcraft production in the country.' In 1954 twenty-five shows were visited by the judges and though their report is quite positive, Muriel could not help harking back (wearing her Country Markets hat, not the RDS one) to the fact that 'the unhappy situation of the country craftsman will not improve until the essential need of universal handcraft training in youth is recognised in this country, and an appreciation of craftsmanship fostered.' In 1953 a judges' school was set up and a workshop was held in The Country Shop where craftworkers were invited to demonstrate in front of the prospective judges and explain their craft. A junior category at Shows was also introduced for the under-seventeens. Metal *brannra* badges – a black bread-iron on a silver background – were introduced in 1951 as awards for craft tests, with a bar at the bottom of the badge to carry different coloured ribbons which would represent tests passed in the different crafts. From sixteen *brannrai* in 1952, 260 were awarded in 1956. By 1966 the number was up to 434.[7]

In 1957 Muriel was elected to the Council of the RDS in recognition of her work. By 1962, handcraft schools were being held in country towns with overwhelming success, while the numbers of candidates for the various tests just grew and grew. Muriel's crusade involving the combined effort of Country Markets, the RDS and the local branches of the Irish Shows Association, not to mention the extraordinary commitment of her voluntary workers, would keep marching from then on, with stringently judged teachers' tests introduced by Country Markets in 1968, the logical extension of the *brannra* tests and demonstrators' bars.[8] Also in that year a new crafts competition was introduced by the RDS to be held annually at the Horse Show.

In 1964 one of Muriel's dreams had come true: a co-operative of craftworkers, the Slieve Bawn Co-operative Handcraft Market, was set up in Strokestown, Co. Roscommon, led by two strong and committed women, Patsy Duignan and Peggy Farrell. They amalgamated two separate craft-producing groups, one in Strokestown (where a third powerful woman, the local rector's wife, Joan Norman, was teaching rushwork with missionary zeal) and the other in Roscommon. It was Peggy Farrell's husband who came up with the title 'Slieve Bawn', since this hill could be seen from both towns and thus united the two groups and the surrounding area where co-operative craftworkers lived. So impressed was Muriel with Peggy Farrell's energy and powers of organisation within the Strokestown co-operative that she pressed her to go forward for the national presidency of the ICA. She was duly elected to the position in 1967 after just five years in the association. Patsy Duignan would soon be playing an active part in the Crafts Council of Ireland.

It is not hard to see how Muriel would become one of the prime movers behind the creation of this all-Ireland body to promote the crafts and protect the interests of craftworkers, a body which would somehow look after all the people she had been encouraging down the years. When Muriel was in the throes of creating the Irish Homespun Society in 1935, she had thought how wonderful it would be if Ireland had the equivalent of England's Rural Industries Bureau. In 1950 she went across the water to study their set-up and found, for a start, that they had an annual government grant of £60,000. Muriel knew this was wonderland by Irish standards and yet she remained convinced that 'for any large scale development of country crafts such a nationwide organisation was necessary.'

In November 1966 she wrote, as the chair of Country Markets, to the registrar of the RDS suggesting that the RDS should play a greater part in promoting the crafts. She suggested that they take the initiative in the creation of a representative national association 'on the lines of such organisations of long standing in England and Scotland, representative of all sections and Societies – voluntary, trading, statutory, Governmental'. Another important lobby was at work in parallel. In 1961 the Scandinavian report on *Design in Ireland* had caused both delight and anger when it appeared. Paul Hogan of the Irish Export Board (CTT) had been responsible for getting it between covers and the director of CTT, Bill Walsh, had the bit of better Irish design firmly between his teeth. The government-sponsored Kilkenny Design Workshops, officially opened in November 1965, were the exciting result of his persistence. Ireland had never had anything like it before. The mood was ripe for further interesting developments in the area of the crafts and design.

In September 1970, thanks to the efforts of those Paul Hogan called the 'founding fathers and mothers' of the Crafts Council of Ireland – Muriel Gahan, Peter and Helena Brennan, Frank Sutton and, of course, Paul Hogan himself who insisted on the inclusive, all-Ireland title – a seminar was held in Greystones. In August the World Crafts Council had held its conference in Dublin, accompanied by a major exhibition of crafts in the library of TCD which had drawn huge crowds. The mood was buoyant and over one hundred craftworkers and representatives of craft organisations from all over Ireland attended the one-day Greystones meeting which addressed the 'possibility of forming an organisation which would concern itself with the cultural, educational, social and economic aspects of handcraft in Ireland, north and south.' The Crafts Council of Ireland was established in October 1971 and incorporated in 1976.

It was to become yet another area where Muriel's energy seemed to defy the laws of nature and grow exponentially with the advancing years. Although it was she who insisted that the first chairman should be James Warwick, former principal of the Ulster College of Art and Design (she saw his representing design *and* the North as equally important to the fledgling Council), it was not long before she found herself in the chair herself, a position she held from 1976–78. But her involvement was total, in the chair or out of it. It was she who persuaded the RDS to give the Crafts Council a free home and secretariat in its early days, with Betty Searson, then assistant to the RDS librarian, later arts administrator, writing and answering letters, minuting meetings and travelling the country with Muriel encouraging craftworkers to form guilds and join the new Council.

Country Markets, meanwhile, went from strength to strength. In 1974 another, larger, department of agriculture grant was obtained and a full-time organising secretary could be appointed. Mary Coleman, with a strong background in the crafts, started her work in July 1974 and the following January the Country Markets office which had been a rent-free room in 23 St Stephen's Green since 1946 moved to the ICA headquarters in Merrion Road, 'by kind invitation of the Association.' In April 1975 Muriel finally relinquished the chair which she had occupied for nearly twenty-nine years, personally nominating her successor, Rita Rutherford, controller of Kilternan Country Market. In 1981 a new position, that of president, was created for Muriel who remained very much in control for years after her functions had officially been taken over. Adored by the markets around the country, Muriel would continue to visit as many of them as she could as long as her health allowed and would attend the AGM where she would invariably surprise delegates by her pertinent and informed remarks. Her only sadness was the growing distance between the ICA and Country Markets, a distance which was never meant to exist and which Muriel would have loved to be able to heal.

Notes

1. When Ann Roche had the occasion to tell Fianna Fáil politician Brian Lenihan what Muriel's nickname for her was he replied: 'Good Lord, isn't it as well it isn't my past!'

2. Craftworkers could become shareholders if they were country workers using native raw materials; country tradesmen; a traditional country industry derived from native products. (Country Markets Ltd Minutes, 4 October 1946)

3. In October 1945 Muriel had told her fellow Country Workers directors that 'future judges should have a higher standard of taste than the average ICA member.' By July 1950 ICA members were complaining that the crafts tests were too difficult. The raising of standards was always central to Muriel's approach to the crafts.

4. Russell, George W. 'Ideals of the Rural Society' from *The United Irishwomen: their place, work and ideals*, 1911. Reprinted in Bolger, Pat (ed.) *And See Her beauty Standing There*, Irish Academic Press, 1986.

5. In his paper, 'The Pillars of Engineering', Hackett himself quotes Whitehead without crediting his source.

6. Author's conversation with Sheila Findlater, 1 September 1995.

7. By this time production tests – organised by Margaret Long – had become equally sought after with 412 taken in 1966, the majority in gardening and cookery.

8. To obtain a *brannra* (at pass, good or excellent grade) a candidate must submit three articles in a given craft. With five 'excellent' grades in five different crafts a demonstrator's bar is obtained, giving the candidate the right to demonstrate those crafts in public. With three demonstrators' bars, the candidate may proceed to the teachers' test. This is comprised of two written papers and a practical part where the candidate's teaching methods are judged by external, university judges.

— 14 —

From Slievenamon. . .

Terence de Vere White, a good friend of Muriel's and an habitué of The Country Shop, once wrote that her achievements were governed by 'a serendipity which beats any story teller's invention'.[1] Yet although it does often appear that she just happened to be in the right place at the right time – a myth she was always the first to sustain – nothing could be farther from the truth. Muriel was a person of both vision and focus. She always had a very clear idea of what she wanted, did her homework and was alert to the right moment to strike in order to achieve optimum results. Above all, she did not hesitate. Later she would shrug off her achievements lightly, leading others to believe that they had all been one colossal stroke of luck. The ICA's magnificent residential college at Termonfechin, Co. Louth, is a case in point. There is no doubt that without Muriel there would be no college today. But that she 'happened' to secure An Grianán for the ICA because she 'happened' to be invited to lunch with the head of the W K Kellogg Foundation and, in a blinding flash over soup, thought a residential college would be a nice thing for the ICA to have, is nonsense. The only serendipitous element in the tale lies not with Muriel at all but in the happy irruption of a fairy godfather from America – the Kellogg Foundation's president – on the lookout for a suitable beneficiary in Ireland of his organisation's largesse.

An Grianán was the result, not of lunch in the Shelbourne Hotel, but of twenty years' single-mindedness. Poverty and dejection, not so different from what she had seen as a child when travelling the west of Ireland with her father, were what Muriel had found when she began her work in the 1930s. In 1929 Lucy Franks' plea had gone out, 'Women to lead are badly needed, women of wide understanding and vision who know what country conditions are, and not what one would like to imagine them to be.' Muriel and a very small number of women obstinately persevered in their chosen, and at first rather amateurish, way of improving lives in the country through 'self help and mutual help'. The 1940s were overshadowed by the war and emergency measures but their work went on and, although the number of committed people now involved in the ICA's project was growing – Kit Ahern and Mamo McDonald, both future national presidents, joined at this time – they still relied almost entirely on hard voluntary effort. Country Workers Ltd, with the money generated by The Country Shop, was their only external funder. In 1945, when Phyllis O'Connell was still the ICA's sole organiser, the cry went up, '. . .we have only one Miss O'Connell, and she has not got a magic carpet, or even a motor car, and already she covers a miraculous amount of ground on her bicycle and by bus and train . . . We want more organisers, we want more money.'[2] The next year the ICA was given the anonymous gift of a van for Phyllis O'Connell but it was not until 1950, as a decade of emigration and despair opened in Ireland, that the plea was finally heard at government level and the first reward came for so many years of invisible – because unacknowledged – work.

There is an almost irreconcilable contrast between, on the one hand the depression eating away at post-emergency Ireland, when figures for both emigration and population transfers from country to cities shot up (especially for women) and, on the other hand the vision and hope embodied by the leaders not just of the ICA, but of such voluntary movements as Macra na Feirme and Muintir na Tíre, as well as the activities of co-operative inspired companies such as Country Markets and Country Workers. All recognised the gaping needs of the country people and their hunger for change, nowhere more acute than in the women. 'No-one has been more sung about, or more written about,' wrote an anonymous ICA member about the rural Irish mother back in 1943, 'and at the same time for no-one has there been less done.' In a paper entitled *The Countrywoman and Adult Education*, which she read to the Annual Congress of the Vocational Education Association in Dublin in June 1950, Muriel herself graphically described the Irish countrywoman as:

> . . . not an abstraction in print, but Mrs Conneely with half a
> dozen children to raise on five acres of rock in Connemara,

Mrs McCarthy of the Midlands, trying to run a big mixed farm with insufficient help and cut off from her sister countrywomen six days of the week. Mary McBride in Donegal, home from service and restless with the thought of opportunities that might be waiting for her in another country; too many of them in the house, her young sister wondering when she too will get away. Nancy O'Sullivan raising chickens in Waterford, her fingers itching to make something pretty for her home, but she doesn't know how. And Mrs Clogherty sitting – just sitting, as I saw her in her little house in Kerry not so long ago; an empty room, no sign of food, no belongings except her spinning wheel, idle in the corner, because she was without the means to buy wool.

In that same lecture she went on:

And Adult Education – not just the phrase of the moment, but something to do, something to see, something to hear and experience, that will unloose the gift of hands, and heart, and mind and spirit, that are locked up in the Mrs Conneelys, the Mary McBrides and the rest, and if they were freed would change the face of Ireland.

Muriel had chaired the ICA's executive committee from 1941 to 1946 and despite her growing workload she once more accepted this position in 1950, backed by an ever-expanding team of determined and increasingly well-informed women. The urgency for something to be done to improve conditions in the country was acutely felt. Fortunately for the ICA the rural electrification scheme, first outlined in a White Paper in 1944, was gathering momentum and the government's campaign for piped water was beginning. *Fortunately*, not because their sisters throughout rural Ireland would be the first to benefit – that went without saying – but because all of a sudden the ICA no longer had to hammer on government doors. Their usefulness had been discovered and their help began to be sought out. They were becoming visible to the male establishment at last.

In a groundbreaking gesture of official recognition – the government's first in financial terms – agriculture minister James Dillon[3], who was trying to implement his own parish plan based on the American model of the agricultural extension service and was thus genuinely impressed by the ICA's structure and aims, offered them an annual grant of £2,600 towards organisers' salaries. It was December 1950. In September, at Dillon's invitation, the ICA executive committee had met with a Food and Agriculture Organisation (FAO) home economics and rural welfare expert, a Canadian woman called Miss Margaret Hockin.[4] Muriel organised an intensive programme for her. In the space of three days she was taken to visit Tramore guild, a South Tipperary ICA rally at Cahir, the Munster Institute, Cork Town Association and Fethard Market. She was also taken to meet Father Hayes of Muintir na Tíre at his home in Bansha and attended a meeting of the ICA executive in Dublin. The immediate effect of her evident enthusiasm for the work of the ICA was twofold: she gave Muriel and her committee official confirmation, only ever afforded them piecemeal from within Ireland, that their work was important and effective and, vitally, she impressed upon James Dillon that this was so. She pointed out the ICA's strengths and weaknesses. On the strengths side, she recognised that the ICA was often the only source of accurate information about country life available and as such could contribute hugely to improving rural housing and in forwarding schemes for bringing both electricity and water into country homes. As for the areas to be developed, Miss Hockin stressed the need for training facilities for country women and for adequate meeting places, too. In October Dillon invited an ICA delegation, headed by Muriel, to come to see him at government buildings. 'The Minister stressed the importance of voluntary organisations,' Muriel reported, 'and asked for the Association's co-operation in making known the Department's Farm Improvements and "Water into the Homes" schemes, and offered his help to the Association in any way possible. . .'

In response to such encouraging signs, Dillon was invited to open the ICA's Country Fair on 8 November 1950. This was a fund-raising event to make money for the organising fund – out of which came Phyllis O'Connell's and Muriel Kehoe's salaries and expenses and central office administration costs – as an alternative to the 'targets' scheme, devised by Grace Somerville-Large in 1948, whereby each guild set itself the 'target' of an annual donation of five pounds[5]. The flamboyant Country Fair was designed and staged by Muriel (plus the habitual gang of willing slaves) in the round room of the Mansion House and the cost of setting it up – £165 – was met by Country Workers. The idea was to simulate a real country fair – coffee van included – and there was music and dancing at a makeshift crossroads as well as a crafts exhibition and both crafts and produce, donated by ICA guilds all over the country, were for sale. Promotions of rural electrification and running water in the home were an important feature. The noisy and colourful fair drew the crowds and well over a thousand pounds were raised. Muriel made a further contribution by buying the best craft exhibits in each category for Country Workers, selling them on at the next year's Horse Show where she replaced them by yet another collection, thus stimulating craft production.

The opening of the exhibition made the front page of *The Irish Times* next day, with a photograph of James Dillon holding a basket of eggs. 'Mr Dillon Will "Stand or Fall" by Eggs' ran the headline, a reference to the fact that the sale of eggs was traditionally the country woman's domain and an area of conflict with successive ministers, including himself, and an implicit if rather patronising acknowledgement of the importance of women in rural life.

> 'I stand or fall by these', said Mr Dillon, Minister for Agriculture, as he posed with a large basket of eggs in his hand to be photographed after the official opening of the Country Fair of the ICA in the Mansion House Dublin yesterday. Remarking on his previous attitude to the Association the Minister said that at one time 'certain public spirited ladies of this century who did not accept that a new day had dawned in the country were closely associated with ICA. Let us not put a tooth in it – there was a very distinct aroma of the ascendancy about it.'
>
> He was at the fair because he was certain that the women now in the countrywomen's movement were truly devoted to the country.
>
> In so far as the Association functioned in bringing the people of the country to co-operative service, Ireland was greatly in its debt.
>
> Miss L Franks President of the Association welcoming Mr Dillon referred to the need of certain amenities such as village halls in rural parts, and the Minister said, in reply, that the country people should ask for all that they wanted, and should challenge the Government to tell them if what they asked for was not provided, why it was not.
>
> 'I can promise nothing but to do my best; I refuse to be restricted in my present ministerial office from saying what I want to do. I am going to go on aiming at stars as long as

I have the capacity to want them.'
Mr Dillon challenged the women with marriageable
daughters to persuade these daughters not to agree to marry
until they had water laid on in their houses, hot and cold.

The barb of Dillon's comments about the early ICA activists, not
to say the insult contained in them, was not lost on Muriel and
her Protestant co-workers standing at the Mansion House
opening. Lucy Franks' deafness may have shielded her from the
minister's words and Muriel probably tossed them off with a laugh
and the suggestion that they should have lobbed a few eggs at the
minister after all, as they had joked about doing beforehand. Livie
Hughes, however, whose mind was constantly exercised by the
issue of religion and national identity in Ireland, could not allow
it to pass and challenged Dillon on the spot. 'Both sides of our
family are pre-Cromwellians,' she later remarked bitterly to a
friend, 'and if it was any other country of the world we would be
reckoned Irish, but now we have to call ourselves West Britons or
Anglo-Irish and feel apologetic for our existence.' Had James
Dillon but looked more closely at such an 'ascendancy' element of
the ICA as Livie, he might well have been alarmed to find that her
radical feminism and socialist views were closer to the bugbear
communism than to any hereditary British oppressor. Democratic
and patriotic were two words Livie invariably used about the work
first of the UI and later the ICA.

Practising Harry Norman's doctrine of 'persistent goodwill',
Muriel remained calm. She got on well with Dillon and, taking
him at his word, she sat down to write a memorandum asking for
'all that they wanted.' On 18 December a detailed request landed
on the minister's desk. Before long the telephone rang in Muriel's
office in The Country Shop. It was Dillon offering a grant for
organisers. Muriel received the news of the grant graciously and
with genuine pleasure. As well as deeds before words, she always
put ends before means. She would laughingly remember the
telephone call. Imitating the minister's booming voice and rather
pedantic delivery, she would make it clear nonetheless that his
generosity had not been boundless. 'Miss Gahan, I'm afraid I can't
give you your college, but I can let you have your organisers. . .'
The department had in fact responded only to the third and least
onerous of Muriel's requests on the ICA's behalf. These had been
for a residential college, home advisers *and* organisers. Still it was
a beginning and thanks to the work which had gone into drawing

up the memorandum the ICA now had a much more precise notion of what sort of a college they wanted. The scene was set and ready for 'Mr Kellogg's' entrance.

There is of course another more colourful strand to the tale of An Grianán and it goes back to Muriel and Livie's youth and the rather hearty camping expeditions they would organise with their friends in summer. In particular it leads to Fethard and to Livie Hughes once again, for that is where the seeds of the long-dreamt-of adult education college were first sown. Livie had joined the UI in May 1928, and in June 1929, while Muriel was still a full-time house painter in Dublin, she put an appeal in the *Farmers' Gazette*. A friend of hers had attended a summer school in an old monastery in the west of England where 'for several holiday weeks gathered women and girls from all parts of the country. . .living was of the plainest, food off long bare tables, long dormitories with twenty or thirty camp beds.' During the day there were craft classes, 'a silver worker teaching his pupils to make brooches and rings and silver spoons. Leather work and basket making were also taught; while out in the garden spinning, carding and wool dyeing were also in progress, the bushes holding skeins of wool fresh from the dye vats; looms in another shed, where the aspiring pupil wove her own jumper and skirt.' In the evening there was dancing.

It is not difficult to see why Livie was excited by the idea and why Muriel would make sure she would be free each summer from 1930 on to take part in such a venture. For Livie, as well as the fact that camping was something she was used to and enjoyed, the idea of a summer camp had both practical and romantic appeal. Practical, because the room where Fethard UI members met was too small to accommodate both the older women who wanted to do basket-making and make lumra rugs and the younger ones who wanted to dance and sing. Out in the open there would be plenty of space. The romantic appeal had to do with Lucy Franks' Aunt Lottie, the suffragist Charlotte Despard, who had allegedly said to her niece, 'Take the women of Ireland up the mountains of Ireland and let them hear the music and the poetry and the old legends.'[6] So Livie launched her appeal: 'If any of our kind friends would guarantee us a small sum towards the expense,' she wrote, 'and that the members would be prepared for camping conditions, there is surely no reason why the UI should not have a Summer School of their own.' Applications from any member who was interested as 'student, craft teacher, lecturer, traditional singer, dancer or, perhaps, all combined', were to be sent to Mrs Hughes at Annsgift. Within weeks, the executive of the UI, to which Livie was freshly elected, decided to support the summer school idea. By 19 July 1929 some twenty women, all but three from Fethard itself, were camping out on the slopes of the mountain of women, Slievenamon[7], 'a mountain famous in legend and song, and suitably enough named for the first Summer School of the UI.' They brought a bell tent up to where the O'Connells had two corrugated iron huts on the mountainside. The 'outsiders' were Lucy Franks, 'an adventuress if ever there was one'[8], who came with a friend and taught people to make cane baskets, and Alice Ryan, one of the 'Ryans of Scarteen', a big hunting family. Livie demonstrated rushwork.

The summer school was a triumph. From then on, wherever an empty castle or big house could be hired, or better still borrowed, a summer school would be held for ten days to a fortnight each summer. 'It is what the Americans call "built-in evaluation"', Livie recalled fifty years later, 'but it really meant: "We must do this again"'. And so they did, again and again, holding the annual summer camp 'for members and their friends'. After Slievenamon came Cappard House, Co. Laois, high in the Slieve Bloom mountains, then Bentley House, Curracloe, Co. Wexford and in 1932 Cappagh, Co. Waterford. In 1933 Vida Lentaigne offered her house at Termonfechin. The house, which twenty years would later become An Grianán, was described that year as 'an ideal place for the purpose. The spacious house, standing in its own park, is within ten minutes walk of the sea, where good bathing can be had and, as well, there are many beautiful walks both along the coast and up the Boyne river.'

Castlefreke, Co. Cork in 1935 stands out as one of the most memorable early summer schools and was typical of the unique, anarchic and thoroughly enjoyable atmosphere that reigned. 'Expect the unexpected' could have been their motto. Castlefreke overlooking Rosscarbery Bay – 'a bare and empty castle on a height overlooking the Atlantic' – was also where Muriel's reputation as an inspired director of improvised drama was established. The castle's flat roof provided her with a sensational stage. Years later Cerise Parker recalled 'a beautiful green dragon winding its ways about the chimney tops and the glorious views of the Atlantic and the surrounding countryside.' In the 1950s Livie came on an old ciné film of Castlefreke with 'MG dressed up as Sir Eglamore dealing with a splendid dragon – mostly Miss Franks' scarlet Lilo.' At the end of a long and energetic day Muriel, Livie, Grace Somerville-Large and other 'hardy folk', including Lucy

Franks' young god-daughter Nonie, climbed the winding stairs to the flat roof and slept there. Helped by members of the local Clonakilty guild Muriel and Grace were in charge as they would be for countless summer schools to come, Muriel on the activities side, Grace organising the catering. Grace and her two sisters, Kathleen and Cerise, had formed an advance party to Castlefreke with the daunting task of making the empty castle – 'no furniture of any kind' – in some way habitable.

For eighteen-year-old Lily Moore (later Harte) Castlefreke was an experience so completely new to her that the smallest details were indelibly etched into her memory. Muriel had decided that three girls from her Country Shop kitchen staff should have a holiday in the country and get a taste of the ICA at the summer school. So into the back of the car belonging to Lily's fiancé, Christy Harte, piled Lily, her sister Kay and Kathleen Bunting. Muriel sat in front beside Christy, 'singing good-o' for most of the journey. The three girls had brought empty sacks with them as instructed by Muriel but had no idea what they were for nor what lay ahead. It was getting dark when they reached the castle. Sixty years on Lily's voice still fills with incredulity. 'We were told to go to the shed to fill our sacks full of straw – to sleep on! There were no lights, we only had candles, only candles. . .' Muriel led them through the dark corridors, stopping every now and then to light a candle which she would leave guttering on a draughty windowsill and then light another to reveal more high ceilings and shadowy corners. Eventually they reached the room where the three Country Shop girls were to sleep. 'Well! I never saw anything like it! It was a huge big barracks of a room, and not a thing in it. Not a thing, only nails all around and nails is what we had to hang our clothes on. We had to make our beds as well as we could, there were quilts for us to cover ourselves with, and when we got up next morning there was a place outside where we could wash and when we'd washed, Miss Gahan said "Follow the arrow when you come out." So we'd follow it twisting and turning, this way and that, until we got where we were to go for our breakfast.' Despite the makeshift arrangements food was plentiful. It was later reported from Fethard that one of their guild members had put on more than a stone in weight at Castlefreke.

As summer schools became more commonplace and the age gap between the organisers and the raw recruits widened, some of the initial sense of excitement was lost and the organisation became more streamlined. 'Pure army' is how a participant in one of the last summer schools before An Grianán remembers it – not without admiration in her voice – run by 'elderly ladies in cotton dresses and handknit cardigans'. By that stage everyone was issued on arrival with a coloured ribbon to wear and chores were listed on a notice board. Each morning you had to check which chore befell your colour group that day. Fifteen years earlier at Castlefreke delicious chaos still had the upper hand.

Several more castles – Coolemaine. . .Kilbrittan. . .Rosturk – were the scene of summer schools over the following years, where 'fun' was without doubt the predominant element with Muriel always in charge of drama and improvisations as well as organising the classes and lectures. When wartime restrictions came the summer school was held closer to Dublin, at Aravon in Bray, Co. Wicklow. Already the numbers had grown dramatically, with eighty delegates from fifty-six guilds at the Bray summer school in 1944. The next year, 1945, was to be pivotal because it was then that it was decided to have a more structured summer course, lasting a month and strictly for ICA members only, more 'serious' than the summer school where the accent was above all on freedom, self-expression and craftwork. Coláiste Charman in Gorey was hired for an extra session and for the first time a 'summer college' was held. It was in 1945 too that Muriel, Livie, Grace and Lucy Franks began to have lengthy discussions at their Country Workers directors' meetings about 'a future ICA summer school and college house.'

By 1947 there was such a demand for places that the summer college, held that year in a school in Galway, was followed by *two* sessions of summer school. Then in June 1948 Muriel and Livie went on a month-long fact-finding trip, financed by Country Workers, to Denmark and Sweden. Their purpose was to study Folk High Schools. On their return they toured ICA guilds widely giving talks on what they had seen, including the Askov Folk High School in Denmark where they heard the founder of the International Folk School in Elsinore, Peter Manniche, speak and where both the principal of the school, Oyvind Arnfred, and the atmosphere impressed them. Their conviction that only in a permanent adult education centre of its own could the ICA achieve far-reaching results was strengthened.

The next year the summer schools and college were held in Sligo Grammar School and another landmark was recorded. For the first time, after much lobbying, the government recognised the ICA's summer college, 'the first college to be recognised by the Department of Education,' reported Muriel, 'who had empowered six domestic science instructresses to be sent by their counties.' Back in Fethard the ICA guild had bought themselves a Nissen hut for £200 in which to hold their meetings. Looking for a name to call the hut, one suggestion was. . . An Grianán.[9]

Notes

1. *Irish Times*, Saturday 7 May 1977.
2. *Farmers' Gazette*, 3 March 1945. At the end of 1945 there were 134 guilds; four years later there were 234 and still only one full-time organiser.
3. James Dillon, Fine Gael, was minister for agriculture 1948–51 and 1954–57.
4. She was in fact Mrs James Harrington but unlike Irish female civil servants she was not obliged to give up her job after marriage.
5. Grace Somerville-Large 'will go down in ICA history as the treasurer who made finance understandable and entertaining.' *Farmers' Gazette*, 8 July 1950.
6. Though Livie had been fired by this idea at the time, she wryly remarked much later in her life, 'I don't know what that was to do to us, but it was to make us better Irishwomen.'
7. The summit of Slievenamon is just six miles from Fethard as the crow flies.
8. Livie Hughes to D Shaw Smith, 1980.
9. *Farmers' Gazette*, 12 March 1949. The name eventually chosen, though little used, was Dun Brigde.

— 15 —

...to Termonfechin

Being spurred into drawing up an official application for a residential college in 1950 was a decisive step. Although the request was turned down, it nevertheless forced Muriel and the other members of the executive to define more closely what exactly it was they wanted. The nature of the ICA itself was changing with increased membership. Once the new organisers began work in October 1951 it expanded even more rapidly. The seven women – Kathleen Gleeson and Ena O'Reilly, full-time; Ann Roche, Kathleen Donnelly, Sheila Connolly, Pauline Frawley and Ena McKeever part-time – had all been scrupulously tested over the summer for the requisite qualities of enthusiasm, fun and initiative. Many women whose names later became prominent in the movement joined the ICA at this time: Aine Barrington, Joan Coady, Margaret Erraught, Phyllis Faris, Joan Norman and Noreen O'Boyle to name but a few. As for the summer school, with two sessions each year as well as a summer college, the original spontaneity of the early days had gone. There were murmurings in the middle ranks and a feeling albeit a minority one that the same people – those 'elderly' ladies in cotton frocks – had been running the show their way for too long. Through the eyes of a woman in her twenties or early thirties Lucy Franks and Alice Ryan were ancient and Muriel and Livie, both fifty-three in 1950, and even Grace Somerville-Large a mere forty-five, were undeniably of another generation. It was a measure of their success in giving rural women a voice that their position was now being questioned.

Ironically Dillon's grant gave rise to further tensions as, firstly, it was paid over late and ended up costing the ICA money since they were obliged to take out an overdraft to pay their newly hired organisers. Secondly, as the grant covered only salaries and not expenses, the 'target' remained in place. At the same time, those 'same people' on the executive committee were finding the workload increasingly heavy with twice-monthly meetings lasting three hours at a time proving insufficient to get through business. In December 1950, within the confines of a Country Workers directors' meeting, Muriel came up with the idea of creating sub-committees at federation level to decentralise the executive's work and of making federation presidents ex-officio members of the executive. Livie suggested they organise a weekend conference in the new year, to be attended by the executive and all federation presidents, to set this in motion. Delegates' expenses would be paid for by Country Workers and the agenda would include not only the formation of sub-committees but 'a discussion of the proposed ICA training centre' as well.

The conference was held in the Grand Hotel in Tramore, Co. Waterford in March 1951 and it was agreed to make a residential college an immediate proiority. Phyllis O'Connell's mother, a widow for over thirty years, had died in 1949 and the three-storey family house in the centre of Fethard was too big for Phyllis and her sister to live in on their own. Since Phyllis was the ICA's chief organiser and Fethard had such a vibrant guild, not to mention Livie Hughes herself, the idea of having a permanent centre there made sense. Country Workers paid to have the O'Connells' house valued and an estimate drawn up of the cost to make it good as a training centre. The idea was subsequently abandoned but in the meantime the application for funds to buy a residential college was once more put in to the department of agriculture. And once more it was turned down. By now it had also been presented to the department of education and 'approved in principle' by both departments.

Muriel had resigned from the chair of the executive in 1951 in order to give more time to Country Markets and the Country Shows Scheme. But then in January 1952 she was invited to become a founder member – and the only female member – of *An Chomhairle Ealaíon*, Ireland's first Arts Council. This was the reward for her years of dogged work for the crafts. Paddy Little, a supporter of Muriel's work since the Irish Homespun Society began in 1935[1], was the Arts Council's first director and it was he who put her name forward for co-option. Muriel must have felt flattered and gratified by the invitation but she also knew this was an honour she would be foolish to turn down. It would be yet another useful platform from which to continue the craft fight.[2]

When she resigned in 1961 she remarked that 'ten years is a long enough time to be on [the Arts Council] and learn in what way it can best be of use. . .for improved craftsmanship.' It was one of the few committees Muriel does not seem to have enjoyed, even using as excuse for leaving it, amusing given her record, that 'some people stay on committees too long'[3]. 'It was to do with an enormously wide range of things, rather abstract things', she recalled years later. 'It occasionally came down to earth and had to do with the kinds of things that one was interested in, but it has left me with very negative thoughts in my mind about what good it is doing. . .I can remember nothing very striking that came out of it.'[4]

Muriel's memory was not usually so poor, but then her meeting with the man she liked to call 'Mr Kellogg' was only indirectly linked to the Arts Council. Early in the summer a fellow Arts Council member, Dr Richard Hayes, director of the National Library, told her as they left a meeting that a Dr Emory Morris of the American W K Kellogg Foundation was expected in Dublin shortly, interested in finding some agricultural project to fund in Ireland. Why didn't she come along and meet him over lunch? Hayes could think of nothing to ask him for, but he knew Muriel's interests lay in the country, if not directly in agriculture.

The Kellogg Foundation had been founded in 1930 by Will Keith Kellogg who in 1906 had set up the W K Kellogg Company to manufacture cereal products, originally promoted as health foods by his elder brother, Dr John Harvey Kellogg, the founder of the Battle Creek Sanatarium (sic) where, amongst its many patients, it once counted Horace Plunkett. Emory Morris, a young dentist, went to work for the Kellogg Foundation shortly after it was created. He was made President in 1943 at the age of thirty-eight. He remained the Foundation's chief executive officer until his retirement in 1970. The Foundation's field of action has always been wide, both socially and geographically. Today their involvement is above all in Latin America, the Caribbean and Southern African countries as well as within the United States, and their field is principally community-based health programmes. In 1952, although the Kellogg Company had been selling their breakfast cereals in Ireland since the 1920s, the Kellogg Foundation had as yet no involvement and Dr Morris's visit was an exploratory one.

Muriel went along to meet him for lunch, still not clear what the Kellogg Foundation was, nor how many of her concerns might coincide with theirs. It turned out however that the Foundation was interested in the development of co-operative programmes in the field of agriculture and that they had a particular interest in adult education. In 1951 they had contributed $1,400,000 towards the seven-storey Kellogg Centre for Continuing Education on the campus of Michigan State University. Once the key words 'co-operative' and 'adult education' had been uttered conversation flowed. A forceful speaker at the best of times, Muriel impressed Dr Morris deeply with her experience and enthusiasm. Described as 'a daring visionary willing to bet on new ideas'[5], with a commitment and capacity for hard work similar to Muriel's, he clearly recognised a kindred spirit in her. He already knew of Denman College, the WI's residential centre in England, established in 1948 and funded by the Carnegie Trust, and Muriel spoke eloquently about the ICA's dreams and desires for a place of their own. It is also more than probable that Morris had been alerted to the ICA's work and Muriel's part in it through the Kellogg Company's contacts in Ireland. Dermot Findlater, managing director of Alex Findlater and Co. Ltd, then Ireland's leading grocery business, had developed a strong friendship over the years with the Kellogg Company's UK representative, Harry McEvoy. Dermot Findlater's sister, Sheila, had joined the Dublin Town Association of the ICA around 1950, becoming its president in January 1952 when the ICA's need for a residential college of their own was top of the agenda. Before lunch was over Emory Morris had asked Muriel to put the ICA's project in writing.

Over the years of the Kellogg Foundation's consistent support – both financial and moral – for the aims and endeavours of the ICA, Muriel was to remain a key figure for them, striking up a strong personal rapport with successive representatives of the Foundation. In 1958 Thomas N Moss, director of the Foundation's agricultural division, reported back that 'Miss Gahan continues to impress as being an exceedingly capable person.' The habit became established of Muriel ferrying visiting Kellogg representatives from Dublin to An Grianán and back by car. In 1971 the Foundation's programme director, Gary W King, referred to Muriel in his report as being 'long a stalwart of the ICA. . .a very delightful lady [who] seems to be going strong'; in 1972 she was 'remarkable and delightful as always'; by 1978, 'Miss Gahan, the stalwart, was very much in evidence and displayed her usual enthusiasm. . .she is really remarkable.' In 1981 King was slightly taken aback that 'the stalwart' should still be playing such an active role: 'We were picked up. . .by Dr Muriel Gahan who forthwith drove us to Termonfechin to tour An Grianán. I must say when I heard that Dr Gahan was to pick us up I had some reservations. She is, after all, 83 years old. I needn't have worried. She is alert, did a good job driving, and carried on a conversation simultaneously practically the whole way. She drives a little red Fiat all over Ireland. Even though she is officially retired, she says she is as busy as ever.' After Dr Morris' retirement as president of the Foundation, his successor, Dr Russ Mawby, also struck up a warm friendship with Muriel.

After Morris' first visit Muriel wasted no time in putting the ICA's desire for a residential centre on paper. On 10 June 1952 she simply posted off to Battle Creek, Michigan a copy of the relevant section of her memorandum to James Dillon, along with the original covering letter dated 18 December 1950 and the original estimate of costs. She also sent Dr Morris, as background, a six-page transcript of a broadcast Livie Hughes had made in 1950 on the subject of Summer Schools. Her covering letter had the tone of a child writing to Father Christmas and not quite believing she will be found worthy of her request:

'

Dear Dr Morris,
At your kind invitation we now have pleasure in sending relevant information about our proposed Residential College, or 'Centre' as we, so far, have less ambitiously called it, in the hope that your Foundation may think it worthy of support.
If our proposals are considered by your Board, would you emphasise that the place we seek is of modest proportions, with low upkeep costs. We do not want anything on as grand a scale as Denman College, because we know that such would be beyond our means to support.
We have no house in view, but houses are constantly coming into the market and it should not be too difficult to get what we want. Its situation near a friendly, helpful guild of our Association would outweigh other considerations. The College must, itself, be in the stream of country life around it. It is not possible to say until our College gets going whether it will, in fact be possible to have a continual series of courses filled by our members alone. Our friendly relations with Macra na Feirma (sic) (Young Farmer's Clubs) suggest that

their members might take advantage of any vacancies in the year's programme, and in planning our house we could see to it that it would be sufficiently adaptable to meet the various needs of the Rural Community.

If your Foundation would consider giving us a grant in aid of buying and setting up our College and contributing to its upkeep during the first testing years you could rest assured that all Ireland's Countrywomen – our most neglected citizens – would gain its benefits. Our Association, affiliated to the Associated Countrywomen of the World, is the only Countrywomen's organisation in the Republic; its membership is open to all women who wish to join, of whatever class, creed or country.

As reference in the United States we give you the name of Dean Carrigan, Home Extension Service, Vermont, Massachusetts, and, in the Food & Agricultural Organisation, Miss Hockin, to both of whom our work is known.

We shall be happy to let you have any further information you may need.

Yours sincerely,

Muriel Gahan

Irish Countrywomen's Association.

In July Dr Morris presented the proposal to his Board with a cost estimate of a maximum of $45,000 for the purchase of a centre and $7,500 as a start-up grant, based on the figures provided by Muriel. In conclusion he said: 'The agricultural problem of Ireland is extremely complicated and the opportunity to assist with programs comparable to those being recommended for the United Kingdom does not exist at this time.' These included collaboration with the ministry of agriculture in England, the department of agriculture in Scotland, the National Federation of Young Farmers Clubs of England and Wales, the Scottish Association of Young Farmers Clubs and the Rowett Research Institute. 'It is our feeling that we should develop over the next few years one constructive program in South Ireland that is sure of success.' As far as he was concerned, the ICA college fitted the bill.

In December, once he had investigated the ICA more fully, Dr Morris wrote a very encouraging letter to Muriel, containing the magic words 'the Foundation will be glad to give further consideration to your request.' He stressed his opinion that 'women in the rural area have a very important part to play in the field of agriculture. . .and this is more true in Southern Ireland than in most any other part of the world.' He announced a return visit to Ireland for the following autumn and encouraged Muriel in the meantime to 'give more detailed attention to the location of the centre, its cost and the personnel needed to initiate the program', so that he could get down to serious business on his arrival in Ireland.

Muriel had got to work even before Morris' favourable reply reached her. The whole question of the future of the summer schools had slowly been reaching crisis point and those who had chiefly been responsible for organising them for so many years – Muriel, Livie and Grace Somerville-Large – were worried. Muriel overheard a disgruntled member say that you had to be either a friend of Muriel Gahan's or an Orpen to get a look-in. Livie had put her mind to the problem of the shape, structure and organisation of the summer schools as they still existed in 1952. As the originator of the summer school she was the most upset and hurt by criticisms of how the schools were run. In 1944 she had written: 'It is grand that our Summer School is truly democratic. Here we have a foretaste of the class-free society of the future.' For her, the same 'work and self-sacrifice and patriotism of un-paid enthusiasts' that had made the ICA such an important women's organisation were central to the summer schools too. Livie felt the demand for greater control of the summer schools by the executive and for a special committee to run them was a threat to their basic spontaneity and, in her eyes, commendable lack of hierarchy. 'Each person at a Summer School stands on her own merit. . .Home circumstances and education mean very little to the fellow-scholars of ten days' endeavour.'[6]

In a note circulated to her friends in the summer of 1952 Livie wrote that 'the S.S. is finished in its present form. . .because every year so many new people are coming into the ICA and onto the Exec who don't know what we are trying at in the S.S., nor how difficult a matter it is to run so unconventional a school.' Bravely, Livie's friend Sarah Ryan responded. 'It looks as if this is the first time your work has ever been questioned', she wrote. 'Your "democracy" was really only surface, as is exemplified by your present rage. . .One can sometimes perceive only too plainly that there is a harking back to those days when you were all equal, all leaving behind the same standard of comfort, all deliberately and self-consciously, and happily, enduring discomfort for its own sake, as only people of a certain development of mind can do. In this atmosphere of deliberate improvisations there are many who don't fit, and to whom formalness is essential in order to keep sane.'

Livie settled her feathers and put her mind to a way forward for education within the ICA. At a summer school conference specially held at 23 St Stephen's Green in December 1952 she put forward the ideas she had been circulating informally for 'small schools, lasting perhaps a week, to deal with certain subjects,' to replace the existing format. 'There would be twenty enthusiasts at such schools and at first it might be possible to get a country house, or technical school in the off season. . .Another advantage of such small one-idea schools is that they would be a try out for a permanent abode of our own along the lines of Denman.' Muriel had in fact held just such a 'one-idea school' the year before through Country Markets when many of those who had applied for posts as ICA organisers, as well as would-be craft teachers and a group of ICA members short-listed for a College of Art scholarship, came together for a Handcraft School in a private house at Annamoe, Co. Wicklow. It had been an outstanding success.

Following the Summer School Conference Muriel moved swiftly to ensure that control of the future of the whole area, with or without permanent college, would remain in her hands, that is to say, within the ambit of 23 St Stephen's Green and the Dublin TA. Before the year was out she had written to Sheila Findlater and 'outlined a scheme for running short courses for ICA members and suggested that as the Summer Schools for many years had been organised by the Dublin TA (ie Grace and herself) that that body would be best equipped to plan these courses.'[7] This is a very striking example of Muriel's political deftness and how different her tactics were from Livie's. Livie felt the need, out of intellectual honesty, to tackle people and problems head-on. Muriel, who because of her high standing within the ICA was almost untouchable, would shrug off the problems but, using great diplomacy, take the *action* necessary to overcome them. Deeds not words again, and a wise combination of 'persistent goodwill' and solid pragmatism.

She was also placing a bet on 'Mr Kellogg'. A ten person sub-committee was formed called the 'Residential Courses Sub-Committee' and it met first on 19 January 1953 by which time Dr Morris' letter had arrived. Ann Blythe, wife of Ernest Blythe, director of the Abbey Theatre, had succeeded Sheila Findlater as president of the Dublin TA and it is she who, in April 1953, is credited with having come up with the name An Grianán for any future and as yet hypothetical ICA residence. The name was variously explained as signifying 'the women's sunny place', 'a bower thatched with feathers' or, following the flight of Maura Laverty's fancy, 'the sunny part of the house where the women gathered to sing and sew and spin, to discuss the tastiest way of cooking the boar killed in the yesterday's chase, the best herbs for curing the chincough, the latest style in sheepskin tunics and the latest news from Tara.' Cerise Parker was elected to the chair of the new committee. The theme of first short residential course was to be drama. The course was held in Ballinrobe, Co. Mayo in a guesthouse run by Livie Hughes's brother- and sister-in-law, Adam and Phyllis Hughes. The next one was held in a hotel in Enniskerry, Co. Wicklow, in June and the themes were interior decoration, taught by Muriel, and outdoor sketching and mural painting with artist Brigid Ganly in charge. A third course on gardening was organised by Phyllis O'Connell and was held in Co. Cork in November, the first to be known as a 'Grianán course'. It was not at all clear that the old guard was loosening its grip.

Muriel had forgotten none of her former skills as a decorator. 'She was workmanlike in a butcher-blue linen smock' in Enniskerry according to *The Irish Times*, while the *Irish Independent*[8] gave a full account of her course describing how she 'showed how to prepare a room for decoration, the washing of the walls, the method of filling holes in wood or plaster.' In typical fashion, since she seemed incapable of travelling anywhere without a collection of things to show, 'She had brought a door from her own home and a few bits and pieces from The Country Shop for her demonstration.' On the five consecutive mornings she led her pupils stage by stage through every aspect of decoration, combining theoretical with practical work and ending with each participant creating 'their own colour circle based on the scientific principles of colour blending'.

'Having seen the response that the first two courses evoked and realising that no hotel or guest house could be as satisfactory as a house of our own, this committee has been very active visiting and looking at houses in various parts of the country', Cerise Parker told a special meeting of the Grianán Committee on 22 September 1953, to which members of the executive and federation presidents had been specially invited. It was a momentous meeting, the purpose of which was to make the final choice. Indeed ever since Dr Morris' suggestion to Muriel that the ICA 'give more detailed consideration as to the location of the centre', members in every corner of the country had been on the lookout for a suitable place. At one stage there was a list of thirty possible properties and this was then whittled down to eight, spread fairly widely around the country. There were two in Co. Waterford and one each in counties Wicklow, Cork, Limerick, Galway, Kilkenny and Louth. Morris' visit was only two weeks away – he was due to arrive on 5 October – and not only had the final choice of house to be made, but depending on this choice the rest of the budget had to be made out too.

The Tearmann Hotel, Termonfechin – formerly Newtown House, home of Vida Lentaigne – was unanimously decided upon. When Morris arrived in Ireland, Muriel and Phyllis O'Connell drove him there. Waiting for them at the hotel (until recently owned by Bord Fáilte) were Bea Trench, then chair of the ICA's executive committee, and her husband. Terry Trench who had known Muriel for more than twenty years was part of the lunch group after the visit of the house and grounds was over. He was struck by the impression Muriel made. 'It was very interesting for me to see the Kellogg representative at the lunch,' he remembered, 'sizing up Muriel in particular, and Bea to some extent, and deciding that he was never going to find anyone who was more positive about what was required than Muriel.' Dr Morris' impression of the property was good too. Muriel always maintained it was the view of the mountains of Mourne that clinched it for him. In 1958 Bea Trench painted the scene and the picture was presented to Morris.

Despite Morris' surprise that the property had not yet been valued his mind was made up in the ICA's favour and things went remarkably fast from that day on. By mid-November the Kellogg Foundation had sent a cheque for the deposit on the Tearmann Hotel which was to cost a total of £24,750. With the exchange rate at $2.81 the Kellogg commitment was almost double the initial sum indicated by Muriel in June 1952. A further sum was allotted over five years as an annual operating budget and a request for money to build on a hall ('an example of what an ICA hall should be to give members an idea of what to work for in their own localities') did not meet with so much as a raised eyebrow from Dr Morris and his board. 'We feel your plans are sound', wrote Dr Morris, 'and concur in them.' As Cerise Parker remarked and in the light of the Irish government's slim contribution to the ICA to date: 'This was generosity indeed.'

When Morris' letter of 18 January 1954 reached Muriel she was lying in bed recovering from a minor operation. Her friend Beatrice (Sammy) Somerville-Large, wife of Paddy's brother Becher and later to become chair of Country Workers Ltd (from 1969 until The Country Shop closed), was looking after her at her home in Palmerstown on the outskirts of Dublin. Livie had also been in the wars, having broken her hip in a fall on New Year's Day. Already An Grianán was coming to life for the ICA. Margaret Long had been 'lent' to look after the garden there once a fortnight and in a letter to Livie from her convalescent bed Muriel reported that 'we are selling snowdrops from it to The Country Shop – our first earnings.' Here is how she began:

Dearest Liv,

Delighted to hear you are on the feet again. I hope it's not too much misery trying to walk. Here am lapped, cushioned, cosseted. Books, books, books. Rich food arriving at appropriate intervals – otherwise complete peace – lovely. All I can see from my bed are the tops of waving trees. They only want a curling elephant's trunk or a giraffe's head to complete the illusion of an oasis in the desert.

This morning I got a letter from my pal Dr Morris which also might be an Arabian Night's Tale. He agrees to everything we ask & has increased our 5–year endowment to up to £5,000 a year. We have got to send him plans of our hall and to agree to certain conditions – but these are the most harmless, obvious ones to do with the actual £.s.d. Now that our annual endowment has been increased (we had budgeted it at £3,000 but I think this was too low) we shall have to consider the question of training some experts for the time when we won't have this money at our back. Have you any notions about this? We did put in a couple of hundred pounds for this in our original estimate, but we will be able to afford more than this now. Subjects that come to mind are fruit bottling etc, dietetics, housing, drama production, public speaking and there are hosts of others – wonderful to have this chance.

The triumphant year of 1954 was overshadowed and saddened for Muriel by the death of her mother on 3 June. The house at Termonfechin had been taken over by the ICA in March and the first course was held there in June, without Muriel. She was however able to attend the official opening of An Grianán by President Seán T O'Kelly on 14 October. When the Kellogg Foundation suggested that she be invited on a four-month fellowship programme 'relative to programming in continuing education' she had to turn the opportunity down as she felt she could not leave her father. Instead Livie, who had been made ICA national president in March 1955[9], took off on the study tour in her place with Doreen Smith, formerly secretary of the ICA and now the first principal of An Grianán. They spent from July to November 1955 touring the United States and Canada. On 31 August 1955 Muriel's father, who had held such a pivotal place in her life, died.

Notes

1. P J Little (1884–1963) was Fianna Fáil TD for Waterford from 1927. From 1939 to 1948, when the Fianna Fáil government fell, he was minister for posts and telegraphs. At the Homespun Society's first Spring Show exhibit in May 1936 Paddy Little and his wife had generously supported the new society by buying twenty-nine yards of 'bawneen' at 4/- a yard and two floor rugs.

2. Two issues for which she used the Arts Council as a platform were the establishment of an official Irish national folk dress (in an effort to oust the historically inaccurate kilt and to honour some of the clothes still worn in the west of Ireland in the 'fifties) and of a folk museum for Ireland. In 1955 she backed a proposal to use the Royal Hospital Kilmainham, once restored, as a national folk museum. Initially she did not see the space as ideal – too small – but on learning that the government had plans for turning it into offices and a conference centre she was so aghast that she was prepared to back the folk museum idea. She told her great-nephew Peter in 1986 that when she heard that Kilmainham was going to be a museum after all – the Irish Museum of Modern Art (IMMA) – 'few things have given me so great delight as that'.

3. In conversation with Brian P Kennedy, assistant director of the National Gallery of Ireland, in March 1987.

4. From conversations with Peter Gahan, 31 July 1986.

5. 'Emory Morris prided himself on assembling a highly qualified staff. He sought people with imagination, energy, commitment, fortitude and "just plain common sense". He wanted colleagues who would care enough for the goals and work of the Foundation to immerse themselves in its mission. He believed in delegating duties and decision-

making opportunities. . .He was a daring visionary willing to bet on new ideas. He didn't require his staff to do any more than he would do himself, but that included painstaking gleaning of facts to avoid mistakes. Only after an issue had been thoroughly researched was he satisfied.' From a tribute to Emory W Morris (1905–1974), published by the W K Kellogg Foundation.

6. 'The advantages of attending a Summer School of the ICA': report on the winning essay by Olivia Hughes in ICA inter-guild competition. *Farmers' Gazette*, 20 May 1944.

7. *Ár Leabhar Féin – Our Book: Golden Jubilee 1910–60*, ICA, 1960, p 73.

8. Both newspaper reports on Saturday 6 June 1953.

9. Livie had tried to persuade Muriel to stand as president instead of her. '. . .it seems to me that in the present tricky situation MG would be the most suitable candidate. All eyes are on Termonfechin and not Rural Ireland which is my line of country.' Private correspondence, September 1954.

— 16 —

MG and the ICA

Muriel's excitement over An Grianán and the possibilities it opened up for Irish women was not unlike what she had felt over twenty years before on opening The Country Shop. Except that now she did not feel in any way that it was *her* place in the way she had about 23 St Stephen's Green. This was a collective joy she shared with her outer family, the ICA, and it was all the richer for that. From 1929 on part of the permanent landscape in Muriel's life was the UI and later the ICA. From a total outsider she very quickly became central to the countrywomen's movement. In 1935 she had been chiefly responsible for setting up the Dublin Town Association and, with the central office of the ICA under 'her' roof for thirty years, it is not surprising that many of the ICA's achievements bore the stamp 'MG'. She was so much a part of everything that was going on behind all the important ICA achievements in the 'fifties and 'sixties that to give a full account of her work would be to write the institutional history of that period. Muriel always shunned credit for herself and as her life became increasingly given over to co-operative work she no longer even thought in personal terms. 'It was everybody together. . .I was just one and just so lucky to be involved' was a typical remark.[1]

When one does extricate Muriel's own life it becomes clear that by 1954 there was very little room in it for anything which was not tied in with her work in some way. When her brother Teddy retired from Africa and returned to live in Ireland in 1952, Muriel managed to dragoon him into helping her with an ambitious travelling exhibition. This was the Good Work exhibition, the best of ICA members' craft and art work, which toured ten Irish towns, ending up in Waterford for An Tóstal week in 1953. Teddy helped put up and take down stands. When in 1955 Muriel and Lillie Curtin bought their cottage in Roundstone, Co. Galway (chosen because it was close to where Teddy and Vera had taken over the management of the Guinness-owned Zetland Hotel) it immediately became available for all sorts of ICA and Country Markets activities.

As for Muriel's public profile, in many ways it echoed the ICA's development. In the 'fifties she too won the respect of the male establishment and her authority grew just as the ICA's authority as a major force to be reckoned with grew. From her central position in Dublin and through her dominant role at An Grianán – where as well as planning college policy and organising conferences she would, when there, welcome groups like a gracious hostess at a house party – she increasingly became a point of reference for those outside the movement. For those within it she represented continuity in a quickly changing ICA. Muriel and Livie stood out as the 'two pillars and pioneers'. Their input in terms of ideas and projects was enormous even though, with the growing momentum generated by the ICA's success in a widening field of action, there was less and less need for them to be directly involved in their actual execution. The next generation looked after that. But they were there to steady the boat when it rocked or to advise younger leaders on procedure. They were also the association's conscience, a constant reminder of the early ideals.

Muriel's own wider recognition began in January 1952 with her co-option to the Arts Council. Throughout the 'fifties, while continuing to chair the Irish Homespun Society and Country Markets Ltd as well as remaining managing director and secretary of Country Workers Ltd, a member of the ICA executive and of the RDS Arts and General Purposes Committee, Muriel's responsibilities continued to grow. In 1956 she was appointed to the council of the Arts and Crafts Society of Ireland and to the National Savings Committee. In 1957 she was elected to the Council of the RDS. Before that, in 1954, she had been appointed as the ICA representative to Forás Éireann, an umbrella group of rural voluntary organisations which had been set up early in 1949. She was also appointed to the Charlotte Shaw Bequest Committee whose job it was to administer the £94,000 left by Mrs Shaw on her death in 1944 and released when G B Shaw died in 1950. The generous bequest, more than a million pounds in today's money, was not universally welcomed. One of the conditions attached was felt to imply an insult to the Irish since, as well as 'bringing fine art within the reach of Irish people',

Charlotte Shaw had designated the money for 'the teaching of self-control, elocution, oratory and deportment, and the arts of personal contact and social intercourse and the other arts of public, private, professional and business life.'[2]

Muriel, however, was quick to spot the potential of this windfall and by January 1951, before the contents of the will were widely known, she was already making discreet enquiries. A memo to the trustees of the bequest outlining the aims of the ICA was drawn up by Muriel, Livie and Sarah Ryan. As early as February 1954, only three months after the money became available for distribution, Muriel was encouraging Forás Éireann to make use of facilities at the newly-acquired residential college[3], and the first project combining the Charlotte Shaw Bequest, Forás Éireann and An Grianán took place in August. This was a week long course in speech, deportment and public speaking open to primary, secondary and vocational teachers, as well as to 'organisers of rural and cultural bodies, including the Irish Countrywomen's Association, Macra na Feirme, Muintir na Tíre, Conradh na Gaedhilge and the Civics Institute.'[4] According to Shaw's biographer, Michael Holroyd, Forás Éireann remains to this day the only beneficiary of the Charlotte Shaw legacy.[5]

Just as with the Charlotte Shaw Bequest and the John Conor Magee Trust, Muriel would repeatedly ferret out little-known sources of funding, sometimes lying dormant for decades, and put them to good use. Amongst these were the Branchardière Trust[6], set up in the nineteenth century 'for the benefit of poor Irish female workers' employed both designing and making lace and crochet, and the Women's National Health Association, founded by Lady Aberdeen in 1909, which provided College of Art scholarships in embroidery and weaving from 1951 on, when Angela Coen of Gort was chosen. Muriel's forceful personality and wide contacts – 'there was nobody she didn't know that had any kind of influence in the country, from the President down, and she never missed an opportunity', according to former An Grianán staff – contributed to the college's success in securing many generous sponsorships, in particular from the ESB with whom the ICA worked closely and most fruitfully over many years. P J Dowling, one of the ESB's key people involved with rural electrification, was a good friend of Muriel's as was Paddy Ennis, their publicity officer for the scheme. When Muriel and Lillie Curtin bought their cottage the ESB insisted on installing electricity in it for nothing.

Though Muriel was the one who had the public profile most of the new schemes she set in motion bore Livie's mark as well as hers. Livie freely recognised the advantages of her friend's winning way with people over her own more abrasive approach. 'My scowls arise when seated with Big Business and Men in the Know,' she told her friend Sarah Ryan after visiting the Kellogg Foundation headquarters at Battle Creek in 1955, 'they decide, I am sure, that I am snooty.' Livie had learnt much on her American trip and as usual shared her enthusiasm with Muriel on her return. Rural youth groups – the 4H Clubs of America – were one of the discoveries that she wanted to start up immediately in Ireland. As a result, Muriel chaired a conference on Rural Youth Work at An Grianán in February 1956, which in turn led to the formation of Macra na Tuaithe of which the ICA and Macra na Feirme were joint founders.

Muriel knew from her father about the Co-operative Agricultural Banks set up by Horace Plunkett and AE on the Raiffeisen system in Ireland in the 1890s and early 1900s. Livie and Doreen Smith had ended their four-month study tour with a trip to Nova Scotia and Livie had come back full of Father Coady (whom she felt supremely privileged to have met) and the Antigonish Movement. So, when during a Folk School which Livie and she both attended in Red Island, Skerries in 1957 Muriel met three Dubliners passionately advocating credit unions for Ireland as a means of seeing off the usurious moneylenders who were having a heyday in the severe poverty of the 'fifties, she joined up with them at once. Amongst those she already knew at Red Island were Lieutenant General M J Costello with whom she always got on well ('a great pal of mine'), Father Peter Mc Kevitt, parish priest of Termonfechin, a firm supporter of the ICA, and Canon Cormac Lloyd and his Danish wife Signe, an ICA member since 1951, both folk school and co-operative enthusiasts. But the three who were talking seriously about re-establishing co-operative banks in Ireland were Nora Herlihy, Seán Forde and Seamus McEoin and the unregistered body they had already formed was the Credit Union Extension Service. Here is how Nora Herlihy herself remembered the beginnings of the Credit Unions in Ireland and Muriel's part in it, in a letter to Muriel dated 25 November 1985:

> The Credit Union Extension Service. . .was originally a sub-committee of the National Co-operative Council, appointed

to examine the possible development of credit unions in Ireland and make recommendations on how they could be developed. Seán Forde was the Chairman appointed by the Council in April 1957. It held its first meeting on June 14th 1957. Present were Miss Gilvarry, Miss Herlihy, Tomás MacGabhann, Michael Callanan, Seamas MacEoin and Seán Forde. You attended the third meeting on June 27th, 1957. As the Folk School was held in Red Island towards the end of May, 1957, I presume that you agreed to join the Credit Union Extension Committee when you met some of the members at the Folk School. At its fourth meeting on July 4th, 1957, you proposed that each member pay a subscription and said you were prepared to pay £5 yourself at once to defray secretarial expenses which up to then had been met by the National Co-operative Council. At the fifth meeting held on July 11th, 1957, you donated £5 to the CUE Committee on behalf of the "Country Workers" of the ICA (Should that be "Country Markets"?) At the seventh meeting, on 25th July, 1957, you reported that the "National Savings Committee" approved of credit unions as described in a paper which I had written ("Credit Unions Old and New") a copy of which you had supplied to each member. You also said that the Irish Countrywomen's Association were actively interested in the subject. . .

On 24th September, 1957, I had a letter from Miss Anne M. Swanton, secretary of the ICA, together with a copy of your letter to the Department of Industry and Commerce concerning my nomination as your representative to the proposed committee to enquire into alterations to the law relating to Friendly Societies, Industrial and Provident Societies, etc. This appointment I owe entirely to you personally, and my work on that committee, from January 1958 onwards, produced fruit eventually in the passage of the Credit Union Act in July, 1966.

Nora Herlihy's confusion as to who exactly Muriel was representing when she put the first ever money into the Irish credit unions (Seán Forde called it 'manna from Heaven, making it possible to purchase 1,200 penny postage stamps') reflects once again the diversity of Muriel's activities. The fact that it was neither the ICA nor Country Markets, but Muriel's Country Workers Ltd who were providing the five pounds is not surprising, either. By

1957 Country Workers were spending £1000 a year on development work: £500 on craft and production; £300 to An Grianán for youth work and travel aid; £100 for a Donegal organiser; £60 towards the development of rushwork and a loan of £40 to Dunlewey towards transforming an ESB hut into an ICA hall.

But proud as she was of Country Workers, as far as Muriel's work with the ICA was concerned far better was the fact that at last outside funders had materialised and were eager to help. Late in 1955 more support from America came in the shape of the Grant Counterpart Fund – part of the Marshall Aid Programme – providing the ICA with £10,000. Once again, this was not serendipitous but the fruit of lobbying the department of agriculture who were administering the fund and of the good name Muriel had already established there for the ICA. A sub-committee was set up with Esther Bishop in the chair and a three year pilot scheme of advisers for countrywomen on production, housing and home economics was worked out. Here at last was the opportunity to realise the third item on the original memo to James Dillon: home advisers. The importance of providing such a service had been reinforced by what Livie had seen in the United States, as can be seen from the following extracts from an irate letter she wrote to the papers on 23 December 1955, provoking a public exchange of letters with Louis P F Smith, agricultural economist, and an editorial in *The Irish Times* on 29 December. She had just learnt, on reading a joint report by the National Farmers' Association and Macra na Feirme, that a proposed Agricultural Institute for Ireland, in the planning stages at the time, made no provision for the education of countrywomen:

> . . .The money for the founding of the Institute is coming from the USA and I have no reason to believe that it has been earmarked 'For Irishmen Only'. . .In every State of the USA there are schools of Home Economics; and in the same way that Agricultural Agents are employed in the counties, there are trained women helping the women on the land in all the problems of Homemaking; and working with the Youth Clubs to build up a healthy interest in agriculture and in life in the Farm Homes. Many of these women are Research specialists in such subjects as Nutrition and Clothing. It is thought quite as important to carry out research into the correct feeding of the Human animal as of

the Farm animal. . .The progress of agriculture is not built
in a vacuum of specialists and scientific research. In the end
it depends on the farmhouse and the people on the land. If
there is one job on earth where men and women must co-
operate for success, it is farming. Any report on any plan for
agriculture which leaves out women altogether is one-sided
and unrealistic. I have recently returned from four months
study of Adult Education in rural communities in the USA
& Canada, and I have seen what the work for Women and
for Youth has done for Agriculture in America and I feel like
saying to my fellow countrymen – 'Take off your blinkers. It
is not only men who need the help of Research and
Education in Rural Ireland.'

In the ICA scheme three advisers were appointed at first. Ann
Roche was given the job of production and marketing adviser and
Eleanor Butler, later Countess of Wicklow, an architect with
strong Labour and trade union sympathies, became the home
planning adviser and housing consultant. A little later Margaret
Crowley was made home economics adviser. The three, whose
scope was to be countrywide, were actively encouraged by Muriel
and Livie to go abroad for further training and to see how things
were done elsewhere. Ann was sent to England to see how the WI
production advisers worked and then to Denmark to work on a
farm. Towards the end of her term she also travelled to the Scilly
Isles and Cornwall to study the growing and marketing of early
flowers and vegetables. Eleanor Butler spent time in Holland,
Denmark and Norway and Margaret Crowley went on a Kellogg
Foundation fellowship to Kentucky University and the US
department of agriculture in Washington. In 1960 further funding
was procured to appoint a fourth adviser, Valerie Bond, in what
had until then been Muriel's bailiwick: home decorating.

The pilot project under the Grant Counterpart Scheme came
to an end, but the ICA was determined to keep the government
involved. In 1959 Kathleen Delap chaired a high-powered four-
day conference in Rathmines Town Hall in Dublin, called 'Rural
Family Week', stressing the need for a home economics advisory
service in Ireland. The FAO was the sponsor and Margaret Hockin
was back to give her full support to the ICA's resolve not to let the
benefit of the pilot scheme dissipate. The result of the conference,
which for the first time brought together the departments of
education and agriculture with the participation of Maura Bonfil[7]

and Harry Spain respectively, was that the department of agriculture agreed to set up a farm home management service, appointing farm home advisers to every county.

When Marie Lewis, director or *maoirseach* of An Grianán from 1958 until 1965, took over the job from Doreen Smith she was disappointed at how many cookery courses there were on the programme of studies. Until, that is, she realised just how essential they were and how many women needed help in making the transition from open turf fire to electric cooker. When An Grianán opened, the press reported that it had a kitchen that 'will bring enraptured sighs from many a countrywoman – perhaps even gasps of disbelief if the Rural Electrification Scheme has not yet reached her.' This period is perhaps at the origin of the prejudice which clung to the ICA for so many years – and which infuriated Muriel – that members were mainly preoccupied with baking cakes and drinking tea. In the 1950s farmhouse design and above all kitchen design was a logical starting point for the radical improvement of rural women's living and working conditions. As Harry Spain, the ICA's most loyal ally in the department of agriculture, was to say, 'unless there is parity between housing conditions of town and country it is foolish to expect that young people will stay on the land.' The story of the returned emigrant who was so delighted with his trip back to Ireland was all too representative. He told his friends back in Boston how wonderful it had been, there was every sort of modern contraption on the farm now, Johnny didn't have to lift a finger any more. 'But what was wonderful too,' he said, 'was to lift the latch and go into the house and find everything just as it was before: the old fireplace and the chair where grandmother used to sit and the pump out in the yard still . . .'

Even before the ICA learnt about the Grant Counterpart Fund which would get advisers into rural women's homes, Muriel was thinking of ways of showing a modern kitchen to as many women as possible. In April 1955 she was in correspondence with James Dillon about displaying a model kitchen at the 1956 Spring Show. She got architect Wilfrid Cantwell to design a space based on the dimensions of a traditional farmhouse kitchen and then with the help of the ESB for modern appliances and with Kathleen Delap's help in collecting up more old-fashioned elements – a pair of china dogs was always to be found in the ICA model kitchen – she showed how it could be updated. In the back kitchen, for example, was a grain-dryer which had been adapted to dry clothes.

After a sensational reception in 1956 the ICA kitchen was then further developed with even greater assistance from the ESB and under the supervision of Eleanor Butler a more ambitious electrified, labour-saving kitchen exhibit went on view at the 1957 Spring Show. By 1958 it had been put on wheels and the 'ESB/ICA Mobile Farm Kitchen' took to the roads and for years travelled to towns big and small showing women just what they had a right to aspire to.

The ball was rolling and nothing could stop it now. Taking her notion of the modernised farmhouse one step further, Muriel had the idea of training women in farm guesthouse management, a totally new idea in Ireland. A first course was held at An Grianán in 1957 and was so successful it was decided to repeat it. Muriel arranged for the Conor Magee Trust to provide twenty-four scholarships a year for women from the Gaeltacht areas to come and study at An Grianán for four weeks at a time. Soon both the ESB and Bord Fáilte were co-operating in the scheme.

By the 1960s An Grianán had become the proverbial bee-hive. There was an all-electric cottage where courses in home management were held. Not to be eclipsed Kosangas had also become substantial sponsors of the college. There was a home furnishing room, a sewing room, a potter's shed, a weaving room, a general craft room and a fabric printing room. Outside, 'the two Rosemaries' – Rosemary McVitty and Rosemary Hyde – were busy organising the walled garden and producing food for the house, and 'Mary in the Dairy' – Mary Guilfoyle – was raising ICA cattle and poultry and teaching butter and cheese-making. As for the courses organised within the house itself, as well as those connected with home-making and the crafts, the programme was ambitious and varied and always involved the best teachers in whatever area was being taught. 'Always go to the top', was one of Muriel's maxims. There were courses in music, drama, puppetry and photography, in leadership, public speaking and in 'organising', the forerunner of community development. Local history was one of Muriel's pet hobby horses and she would do all in her power to encourage ICA members to get to know the Boyne Valley while they were at An Grianán. For five pounds ICA members could spend from Monday to Saturday learning new skills and letting their hair down in a rare escape from husband, children and chores.

If rural electrification lit up the 1950s and made so much possible for the ICA, the 1960s began with a splash. Muriel's close working relationship with the ESB and their piped water campaign, a logical extension of the rural electrification scheme, led to her suggesting to the ICA quarterly council meeting in Galway in June 1960 that a committee be set up to boost the installation of rural water supplies. The figures told their own story: only 15% of dwellings had piped water while a quarter of a million rural houses still depended on a well, stream or pump. In August the Campaign for Rural Water Supplies Committee was formed with Aine Barrington in the chair. As well as six other ICA members, including Muriel, there was PJ Dowling for the ESB and representatives of a wide spectrum of voluntary, political and commercial bodies as well as journalists from both the *Farmers' Gazette* and the *Irish Farmers' Journal.*

In October over 200 people gathered at An Grianán for a one-day conference: 'Water in the Rural Home'. Eamon de Valera had addressed the ICA's Golden Jubilee year AGM in Dublin's Mansion House the previous April and now they had the minister for local government, Neil Blaney, to address delegates at the conference which brought together such pioneers of group water supply schemes as Father Joseph Collins and Dr J G O'Flynn. They had been doing similar work, one in Co. Wicklow and the other in Co. Cork, each ignorant of the other's efforts until the ICA brought them together. The campaign produced results. 'It is quite a triumph for the ICA that the minister for local government has announced that his department is pushing ahead with rural water schemes just a few months after they started their campaign', wrote Michael Dillon in *The Irish Times*, '. . .such speed in getting government support can seldom have been achieved by any association.'

The 1961 AGM was held in the midst of an exhibition – 'Turn of the Tap' – which Muriel had designed and organised in the Mansion House. The Taoiseach, Seán Lemass, was guest speaker this time. Surrounding him as he spoke were 'model bathrooms and kitchens, stands showing you or your husband how to fit water appliances yourself and how to decorate to the best advantage'. And, of course, this being a Muriel Gahan creation, there were thirty craftworkers who had travelled specially to Dublin to demonstrate what women *could* do in the time that would be theirs to spend once running water and electrical appliances were fitted in their homes.

Having been an active source of support for Kathleen Delap and Aine Barrington in their important and successful projects,

A dream come true. The ICA's residential college, An Grianán, was bought for the Association by the WK Kellogg Foundation in 1953.

President Seán T O'Kelly, accompanied by ICA National President Alice Ryan and followed by Mrs O'Kelly and Muriel at the official opening of An Grianán, 14 October 1954.

1961. Dr Glenwood Creech *(centre standing)*, one of many regular Kellogg Foundation visitors to An Grianán, seen here with Dr Jerry Douglas and Dr Harry Spain. *Seated (left to right):* Kit Ahern (ICA National President 1961–64), Marie Lewis (Director, An Grianán 1958–65) and Muriel Gahan.

1962. Muriel's enthusiasm for the emerging Credit Union movement did much to encourage its founder members, seen here at a meeting of the Credit Union Extension Service in The Country Shop. *Left to right:* Seán Forde, Muriel Gahan, Seamus MacEoin and Nora Herlihy.

Livie Hughes, Muriel's closest friend, was a
constant source of original and challenging
ideas.

Muriel was the first woman ever
elected as vice-president of the RDS.
Her portrait, by Edward Maguire,
hangs in the council chamber of the
Society.

Felix Hackett, Muriel's mentor.
Portrait by Muriel Brandt.

The Country Markets team in the mid-1970s. *Seated (left to right):* Muriel Gahan, Cerise Parker, Margaret Long. *Standing:* Ann Roche and Mary Coleman.

1978. Muriel at her desk in the 'boardroom' of The Country Shop shortly before it closed. On her desk is a copy of the *Guide to the Redundancy Payments Scheme.*

1984. Muriel accepting the Plunkett Award for the Co-operative Endeavour from Justin Keating.

Members of the RDS Crafts Committee with award-winning work at the Horse Show annual crafts competition. *Left to right:* Muriel Gahan, Blanaid Reddin, Geoffrey Healy, Nancy Larchet, Veronica Rowe, Lady Mahon and Evelyn Greif.

Muriel and ICA National President Ina Broughall cut the ribbon at the official opening of the Muriel Gahan Museum at An Grianán on 2 September 1985. Eva Coyle (in check dress), elected ICA National President in 1997, looks on.

President Mary Robinson receiving Muriel at Aras an Uachtaráin with Monica Prendiville, ICA National President (1991–4).

October 1994. Muriel celebrates her 97th birthday at St Mary's Home in Dublin.

Muriel came into the forefront again in 1963 when she presented a government backed five-year rural development programme for the ICA. This had three principal goals – expansion, co-operation and education – outlined in a booklet which Muriel produced. The idea was to make the most of the energy the association had accumulated over the previous ten years in order to go even further. First she planned a concerted recruitment drive so that at the end of five years every woman and girl in rural Ireland would have been given the chance of joining the ICA. By co-operation Muriel had in mind even greater interaction with other rural voluntary bodies, especially Macra na Feirme and Macra na Tuaithe as well as with county services, so as to pool and share facilities and expertise. The heading 'education' was perhaps her most ambitious. This covered economic, cultural and social educational activities. On the economic front this meant coming together to learn how better to raise farm incomes by producing for markets and running farm guest houses, for example, with special emphasis on small farm areas in the west and in Gaeltacht areas. As for cultural and social activities, Muriel had uppermost in her mind the need to foster leadership within the association. By highlighting the self-development and self-expression afforded by group activities, for her perhaps the greatest advantage of ICA membership, she appealed to 'members of long-standing to make room for the newer members of committees and in office, and to give their share of responsibility to all members, and special thought to the younger ones.'

By 1965 the ACWW had grown to represent over six million women in 176 constituent societies around the world. Their eleventh triennial conference, held in the RDS from 14 to 26 September 1965, was to prove a supreme affirmation of the ICA's strength and efficiency. No such large-scale conference had ever before been held in the RDS, nor indeed in Dublin. The UN had declared 1965 'International Co-operation Year' and the title of the conference was 'Working Together'. Organisation of the conference was along the lines of a major military campaign – a living example of successful co-operation – and involved a shift into larger headquarters for the ICA. The prospect of receiving over 1,200 delegates from every corner of the globe over a two-week period – there would be 3,000 delegates and guests at the opening ceremony – and having only the top rooms of 23 St Stephen's Green as base camp, precipitated a move which would have had to happen sooner or later. Muriel and Kay Hogan did the house hunting and had great luck. According to Muriel the house at 58 Merrion Road, still the ICA headquarters today, was the first they saw and the one they thought most suitable. They made an offer of £7,000 as the maximum the bank would allow. Their offer was refused and the house went to auction. In the light of today's property prices it seems incredible that the house had to be withdrawn because bidding did not reach the ICA offer. As a result the house subsequently became theirs and the new offices, just across the road from the RDS, were opened by Charles Haughey and occupied by the ICA in January 1964 – in plenty of time to prepare for the big event.

Muriel was not on the eight member co-ordinating committee for the conference, but chaired one of sixteen organising sub-committees, her responsibility being to organise Ireland Day on 16 September. It is obvious, however, given the theme of the conference and her expertise and passionate interest in the field, that her involvement went beyond that sub-committee. One event to be opened on Ireland Day particularly interested her. This was an exhibition on the history of 'Rural Co-operatives in Ireland' organised by the IAOS. Muriel's personal contribution to the exhibition was a *tableau vivant* made up of six of her old Dunlewey friends: Mary Roarty, Nora O'Donnell, Sheila McFadden, Maggie Gallagher, Annie Ferry and Mary McClafferty. She dressed them up in clothes their grandmothers would have worn and with the help of Valerie Bond decorated their space in the exhibition as an old country kitchen complete with bread iron and salt box. The women thoroughly enjoyed themselves taking turns carding and spinning and talking to the visitors as they filed through the stand. Even though Muriel had failed in her ambition to start a co-operative in Dunlewey twenty years before, she had never lost touch with these women, all ICA members as well as skilled craftworkers.

Muriel was made Buan Chara (honorary life member, a sort of 'national treasure' within the ICA) in 1965, following the death of Lucy Franks the year before. There was then a rule that there were never more than three Buan Chairde at one time and so it was not until 1970, following the death of Josephine MacNeill in 1969, that the honour was bestowed on Livie. The third Buan Chara was Alice Ryan. Muriel and Livie's elevation to the status of Buan Chairde, giving them ex officio membership of all committees and sub-committees of the ICA, can in retrospect be seen as a milestone, a boundary marker between their past and future roles in the association. At the time any notion that this honour might represent a form of 'retirement' would have seemed absurd. After all, in the mid-1960s Livie and Muriel were in the thick of planning and plotting a Horticultural College for girls at An Grianán. This was an inspired idea of Livie's and despite initial scepticism from all sides it proved an unqualified success. The college was also backed most generously by the Kellogg Foundation.

A milestone can nevertheless be discerned. The ICA no longer met under Muriel's roof and from the end of the 1960s there was also a change in the sort of issues increasingly facing the association. Most of Muriel and Livie's early goals had been achieved, membership had never been so high and leadership was strong. In 1967 the visiting Kelloggs representative found the ICA's leaders 'articulate, well informed, and dedicated, with members of its Executive group at the national level including some of the most able women in the country. Both as representatives of the ICA and in their other capacities of leadership, these women are involved in dealing with problems of economic development, social improvement, health and education, and other significant items in Irish life.' How Muriel and Livie would have purred to read that! They could relax. As Livie had quipped back in 1961 on recognising the worth of a group of younger leaders ('they are working hard and they have enterprise, they are not climbers or battlers or self-seekers, they have the kind of spirit the summer schools promoted'): 'Lord, now lettest thou thy servant depart in peace.'

But it was not just the satisfaction of having achieved so much of what they set out to do that allowed these pioneers to take a back seat. Instead of co-operative marketing or labour saving houses, self-expression and personal growth, diet and nutrition, the ICA now had to deal with issues such as contraception and divorce or violence in television films, all of which made their appearance on the agenda for the first time. A more aggressive urban women's movement was gaining ground in the cities and presented an inevitable challenge to ICA positions and aims. Muriel retired from the thick of the action, her energies going more to Country Markets, the RDS and the Crafts Council of Ireland from 1970 on. She would still attend ICA meetings, sitting in the front row, no longer on the platform. She would participate less yet she always commanded great respect. When she did speak there would be dead silence. When she sat down again, huge applause. What she had to say always made sense.

In 1970, the ICA's Diamond Jubilee year, we can see a relaxed Muriel behaving with all the confidence that age and success bring. There were four Field Days that year organised by Country Markets to celebrate the ICA's anniversary. As organiser of the events, Muriel had the RDS involved too. The Field Days were at Fethard, opened by the well known cookery author Theodora Fitzgibbon; at Kells, opened by National Farmers' Association president, T J Maher; and at Boyle where Muriel's friend, General Costello, did the honours. The last field day was held in Ennis and this time it was the turn of Patrick Hillery, future president of Ireland, then minister for external affairs. Muriel recalled the scene with great amusement: 'Dr Hillery started reading some wretched little thing someone had written for him in his office so I said to him, lowering my voice, "Would you mind putting that down and just talking naturally yourself?" And he did,' Muriel would chuckle gleefully as she told the story, 'he did!'

Notes

1. Interview with Hilary Orpen, RTE Radio One, 1984.
2. For the full text of Charlotte Shaw's will see Holroyd, M. *Bernard Shaw Vol 4: The Last Laugh* Chatto and Windus, London, 1992, pp 95–104.
3. Letter from Muriel Gahan to Maurice Fitzpatrick, 10 February 1954.
4. *Farmers' Gazette*, 3 July 1954.
5. Holroyd, M. op cit pp 8–9.
6. 'What a happy sound Branchardière has to those hundreds of lace makers who have taken part in the Society's lace competitions and in so many different ways benefited from Mlle. Eleonore Riego de la Branchardière's bequest. . .In the Society's records the earliest word of the Branchardière Trust Fund for improving and encouraging the making of lace and crochet is linked with their first Arts and Industries exhibitions starting in 1888 for which the Society granted space each year on the request of the Irish Industries Association.' From 'The Development of Crafts' by Muriel Gahan in *The Royal Dublin Society 1731–1981*, Meenan J and Clarke D (eds), Gill and Macmillan, Dublin, 1981, p 264.
7. Maura Bonfil was chief domestic science inspector at the department of education; Harry Spain, a founder member of Macra na Feirme, had joined the department of agriculture in 1949, recruited by James Dillon to oversee his parish plan. Spain was promoted to senior inspector, becoming, in 1965, chief inspector.

— 17 —

Why Did You Close The Country Shop?

W hen customers came into The Country Shop on 25 July 1978 a sheet of paper lay on each table. It was signed 'Muriel Gahan' and it read:

In two months time The Country Shop in St Stephen's Green, Dublin will be closing down. This inevitable end to a much loved institution will bring sadness to many people, and not least to its Directors and staff.

From its start in December 1930, The Country Shop has been a family rather than a business, and, as with all families, the increasing years have taken their toll of its personnel, including retirement age becoming more and more the pattern of one after another of its members, with this a crisis year for several in key positions whose impossibility of replacement has long been recognised.

No words can adequately express the Directors' appreciation of the dedication over the years of each member of The Country Shop staff in carrying out her part of the work to be done so that the Shop – homely restaurant, sought after cakes and bread, produce, and countrywide traditional crafts – should continue to flourish in its own right, and continue to be the financial means whereby its non-profit private company founder, Country Workers Limited, has been enabled to pioneer and involve itself in one rural programme after another for the benefit of Ireland's country men and women with emphasis on their traditional and home crafts, and their small farm products.

The Country Shop's closing marks the end of an era for many, including the Company of Country Workers. Linked with the sadness of this however, gladness remains in the fact that those who have been involved in the Company's development programme in the past will continue to work for it as members of one or more of the co-operating organisations with which they have been so happily associating for up to 48 years – The Royal Dublin Society, The Irish Countrywomen's Association, Country Markets Co-operative Society and The Crafts Council of Ireland.
And so the work goes on.

A special meeting of directors and shareholders had been held in June and the closure was unanimously agreed to. Though the business was still financially sound, the staff, many with The Country Shop for over forty years, were quite simply tired and wanted to retire. It was increasingly difficult to find replacements who would both respect the ethos and accept the low pay of this unique institution. Muriel's good friend Lillie Curtin, company director, chief cook and manager of the catering department, had not been back to work since a car accident in 1974. She was in her early seventies and had worked in The Country Shop since 1931. Kathleen Muldowney, baker of The Country Shop's incomparable breads, had finally been forced to retire because of ill health in 1969, after thirty-four years on the job. Angela Kehoe, the other weight-bearing pillar, along with Lillie, was seventy-five and longing for a rest. Her sister, Muriel Kehoe, who for so many years had been the ICA's itinerant craft teacher had already retired and Angela wanted to join her. A great number of The Country Shop's most faithful staff were well over sixty-five. Muriel, a mere eighty-one, was not tired but could not carry the burden of the business on her own.

It was back in 1959 that the question of a pension scheme for Country Shop staff first made its unwelcome appearance on the agenda. Saving for a rainy day had never been Muriel's priority in life. But as the years went by and people got older this whole area took on increasing importance. A pensions scheme was set up and later a trust. It was revealed to shareholders in 1961 that while social insurance contributions had been made for all ordinary members of staff, no such payments had been made for Muriel. The combination of an ageing staff and worries about providing adequately for their old age must have been weighing heavily on the directors when, in 1973, they virtually agreed to the end of The Country Shop. The question of leases arose and the decision was taken to sell 'within a period of ten years their interest in the property including the basement at the then full market value' to another tenant in the building. By 1975 this Faustian pact appeared to have been undone and the only space which had to be vacated was the second floor where Country Markets were housed and where *Saor an Leanbh* (Save the Children Fund, Ireland) held their meetings. Country Markets moved in with the ICA. A twenty-one year lease opened into the future for the basement and first floor rooms.

Changes in social patterns had already made a dent in 1968 when a drop in lunch sales was seen to coincide 'not only with our raised prices, but with the time the traffic was re-routed round the Green and taxis lined the footpath in front of us. The majority of our customers are now from the middle or low income group who travel by bus. Now, no buses from either direction stop opposite or beside us as they used to. Our motoring customers also fail to reach us because of the impossibility of parking their cars and their terrorisation by the taxi men. We miss the numbers of country people who regularly had lunch here. Others we miss are the Civil Service and other office employees. With the five day week they now only get one hour for lunch instead of their former one-and-a-half hours. They made up the bulk of our regulars for our set lunch. Now, they either boil a kettle in their office or they have a quick snack lunch outside.'

Alarm bells rang in 1968 where staff recruitment was concerned too. 'No year has been so difficult for Miss Curtin engaging kitchen staff and Miss Kehoe engaging waiting staff. It has been Miss Curtin's experience that it is impossible to get any kind of staff at previous rates, and the salaries looked for by trained staff are higher than the salaries of either of the Company's working directors.' From then on staff problems were a constant headache. In 1972 shortages were reported to be 'endemic in all departments'. When staff could be found – part-time workers and foreign students – they were 'unreliable and unpredictable'. Cooked teas had to be dropped and The Country Shop closed at half-past-five instead of six o'clock. Since 1971 it had been closed on Saturdays, for the first time in its history going over to a five-day week. Then in 1976 the unheard-of problem of 'pilfering' arose. The Country Shop which had pioneered the sale of charity Christmas cards had to abandon selling them that year because 'the pilfering of everything else in the cottage and porch is almost impossible to deal with'.

Whatever the internal reasons for its closure, the news came as a total shock to customers who could see no logic in the decision. The question 'Why did you close The Country Shop?' was to haunt Muriel until the end. The newspapers were full of laments. In valedictory tones *The Irish Times* 'Pro-Quidnunc' mourned its passing, having gone there for the last time on 18 October, the day before the contents were sold at auction:

> Irishman's Diary went to a wake yesterday for an old and greatly loved Dublin institution, which went to every possible length to disguise the fact that the big grey city lay outside its walls.
>
> This morning the fittings, china, tea urns, those so familiar green and red chairs, the glossy oval black tables, the ovens and sinks and cake tins, even the last craft items left in the craft shop of The Country Shop in St Stephen's Green will be auctioned off.
>
> Yesterday, the curious were allowed in to poke and root in the sad debris of almost half a century of a unique institution, a part of countless Dublin childhoods. The cavernous kitchens, the servants' quarters that once were of a great town house, were laid open to the vulgar rabble for the first time, astonishing lengths of red-tiled corridors with pantries and washrooms and larders and wine bins opening off them. A newly-moved-in mouse crept out from under a grain bin, not yet believing that the good times are gone for ever. The cat has gone, leaving a trail of muddy footprints across a white ceramic counter to a broken window.
>
> Pro-Quidnunc poked and wept, for even Diarists have vanished childhoods. The aged parent used to work two doors up from it, in a house straight out of Dickens with a great coach house and servants' entry for the much-more-civil-than now servants to creep deferentially into Estate Duties. It was a fascinating place to be brought as a child, perpetually associated with fog curling up from the back-yard cobbles and frightening shadows from the ruin at the back, the tall house itself smelling of dust and sealing wax and old offices. From there it was a minute's dash through the rain to the open fire in The Country Shop, hot buttered toast and fresh scones, potato cakes and fresh crumpets, and

cakes to make a child's eyes pop. Downstairs was the place for a winter's afternoon, but on a spring morning the seats by the window, with pale sunshine slanting in over the primroses and crocuses in the window boxes, were the best place in the city to sit and drink coffee.

. . .It seems impossible, both to me and to the many familiar faces guarding the contents yesterday, that it should all be gone - just two years short of its half century. Four of the staff members yesterday had about 140 years of service between them, and it is just because we shall not see their like again that the place is closing. The staff are irreplaceable, and tired, and it was decided it was better to close now, on an up-note, rather than to see standards slip.

If the general public was shocked and saddened by the news of The Country Shop's imminent closure the shock was even more cruel for the staff, many of whom had arrived back from their two weeks' annual holiday ignorant of what lay in store. Muriel called a staff meeting just days before the public announcement was made. Still a lot of the staff had no idea what the meeting would be about, only that it was important and everybody had to attend. Kay Tyrell, a Country Shop waitress for over twenty years, had brought in a pottery jug she had bought on her holidays, thinking that Muriel would be interested. Uncharacteristically, she was not. When the announcement was made by the company's accountant and auditor, Harry Forsyth, 'everybody burst out crying,' Kay Tyrell remembered. Mr Forsyth, the gentlest of men, was aghast at being the cause of so many tears. After the auction there was just a tea chest left on which the last ones to leave – Betty Irwin, Angela Kehoe, Deirdre Ennis, Kay Tyrell and Muriel – spread a plastic bag and ate their lunch. 'I couldn't bring myself to say good-bye to the others when we had finished clearing up,' Kay said, 'I just walked out the main door of number 23 St Stephen's Green and got a taxi to the dole office.' Everyone felt numb.

Shanagarry potter Stephen Pearce, whose sienna-and-white pottery was becoming increasingly successful by 1978, came very close to offering to take over The Country Shop from Muriel. 'And then I thought to myself, no, this is a period in history, this is Muriel's thing, she has done it, it really has come to an end. . .it should be let quietly go into history as a happy memory in everybody's mind.' Stephen's connections with The Country Shop were strong. He had been a constant visitor since childhood when his parents, Philip and Lucy, up in Dublin from Co. Cork, would always spend time with Muriel. Stephen's father had set up his own pottery in 1953 thanks to Muriel's encouragement. 'I think about the only person who took him seriously was Muriel.' She told him where to find a country potter who would teach him the craft. The choice was not huge. Muriel had found only three traditional Irish potteries down the years: Joseph Greene's in Youghal, Co. Cork which she had 'discovered' in 1932, Carleys Bridge in Co. Wexford and the third in Coalisland, Co. Tyrone. In 1948 Grattan Freyer had started up the Terrybaun Pottery in Co. Mayo, he too becoming a friend of Muriel's. Philip Pearce spent six months at Carleys Bridge and then got in touch with Joseph Greene whose family had been making pots from the local red clay (still used by Stephen Pearce today) for four hundred years. Greene showed Philip Pearce the field where the clay came from and was even persuaded to come out of retirement for a time and work with the novice potter. 'When my father had made a few pots he went along to Muriel and said what do I do now?' She told him to find a Country Market. So off they went to Dungarvan where, on the first day, they sold one mug for 1/3d and went home 'over the moon'. Their next selling point was The Country Shop. 'They were the first, they were the pioneers, and they stuck with us through thick or thin,' Stephen Pearce says. 'Without The Country Shop my father's pottery probably wouldn't have got going, without my father's pottery, (modern) craft in Ireland probably wouldn't have started. When my brother and I got going in 1973 nobody believed there was anything in crafts – and yet handmade pottery in Ireland today is retailing at a value of around £10 million a year. All from Muriel encouraging Philip.'

Countless are and were the craftworkers who like Philip Pearce had been helped by Muriel and for whom the closing of The Country Shop marked the end of an era. By 1978 craft shops were commonplace – thanks again to Muriel's work – and to the untrained eye The Country Shop's cottage probably looked rather cramped and small in comparison. But for those craftworkers who remembered the time when *no-one* took an interest in their work, The Country Shop was unique. From the Aran knitters and crios weavers who awaited their Christmas bonus with such anticipation to those other knitters in Cruit Island, Co. Donegal, who for years had made slippers, known as 'Donegal pampooties', for The Country Shop on a pattern Muriel had brought back from Austria in 1936[1]; from the Quinlan brothers of Tallow Bridge,

Co. Waterford, traditional rod basketmakers who thanks to Muriel survived a time when 'you couldn't give away a basket on the streets of Cork', to small family weaving businesses such as the Farrells' Crock of Gold and the Wynne sisters' Avoca Handweavers who could always count on sales through The Country Shop, there could never be a place like it again.

All these craftworkers had one thing in common: Muriel had singled them out, recognised their skill and found a market for their work. She saw, for example, the beautiful St Brigid's crosses young Manus McFadden from Glenthornan beside Dunlewey was making from the corn that grew on the sandy shore of the lake. The arms of the crosses were tied with the wool his mother, Sheila McFadden, dyed with crottle and the corn shone a beautiful pale gold. Not content with admiring the young boy's work, Muriel put in an order for The Country Shop and Manus still remembers how his ambition to make a thousand crosses in one batch was never achieved, but to a schoolboy in the 1950s his last cheque for £41 (820 crosses at one shilling each) was memorable enough.

Traditional chairmaker John Surlis was first discovered by Chrissie O'Gorman in November 1945. He owed his success to Muriel, culminating in the Toronto International Craft Fair in 1974 when he represented Ireland and his Leitrim chairs figured on the cover of the catalogue and in the *New York Times*. 'You asked me what nice things I had to say about Miss Gahan,' he wrote to David Shaw-Smith in 1979. 'Only for her I would not be on television. She sent an organiser by bye-ways and highways looking for craft workers and she came to Monasteraden. Some years later through Miss Gahan I gave a demonstration at the Dublin Horse Show in 1951. I was treated so well before leaving Dublin that I promised her that anything I made in the future would be better each time I made it. . .' Betty Searson, who worked closely with Muriel at the time the Crafts Council of Ireland was being set up, remembers vividly John Surlis's visits to the RDS. 'Muriel met him at the train and if the president of Ireland had come visiting the RDS she couldn't have given him better treatment – VIP treatment. She entertained him to lunch in the members' restaurant and then brought him on a royal tour of the craft exhibition.' When John Surlis sent his sturdy ash chairs and stools up to Dublin they sold as fast as The Country Shop's own hot cakes.

Unlike Surlis, Patty O'Flaherty of Cloonshee, Co. Roscommon, was not a traditional craftworker but is equally unstinting in her recognition of Muriel's special qualities. Patty was a founding member of the Slieve Bawn Co-operative Handcraft Market in Strokestown in the early 1960s. Like hundreds of other women throughout Ireland, Patty discovered rushwork through the ICA. What marks her out from most of the others, however, is that rushwork is Patty's successful livelihood today. Of Country Workers Ltd Muriel had written: 'We shall never know the intangible results of our Company's work – the creative gifts it has developed, the self-confidence it has engendered, the lives it has enriched. But of all that we have succeeded through Country Workers, we have no doubt that these results are the most rewarding of all.' They certainly were for Patty O'Flaherty. Speaking of Muriel she said:

> She encouraged you if you had an idea. She brought out the best in everybody, she could probe into you and she made you feel important. Maybe your idea would be nothing. Or maybe you started off by thinking that but, by the time she'd finished with you, you had a good idea, you had developed it into something good. With her little word here and there. . .she made you think, she elicited some ideas from you without you knowing it. She was like a mother in a sense, but not motherly. She was somebody you could go to, you knew the door was open – she had this great openness about her that you could go to her and chat about things. This was why everybody loved her. No matter that she was in the middle of something, you never felt you were interrupting her. You always came away happy and satisfied and with new initiative and a new kind of gusto.

Patricia D'Arcy is another rushworker who thanks to Muriel's belief in her also makes a living from baskets today, having set up a basket museum in Mountnugent, Co. Cavan. In 1966 Muriel had come to the Mountnugent Guild of the ICA and had convinced Patricia that her baskets were good enough to sell. So she would make a dozen at a time and give them to a local man to take up to The Country Shop. By the 1980s she was employing five local girls making rush baskets and toys, getting her orders from the annual craft trade fair organised by the Crafts Council in Dublin[2]. 'Muriel Gahan never forgot people, she was always encouraging them, up and down to the country to see how things were going, getting people to believe in what they were doing.' Thanks to Muriel's encouragement Patricia combined the teaching of the craft with selling and was able to continue making her living from rushwork after her husband died in 1978, putting her three children through college thanks to the crafts.

Muriel did not just mete out encouragement. She was a tough judge of standards, too. You had to earn your place on her list of suppliers for The Country Shop. Patrick O'Connor who came of a long line of Nenagh basketmakers had accompanied his father to the 1930 Spring Show to demonstrate when he was just seventeen. He remembers how Muriel had taken a group of craft demonstrators to the pictures in Dublin that week. He also remembers with affection and respect the genuine interest she took in his craft over the years when others ignored it. Once when in Dublin to demonstrate at a show he earned special regard from her because he found time to go to the Botanical Gardens to get some new types of willow to plant at home. That was the sort of initiative Muriel loved. Yet he gave up the uneven struggle to make a living out of baskets in 1950, becoming a travelling salesman and later a shopkeeper instead. Before he gave up he experimented with cane in an attempt to increase his sales and he still remembers Muriel's stern disapproval: baskets had to be made of 'native materials' only.

The Quinlan brothers of Co. Waterford, amongst Muriel's most regular basket suppliers in the 1950s and 1960s, were also surprised at Muriel's insistence on high standards. 'They want good baskets up there in Dublin', Tom Quinlan would say in amazement, more concerned himself with keeping the price down even if the quality suffered a bit. But Muriel wanted the quality and she would think nothing of letting Tom and his brother Michael know if a basket wasn't up to standard. They'd have to make sure the next batch were better.

Patrick Madden, Muriel's old friend, never needed to be reminded about quality, but times were hard for him too over the years he supplied The Country Shop. Over a period of thirty years, until his health began to fail in 1960 and he was obliged to give up almost entirely, there were several occasions when his livelihood from weaving was touch and go. Muriel never let him down and whatever his problems would always do her utmost to help him and his family and get him back into creative production. When Madden and his family moved inland from Ballycroy to Charlestown in 1946 Muriel arranged for Country Workers to lend him £200 to buy a new house. Muriel was impressed by Patrick Madden's eldest son, John Patrick, then a boy of ten or eleven and wanted Country Workers to contribute to his education. In 1952 when Madden's cow died, the company lent him the money to buy a new one. Both the Madden sons – John Patrick and Michael – became skilled weavers, no doubt in part thanks to Muriel's constant interest in their father's craft. Michael is currently weaving on his father's old loom in Vermont, USA. Patrick Madden's death in 1968 was a cause of real sadness to Muriel. 'With the death of Patrick Madden', she recorded, 'we have lost the last of our traditional handweavers. More than anything else it was his enthusiasm for his weaving and his dauntlessness in the face of every difficulty. . .' which had decided Muriel to start a shop in Dublin where the isolated craftsman could sell his work.

Notes

1. The slippers, like socks cut off around the ankle, were knitted in fairisle pattern and had a leather sole. For many years the soles were put on by refugees living at The Haven in Clonliffe Road. This was organised by Muriel Kehoe who also, at one point, taught crafts to women prisoners in Mountjoy jail.

2. The first national crafts trade fair was held in 1976. There were 35 entrants and sales orders were worth £50,000. In 1996 the fair, now called Showcase, was visited by over 11,000 buyers and according to a survey commissioned by the Crafts Council of Ireland sales orders were worth £17.2 million.

— 18 —

Keep Right on to the End of the Road

Tributes to Muriel's work had begun to arrive before The Country Shop closed, softening in a way the transition from 'before' to 'after' and the loss of her power base. In 1974 she was chosen for the Allied Irish Banks community development award for her contribution to developing the crafts. Then in 1976 the RDS bestowed on her a great and wholly deserved honour when they made her a vice-president of the Society. It was the first time a woman had ever been appointed to this position. Her portrait, painted by Edward McGuire in 1979, a curiously harsh, masculine image of her, hangs in the RDS. In 1978 it was another, even older Irish establishment that paid her a special tribute. In July 1978, months before The Country Shop closed, Miss Gahan became Dr Gahan LL D when Trinity College Dublin gave her an honorary doctorate. More rewards for Muriel's dedicated work would follow. In 1978 she was made one of the Rehabilitation Institute's 'People of the Year' and in 1984 she was given the Plunkett Award for Co-operative Endeavour. In 1982 the Irish-American Cultural Institute endowed an annual development grant in her name. The Muriel Gahan Scholarship, worth £1,000, is awarded at the RDS National Craft Competition held each year at the Horse Show. To celebrate her ninetieth birthday she was Gay Byrne's guest on the *Late Late Show*.

Muriel had lost her city centre headquarters and was being heaped with honours for her past achievements, but she had not the slightest intention of slackening her pace. When Mamo McDonald was elected ICA national president in 1982 she said, 'I have somebody who above all others is my sort of person and that's Dr Muriel Gahan. She has a great mind and has as much go in her now as women half her age. . .She's the greatest woman in the country.' 'The time to ring me up is round midnight', Muriel told Mary Mullin, formerly of the Kilkenny Design Workshops and co-founding member of the Crafts Council of Ireland, in 1983. Muriel was fortunate in being able to keep her driving licence for almost ten years after The Country Shop closed because, living in Shankill, ten miles from the city centre, she would have found the sudden isolation difficult to adapt to. Difficult but not impossible. When she was finally forced to give up her car at the age of ninety she was doubly indignant because Teddy, at ninety-one, was still allowed to drive. However she swiftly moved to public transport and would cheerfully get the bus to the RDS and ICA headquarters in Merrion Road. It was at some point during her last ten years at the wheel that 'The Accident' happened. This is another story which has become apocryphal, occurring at several different locations around the country. Most likely Muriel was on her way from a Country Markets meeting in Westport to see friends in Achill when her car left the road and was found upside down in the ditch, Muriel suspended by her seat belt. A fearful young garda put his face to the window of the car and asked if she was all right. 'Of course I'm all right,' came the impatient reply, 'Just get me out of here, will you?' Asked by her friends later if she had not been frightened when the accident happened Muriel answered, 'How could I have been frightened? I was asleep when it happened.'

Over several years Muriel would hold reunions for Country Shop staff out at her house, catching up with what each former worker was doing, keeping track of their families. Withdrawal from 23 St Stephen's Green was a traumatic process and her characteristic resilience was put to the test. 'I never have any regrets,' Muriel told David Shaw Smith in 1980. 'I think it is one of my tenets that if a thing has happened it has happened, forget about it and start something else. So I never look back with any regret on anything for that reason – you can't change it now. . .I look forward always, what can be done in the future about something or other. Always something to be done, something to look forward to, and that is my great pleasure.'

Almost immediately Muriel started researching what was to be an excellent contribution on 'The Development of Crafts' in *The Royal Dublin Society 1731–1981*, a history of the RDS made up of chapters by sixteen different specialists in their various fields.[1] In

June 1984 an important one-day conference was held in the RDS with the title 'A Folk Museum for Ireland'. Anne O'Dowd of the National Museum's Irish Folklife Section was on the organising committee and remembers how suddenly, without anyone quite understanding what had happened or how, Muriel had taken charge, organising the venue and chairing the conference. The following year, 1985, saw the inauguaration of the 'Dr Muriel Gahan Museum' at An Grianán. Here was displayed the best of what Muriel had collected down the years and which had been too precious to sell off at The Country Shop auction. It had all been stored under friends' spare beds and in their garages while the plan for a permanent home in the old basement kitchen at An Grianán took shape.

Muriel continued to attend meetings of the ICA, Country Markets, the RDS and the Crafts Council of Ireland until 1992. Separate accounts from all of these bodies tell the same story. Muriel remained focused always even though she herself was no longer 'getting things cracking' to the same extent and the value of money was changing faster than she could keep track of, restricting each organisation's activities in a way she was not always prepared to accept. She might sit with her eyes closed throughout a meeting but she was not asleep. Just as people thought that she must finally have nodded off, she would come out with a totally apposite comment. Just like her mentor, Felix Hackett, in his old age. '*Dear* Dr Hackett', Muriel told Mavis Arnold in 1983, 'He would sit at committee meetings with his eyes closed and we would think he was asleep but of course he had been listening all the time.'

In 1992 Muriel's brother Teddy died. He and Muriel had been living alone together in Carrigfern, the gate lodge of the family's former home, St Brendan's, since Vera died in 1980. Teddy lived downstairs, Muriel upstairs, happily sharing her room with families of mice. She cooked lunch, he got the supper. Muriel had had a terrific appetite all her life. In particular she loved caragen jelly and would always put a little sherry in her soup, or failing sherry, some sugar. But she was no cook, she had never had to learn. Precarious arrangements of steamers with stones weighting down the lids were what she used at Carrigfern, always delighted to discover some new labour-saving device, whatever the gastronomic results.

Teddy and Muriel both sang in the local choir and belonged to Rathmichael Church of Ireland parish. After Teddy's death,

Muriel soon moved into St Mary's, a nursing home for Protestant women in Pembroke Park, Ballsbridge, where she was extremely content and wonderfully looked after. She felt geographically close to her life-long interests, with Country Markets up the road in one direction and the RDS and the ICA in the other. In her room she was surrounded by her own familiar things: a painting by her father of the spot where the Children of Lir had been restored to their human form; a sketch of the gate of her 'cot' in Roundstone, half-open and inviting you to go down to the sea; a sketch by Liam C Martin of her other favourite cottage, the one that hung outside The Country Shop. On her windowsill were her trophies and around the room bits of crafts of all sorts to remind her of the people who had made them. Down in the sitting room she would entertain the other women with her repertoire of songs or with her favourite party-piece, *The Bears*, a word-and-action game which Livie had learned in America in 1955 and which had been taught to generations of visitors to An Grianán. (*see* Annexe III)

As life finally began to slip from Muriel in the summer of 1995 she was peaceful, drawing on her deep religious faith and reciting prayers and hymns as she lay in bed, such as John Newton's well known lines,

> Amazing grace, how sweet the sound
> That saved a wretch like me
> I once was lost, but now am found
> Was blind but now I see

When Archbishop Caird spoke at Muriel's funeral he reminded her friends of her irrepressible generosity. Days before her death, he told them, when a visitor would go into her room to see her she would first sing out 'Come in!' and then ask, 'What can I do for you, my dear?' Smiles broke out on many faces in the church and that is how Muriel would have wanted it.

Notes

1.   James Meenan and Desmond Clarke (eds), *The Royal Dublin Society 1731–1981*, Gill and Macmillan, Dublin, 1981.

Annexe I

Questionnaire for CDB base-line survey:

1 Extent of district. Whether inland or maritime.
2 Average quantity of land cultivated on holdings at and under £4 valuation, under potatoes, oats, green crops and meadow.
3 Extent of mountain or moor grazing.
4 Whether land could be reclaimed and added to adjoining holdings.
5 Possibility of migration.
6 Method of cultivation etc.
7 Information with regard to livestock and poultry.
8 Markets and fairs for the sale of cattle and produce and for the purchase of supplies.
9 Rail, steamer, boat, road, postal and telegraph facilities.
10 Employment for labourers in the district.
11 Migratory labour and earnings.
12 Weaving, spinning, knitting and sewing.
13 Kelp and seaweed.
14 Sale of turf – and nature and extent of bogs.
15 Lobster fishing; number of men and boats employed.
16 Sea fishing.
17 Number and class of boats employed in fishing or carrying turf or seaweed.
18 Fish – whether used at home or sold.
19 Fish curing.
20 Piers and harbours.
21 Salmon and freshwater fisheries.
22 Banks and loan funds.
23 Mineral and other resources.
24 Dealings – whether cash, credit or barter.
25 Estimated cash receipts and expenditure of a family in ordinary circumstances.
26 Estimated money value of the products of an average holding, with other local advantages.
27 Dietary of the people.

28   Clothing and bedding of the people.

29 & 30 Character, disposition, dwellings, home-life and customs of the people.

31   Organised efforts for improvement of the district.

32   Suggestions for the improvement of the district.

i. Establishment of steam and other communication

ii. Agricultural development

iii. Introduction of good breeds of live stock and poultry

iv. Development of fisheries

v. Provision of industrial occupation for the male population during months of November, December, January and February

vi. Technical instruction of girls in needlework and kindred occupations

vii. Development of tourist traffic

viii. Migration of population and reclamation of land

ix. Promotion of minor miscellaneous occupations.

Annexe II

Tweeds

All Colours and Designs

Light, Medium, Heavy

Manufacturers of Heavy

Hand-Made Blankets and

Flannels

St. Anthony's Place, Ballycroy, Co. Mayo.

12th Feb 1930

Memo from PATRICK MADDEN

Fancy Hand-made Tweed Manufacturer

☛ COTTAGE INDUSTRY

Miss Muriel F. Gahan, 26 Leinster Rd. Dublin

Dear Madam,

With further reference to the carpet I have to explain that our worker although a crack spinner didn't seem to clearly understand the nature of her task. She spun the yarn too fine for your purpose, too soft for mine but something had to be done with it. In rugs as well as tweeds, the warp should be spun hard. The weft in all cloths should be spun much thicker than the warp. Thick, soft yarn 37 ins wide, 20 threads to the inch in warp, couldn't possibly be woven hard. It was woven in fine gear, threw up a surface of white wool which had to be singed – the rough hairs burned off – soaked some hours in soap mash and paraffin and second washed. All this was simply a test to discover the extreme of what a weaver, yarn, machinery, and dyes could do – what strain each and all of them could endure in work of this kind. All the dyes stood well except the centre panel of "Mary Blue" which went off at once. In this case if the warp was spun finer and harder and the weft much thicker you would have a good hard woven carpet showing strong bright colours, and a really decent, durable article. My discovery from this experiment from an afterstudy is that even a learner with a reliable loom and trainer – given hard spun warp and thick spun weft – all mountain wool – on a 29 inch width should be able to market carpets @ between 6/- and 7/- per yard, proper, even fast dyes of course being used. If the yarn is spun hard enough – and in this respect hard spinning is so far as I know master – it is quite possible to weave cloth very thick and close and almost as hard as timber. Notice on or two of the little yellow belts in the carpet how hard they are because of hard spinning. They are not half as hard as they could be with hard warp.

You say that the dyeing question is a difficult one and appear to suggest that it is a business for Dublin. All this is certainly very true. Assuming that we are trying to expedite the economic production on a fairly extensive scale of really saleable articles your question about the dyes has started an argument which may yet give rise to drastic and much needed litigation. Speaking, briefly as possible, for myself alone I cannot venture an opinion about the dyes without first taking up the raw material, the wool itself. At the start let us *hope*, and the same sincerely, that a woollen industrial revival if it ever comes to be will not bring on the stage of the Irish Free State an army of rogues and swindlers, that instead it will help to give us a clean, honest minded, thrifty industrious people. In a previous document I said that the woollen trade, given fair play, is as honourable as any other occupation. I am not dealing with the question of social status, but simply business.

Down here in Mayo if we take a thread of yarn spun from mountain wool, no matter how well the wool or yarn is washed we find it sometimes has a dark shade and this dark shade sometimes draws through the dye no matter how fast, or strong, or how expert the worker. This shade is often taken to be natural because it is coarse mountain wool. Sometimes, *very seldom* I am sure, the darkish shade is natural. Here we have sheep with heavy riddle and bold tar brands roaming miles every day over bog, mire and moss, forcing their way through brush and briar. This mixture of grit, moss, tar, bog thorns & etc is taken with the fleece, all mixed and ground up in woollen cards, and spun into yarn – and so we have the dark shade. You are late now for true, successful cleaning or dyeing. Washing the wool or yarn won't get rid of tar; moss; grit; thorns etc. because all this stuff is mixed in the wool; ground in the hand cards or carding machinery, and spun through every atom and fibre of the yarn. This is no theory at all but what I have often seen and worked at. Now again people have often complained to me about how out of quantities such as 14 lbs of wool they couldn't get 12 lbs of yarn. Added to all this dross and carelessness some stockowners are not above storing their wool in damp places, sometimes sponging it with water to get more weight. What have the Government to say to salesmen of this kind: as between stockowners who fraud; buyers who are mulcted; and workers, firms or Depts, who cannot get the full value of effort and investment, because wool is tumbled into the market, on to the spindle and dyeworks in a damp, dirty haphazard fashion. Fowl owners have been compelled to market clean fresh eggs. Why not deal with wool owners the same way. If the making of law and order was in my hands I would appoint export, or transport agents for different districts and under severe penalty would have these men to get in only bone dry, thoroughly clean wool. Anything else I would regard as a nuisance and prosecute stock owners and agents accordingly. It may be argued that this is carrying the case too far; but if we want firm spinning; successful dyeing; and really clean durable cloth – cloth that won't readily attract disease microbes we must certainly have some such legislation. Taking it for granted that supplies of clean wool are available I still would not have dyeing carried on in the homes of the workers.

Going into the dyeing question we would have to consider a thousand items. Here economy in time; method; machinery; cost of dye and even successful results, is of the utmost importance. Let us parcel out the wool and send it down into the different districts, into the homes of the workers, and now try and get a glimpse of how this method will work out. Our country spinner has water not always too clean; a small pot; perhaps a leaking pail; sometimes a dull fire; intrusion from youngsters and others every moment; a thousand odds and ends of household work to be attended. The dyed article has to be washed and dried perhaps where sheep and cattle or careless youngsters are roaming about. Were she ever do expert the chances are that weeks, perhaps months later the wool or yarn will come back to the weaver or Depot so badly blotched and smeared and burned as to be useless for manufacturing into saleable articles. If safety, success, and satisfaction is to be assured all ideas of local skill and effort must be abandoned so far as the dyeing of wool or yarn is concerned. A dye factory or Depot with skilled workers, under *expert supervision* – for even skilled workers sometimes run the easy way with business – should account for more work in a week, and the same satisfaction, than all the skilled workers of the Gaeltacht could attend in some kind of way in a month. It may be considered rather costly to continue sending wool to Dublin and back again to workers in mayo and Galway. What about the establishment at let us say Castlebar of such a Depot for dyeing the wool of Mayo and Galway? The Mayo wool is much too coarse for fine tweeds. That of Galway is fair enough. Perhaps a blend of both varieties of wool would produce a fairly saleable tweed. It would give splendid results in carpets. This suggestion is only in case of business on a large scale; and when there are plenty of trained hands to take charge of local stations.

I have experience in the tweed line since I was apprenticed to my late father who was a tradesman of the old school specially skilled in all branches of linen and woollen weaving; and strange as it may seem we always found English tourists of every rank, station and creed to be by far the best and surest buyers. Those same ladies and gentlemen have always told us that they could not possibly get tweeds of this kind in their own country where there seems to be a roaring demand for such wear among all classes. I find that tweeds with a light grey, blue or brown background, plentifully sprinkled with strong clear coloured little naps of green, red, yellow, and royal blue, also pure white tweed are in great demand. Hence the grave necessity of expert skill; uptodate machinery; ample convenience in the work of yarn or wool dyeing.

Of course if your question refers only to my own particular work, for so far I have not been able owing to lack of funds to cater for a tenth of my would be clients and am able to manage these small lots myself; and time is too fast running out for sending raw material to Dublin and here again. I sincerely hope that the Dept. of Lands and Fisheries will let me have a substantial loan to get yarn; and the same immediately else it will be too late. The loan of £40 or better still £50 would bring me a very substantial return in a few months and could be merged into a building loan later.

I send your yarns ten lbs white, thick extra twisted, which should be stretched well and put on pegs. If you cannot manage to wind it with convenience I will send revolving hank bars immediately.

Hoping to have your further advice.

I am, Madam, your grateful and obedient Srvt

P Madden

Annexe III

Bear Hunt
Game brought from USA in 1955 by Mrs Olivia Hughes, President, ICA

START: All sit in circle with feet firmly on ground, and *remain seated throughout the game.*

1.   All start 'walking', feet slowly lifted alternately, and knees slapped in time. After about ten paces all stop, and, looking intently in front of them, all speak together:
2.   "What's that?" "It's a tree." "Can't get round it; can't get under it; must climb up it." All climb up, one hand above the other, and, at the top, part the branches.
3.   One hand raised to the eyes and the horizon searched. "Any bears there?" "No bears there."
4.   All climb down (reverse action)
5.   Repeat (1)
6.   "What's that?" "It's a cornfield." "Can't get round it; can't get over it; must go through it." All go through, hands out in front, palms together, swishing from side to side.
7.   Repeat (3)
8.   Repeat (1)
9.   "What's that?" "It's a bridge." "Can't get round it; can't get under it; must go over it." All go over each hand alternate: climbing the opposite arm to the shoulder and down again.
10.   Repeat (3)
11.   Repeat (1)
12.   "What's that?" "It's a river." "Can't get round it; can't get under it; must swim through it." All swim through with both arms.
13.   Repeat (3)
14.   Repeat (1)
15.   "What's that?" "It's a cave." "Can't get round it; can't get under it; must go into it." All go into cave, hands out either side feeling walls of cave, feet moving slowly.
16.   Repeat (3) to "Any bears?" Then feeling their shapes nervously at arms length, all say quiveringly: "Two ears...wet nose...rough fur..." Then they all yell in terror: "IT'S A BEAR!"
17   All actions done as quickly as possible in reverse, in right order (cave, river, bridge and cornfield, tree) until HOME, SWEET HOME is reached.

To make the contrast, all actions on the outward journey should be very deliberate and slow.
A strong 'American' accent is essential to get the right BEAR atmosphere.

Index